# Luke the Composer

# Luke the Composer

Exploring the Evangelist's Use of Matthew

Thomas J. Mosbø

Fortress Press
*Minneapolis*

LUKE THE COMPOSER
Exploring the Evangelist's Use of Matthew

Cover design: Joe Reinke


Hardcover ISBN: 978-1-5064-2557-3
Paperback ISBN: 978-1-5064-2037-0
eBook ISBN: 978-1-5064-2038-7


The paper used in this publication meets the minimum requirements of American National Standard for Information Sciences — Permanence of Paper for Printed Library Materials, ANSI Z329.48-1984.


Manufactured in the U.S.A.

This book was produced using Pressbooks.com, and PDF rendering was done by PrinceXML.

*This work is dedicated to my wife*
*Coral*
*my truest friend, inspiration, and supporter*
*whose tireless help on so many levels made this work possible*

*and to our children and their spouses*
*Christian, Rachel & Joseph, and Arwen & Barry*

*our grandchildren*
*Caitlin, Katarina, Jamie, Michael, Genevieve, and Louisa*

*Our "adopted" daughter, her husband, and their children*
*Susanne & Marcus, Ole, and Martha*
*and all who shall come after*

*With thanks to*
*Michael Sadgrove, David Kennedy, and the Durham Cathedral*
*Community*
*who provided much needed spiritual inspiration during this*
*project*

*and N T Wright*
*who personally encouraged me to pursue this endeavor*

# Contents

# Figures and Tables

## Figures

Note, several of these figures are large, full-color diagrams available online.

# Tables

# Prologue

## *The Synoptic Problem*

Why were the Gospels written?

On the surface this may appear to be a straightforward question, to which the simplest answer would be: to tell the story of Jesus. But when we consider the implications of both the question and the answer, neither turns out to be straightforward or simple at all. As soon as we ask this question, we are immediately faced with all sorts of related and sticky problems. The question of why the Gospels were written also entails further questions about when, where, how, and by whom they were written. But we may also ask, Which Gospels? Do we mean only the four Gospels that form the core of the New Testament? But what about the "other" Gospels such as the so-called Gospel of Thomas and the Gnostic Gospels? Even if we confine ourselves just to the four canonical Gospels, can we say confidently that they were all written for the same specific reason? Did each of the Gospel writers have the same idea about what the story of Jesus was or about who Jesus himself actually was? And were they right? Did they, in fact, faithfully tell the story of Jesus? And just who was, or is, this mysterious person after all?

None of these questions is merely academic, raised by disinterested historians who look back at the past from a comfortable distance with no personal involvement. Yes, for some in our culture all of this may simply *seem* to be a historical curiosity, no longer relevant or important. But even such people must ultimately admit that the Gospels and the religion that arose along with them (and largely *because* of them) have played a large part in shaping the modern world and have influenced in one way or another nearly every aspect of Western civilization and culture—they are hardly just a curiosity. Indeed, no other

1

documents have had quite the impact these writings have had. Therefore we cannot look back at the writing of the Gospels from a comfortable distance, because they are a part of us, and seeking such distance would mean trying to distance ourselves from ourselves.

For the hundreds of millions of people around the globe who call ourselves Christians, these writings and the questions about them penetrate to the very center of how we see our place in the universe. Do these documents express only internal beliefs about what was true for their authors, which we must each individually evaluate for ourselves as part of our own "personal faith"? If so, is such "faith" merely an internal, subjective matter for the individual? Or is it perhaps something that extends beyond ourselves? Do the Gospels perhaps express something that is true about the entire external world around all of us and about the nature of our common human history? Or do they represent a colossal "mistake" that would now wisely be abandoned or rejected? Or do they simply represent one set of resources (among many others) from which we may choose those portions we find comfortable and ignore all the rest?

All of the Gospel writers attempted to tell the story of Jesus. Did they do so faithfully? And if so, are we ourselves faithful to them, and faithful to him (assuming of course that he *is* someone worth being faithful to)?

The answers to all the questions surrounding the writing of these Gospels are therefore intensely relevant for us today, but to answer any of these ultimate questions we must first have some sort of understanding of why and how the Gospels actually came to be written. They did not simply descend from heaven already in their completed form. Instead, they were written by real people living in a specific time and culture (and this is true even if we take the idea of divine inspiration seriously in relation to their writing). Understanding the Gospel writers who laid the foundations of the Christian religion and who thereby have influenced our entire culture is therefore essential for the task of helping us to understand ourselves as well. The question of why the Gospels were written is an important one for us today and can affect the future as we face what it means to be Christians (or, for others, to be non-Christians) in the third millennium.

This book will not attempt to give a comprehensive answer to all of these questions. That is far more than can be expected of one slim volume, especially in light of the hundreds of other books that have already been written on the subject. Instead, it will only begin to lay some of the groundwork necessary before larger issues can be considered, by confining itself to one specific aspect of this matter: why and how the particular Gospel of Luke was written. Here there is still much to be said that has not been said before, and to which this volume can offer its own unique contribution.

Even narrowing the scope of the inquiry in this way, however, does not shield us from the wider issues raised above. The writing of the Lukan Gospel was not isolated from the writing of the other Gospels or from the overall historical environment in which they were written. Luke could not possibly have attempted to tell the story of Jesus unless he had either been personally involved in that story himself or had learned it from others, whether in oral or written form. Hence, the story and its telling involved people other than just Luke himself, and those others must be taken into consideration. Some of those people may well have been other Gospel writers (whether Luke knew them personally or had only read their works). Therefore, the extent to which Luke may have been familiar with other Gospels will be of great importance in our quest if there is any hope of addressing realistically the questions of how and why Luke's Gospel was written.

Two related questions that will not, however, be our focus here are the questions of *when* and *by whom* any of the Gospels were written. Although these are important questions in the larger context of *why* the Gospels were written, they might easily get in the way of the specific issues I wish to address in this book. Ultimately, of course, the questions of *when* and *by whom* are intimately bound up with the questions of *why* and *how*, but it is my position that it is the why and how that will eventually lead to an understanding of the when and by whom, rather than the other way round. I will keep an open mind throughout this book, therefore, regarding the specific dating and authorship of any of the Gospels.

In this light, the use in this book of the names "Luke" or "Matthew" or "Mark" or "John" as the authors of the Gospels is to be understood as a simple convention, not as an assertion that the actual Gospel authors were necessarily those individuals known to us by these names from the New Testament, and to whom the Gospels have traditionally been attributed. Instead, I leave the question of authorship open.

Similarly, the dating of the canonical Gospels will simply be assumed to be sometime after the crucifixion of Jesus (approximately 30 CE) and sometime before the early second century, when other authors began to quote the Gospels. In addition, the earliest extant fragments of Gospel manuscripts can be dated to the early second century. This is not a huge stretch of time, representing only the first and second (and possibly the beginning of the third) generation of Christians. Although this period saw a great expansion of the Christian church from an originally small Jewish sect in Judea and Galilee to an empire-wide movement of Jews and gentiles, this expansion had already begun in the early decades of the Christian movement and was therefore certainly ongoing throughout the period during which the Gospels were written.

So we may speak of a more or less consistent Christian community that existed during this entire period. My discussion of passages in Luke that may point to more specific events, conditions, or locations within this broad time frame will usually not require fixing the date of Luke or any of the other Gospels to a specific point during this period. Yet, once our exploration of Luke has concluded, we will return to some of these issues briefly in an epilogue, since this exploration itself should begin to shed some light on them. Hence, this book will seek to provide a starting point for such considerations, not an ending point for understanding Luke.

What will be necessary throughout this volume, however, will be to address the relationship of Luke's Gospel to the others, and especially to Matthew and to Mark. These three works seem to have a special relationship with one another and share a common viewpoint; for this reason they are collectively known as the "Synoptics" (from Greek, meaning "seeing together"). The relative historical order of these three documents and their possible influences on each other will therefore be important issues in this book, since it is possible that the existence of these other documents influenced how and why Luke's Gospel was written. It is impossible, therefore, to address the writing of Luke without coming face to face with that conundrum known as the "Synoptic Problem."

## Defining the Synoptic Problem

While all four canonical Gospels tell a similar story of the ministry, trial, death, and resurrection of Jesus (including versions of many of the same important incidents and miracles), John's version is quite different from the first three. John focuses on only a few incidents in the life of Jesus and tends to convey long discourses, often dialogues between Jesus and other parties, none of which corresponds exactly with the words of Jesus recorded in the other Gospels. In contrast, the first three Gospels are each composed of a large number of similar brief individual pericopes, that is, short episodes or parables or other sayings, strung together in an orderly fashion in order to tell the story. The Gospels of Matthew, Mark, and Luke share many of the same pericopes and have much in common in approach, structure, and order—and in many cases even exact wording. How do we account for such similar viewpoints? Were these three Gospels written one after the other, each successive author drawing on the work of the previous, or is their relationship more complicated than this? That, indeed, is the problem!

When we look more closely at the content of the Synoptics, we find that many pericopes are common to all three of these Gospels, and most of these common pericopes tend to follow in approximately the same order in each Gospel. Although the exact wording may vary, the general correspondence between them is evident. These common passages are often referred to as the "Triple Tradition," since they are attested in all three Synoptics. Usually included under this category of the Triple Tradition, however, are a handful of scattered pericopes common to Mark and Luke but not present in Matthew, and a few more common to Mark and Matthew that do not appear in Luke, since in total such passages represent a relatively insignificant portion of the Gospels. This Triple Tradition represents nearly the entire Gospel of Mark (632 out of 662 verses), about one half of Matthew (526 out of 1,069 verses), and a bit less than two-fifths of Luke (414 out of 1,150 verses).[1]

The similarity in the order and wording of this Triple Tradition material, the fact that this material appears to provide the basic narrative structure for all three Synoptics, and the further fact that this material makes up nearly the entire Gospel of Mark have suggested to most scholars of the past and present that there is a single common source for all this material. This common source could have been one of the three Gospels themselves (depending on which was written first), or this material could have come originally from some other, now-lost document written before any of the known Gospels.

In addition to this Triple Tradition, however, a significant number of additional pericopes are common to Matthew and Luke that are not present in Mark. These pericopes are often known as the "Double Tradition," since they are attested in only two of the three Synoptics. In

---

1. All figures quoted in the prologue are from Allan Barr, *A Diagram of Synoptic Relationships* (1938; rev. ed., Edinburgh: T&T Clark, 1976).

contrast to the Triple Tradition, however, these pericopes are, for the most part, not in the same order in Matthew and Luke and often vary more markedly in wording and even in emphasis than do the Triple Tradition pericopes. The different ways in which Matthew and Luke present the Double Tradition material illustrate the significant differences between these two Gospels.

Of the three Synoptics, Matthew and Mark are the most similar to each other and follow the most similar narrative pattern (formed by the Triple Tradition material), but Matthew is significantly longer than Mark. Most of the additional material in Matthew that is not found in Mark consists of additional sayings of Jesus, which are grouped into five separate "discourses." These occur at fairly regular intervals throughout Matthew's Gospel, and each ends with the same formula: "When Jesus had finished saying these things . . ." (Matt 7:28; 11:1; 13:53; 19:1; 26:1). The first and by far the longest of these is the "Sermon on the Mount." The discourses are generally mixes of Double Tradition material and material unique to Matthew.

Luke, on the other hand, is organized quite differently. The first third of his Gospel seems to alternate in long blocks between material similar to Mark's and other material either unique to Luke or common with Matthew. The Double Tradition material in this first third of Luke tends to follow closely the same order it has in Matthew and consists of both stories and teachings, including Luke's "Sermon on the Plain," which is shorter but contains much of the same content as Matthew's Sermon on the Mount. The first part of Luke then ends with the story of the transfiguration, which in both Matthew and Mark comes only a little bit before the final entry into Jerusalem and the last week of Jesus's life. In Luke, however, the entire middle third of his Gospel after the transfiguration is dedicated to a series of teachings given by Jesus during his "journey to Jerusalem." This middle section of Luke contains almost no material from the Triple Tradition but includes material unique to Luke plus most of the Double Tradition material. Here, however, the order of this Double Tradition material is completely different from its order in Matthew, and there are significant variations in wording. Then, once we reach Jerusalem for the final third of Luke, the situation is virtually reversed. Here, there is mostly Triple Tradition material mixed with material unique to Luke, with only a tiny amount of Double Tradition material.

The Double Tradition material is therefore much more difficult to account for than is the Triple Tradition, since the Double Tradition material is presented so differently by Matthew than by Luke and is missing completely from Mark. But for all its import in resolving the Synoptic Problem, the Double Tradition comprises only a relatively small amount of material, less than one quarter of Matthew (261 verses), and about one fifth of Luke (245 verses). Did this material come from a common source? If so, why is it in such a different order in the two Gospels? If not, why is so much of it so similar?

The remaining material in Matthew and Luke beyond the Triple and Double Traditions is unique to each of these Gospels and represents a significant portion of each, more than one quarter of Matthew (282 verses) and more than two-fifths of Luke (491 verses). (The German term *Sondergut* is often used to describe such unique material.) Yet not only is this material unique to its specific Gospel, but it often seems to contradict unique material found in the other Gospel. Such divergent material includes especially the birth narratives, the genealogies, and portions of the passion and resurrection accounts. These differences seem to present a significant difficulty for theories that suggest that Matthew or Luke knew of the other's Gospel.

But there is yet one more twist to the whole problem: the "Minor Agreements" between Matthew and Luke. As mentioned above, the entire Gospel of Mark is often equated with the Triple Tradition. As such, it also serves as a "middle term" between Matthew and Luke. None of the Synoptics agrees completely with either of the others, but whenever there are differences, one of the other two almost always agrees with Mark. When pericopes are in a different order in Matthew and Mark, Luke follows the same order as Mark, and in cases when Luke's pericopes deviate in order from Mark, Matthew almost always agrees with Mark's order.

The same is true, for the most part, in the wording of pericopes. When there are differences in wording, Matthew usually agrees with Mark against Luke and Luke typically agrees with Mark against Matthew. This makes it almost certain that there is a direct relationship between Mark and Matthew as well as one between Mark and Luke (otherwise it would be too great a coincidence that Matthew and Luke would agree with Mark in such a way and so consistently). Mark could have been written first and then used by Matthew and by Luke. Or Mark could have been written as an abbreviation of Matthew and then Luke used Mark. Or Mark could have been written as a condensation and reconciliation of both Luke and Matthew.[2]

It is not always the case, however, that Mark serves as this "middle term" between Matthew and Luke when it comes to wording. There are a number of common phrases or sometimes single words that occur in Triple Tradition passages where Matthew and Luke use the same words while Mark gives a slightly different reading. These are known as the Minor Agreements between Matthew and Luke. The Minor Agreements are therefore a particular problem for any theories that suggest that Matthew and Luke wrote their Gospels with no knowledge of each other.

We may now summarize the basic types of material found in the Synoptics as follows:

- **Triple Tradition**: Material common to all three Synoptics, mostly narrative and mostly in the same order in all three. It makes up nearly all of Mark, one half of Matthew, and two-fifths of Luke.

- **Double Tradition**: Material common to Matthew and Luke but not present in Mark, mostly consisting of Jesus's teachings and frequently in a completely different order in the two. It makes up one-quarter of Matthew and one-fifth of Luke.

- **Matthew's unique material** (Matthean *Sondergut*): Material found in Matthew but in neither of the other two Gospels, including the birth and resurrection narratives and some of Jesus's teachings. It makes up one-quarter of Matthew.

- **Luke's unique material** (Lukan *Sondergut*): Material found in Luke but in neither of the other two, including the birth and resurrection narratives and some of Jesus's teachings. A sizable amount of material (longer in Luke than even the Triple Tradition), it makes up two-fifths of Luke.

- **Minor Agreements**: Occasional agreements of wording between Matthew and Luke against Mark in Triple Tradition passages, although in most cases where there is a variation in order and wording Mark serves as a "middle term" between the others, Matthew agreeing with Mark against Luke or Luke agreeing with Mark against Matthew.

These categories, the four traditions and the Minor Agreements, provide the basic "raw material" of the Synoptic Problem, and each of them must be considered carefully when we ask how and why Luke's Gospel was written.

2. As shown by B. C. Butler, *The Originality of St. Matthew: A Critique of the Two-Document Hypothesis* (Cambridge: University Press, 1951).

## Solutions

In what order, then, were the Synoptic Gospels written and what is their relationship to each other? Did their authors work directly from each other's texts, or did they write independently of each other, drawing on similar but now lost sources? If so, were such sources, written or oral? Numerous different solutions to this problem have been proposed, and although it is not the intention of this book to give a history of the scholarship surrounding the Synoptic Problem, or to look in detail at all the various theories that have been proposed to solve it, two such solutions for which there are currently serious advocates provide the two main alternatives that will be considered in this book. As with the "problem" itself, therefore, we need to have at least a basic understanding of these major solutions before we begin our investigation proper.

For more than a century, the "Two-Source" hypothesis has been the dominant theory regarding the writing of the Synoptic Gospels, based largely on the work of C. H. Weisse, H. J. Holtzmann, and especially B. H. Streeter.[3] This hypothesis posits that Mark was the first of the Synoptics to have been written and that the authors of Matthew and Luke worked independently of one another, each using Mark plus a second common source (usually referred to as "Q") in the writing of their own Gospels. In particular, Streeter not only presents his own influential version of this theory but also encapsulates much of the scholarship that preceded it and laid out most of the issues that are still at the heart of current debates about the Synoptics.

Nevertheless, because there are many variations of this theory, including those known as the "Three-" or "Four-Source" hypotheses, perhaps it is best to refer to all these theories together under the heading of the single most prominent feature they all share, the proposed source document known as "Q." The Q solution to the Synoptic Problem is so pervasive that it is the only theory usually even mentioned in most introductory texts on the New Testament and in most commentaries. Indeed, for all practical purposes, it seems that the Q theory is considered by many to be the only "fact" generally accepted as virtually certain within the discipline of New Testament studies, as a brief

---

3. Christian Hermann Weisse, *Die evangelische Geschichte, kritisch und philosophisch bearbeitet* (Leipzig: Breitkopf & Hartel, 1838); Heinrich Julius Holtzmann, *Die synoptischen Evangelien: Ihr Ursprung und geschichtlicher Charakter* (Leipzig: Wilhelm Engelmann, 1863); Burnett Hillman Streeter, *The Four Gospels: A Study of Origins, Treating of the Manuscript Tradition, Sources, Authorship, and Dates* (London: Macmillan, 1924).

excerpt from W. Marxsen's *Introduction to the New Testament* exemplifies:

> This Two-Sources theory has been so widely accepted by scholars that one feels inclined to abandon the term "theory" (in the sense of "hypothesis"). We can in fact regard it as an assured finding--but we must bear in mind that there are inevitable uncertainties as far as the extent and form of Q and the special material are concerned.[4]

In its simplest form, the Q theory may be depicted as follows:

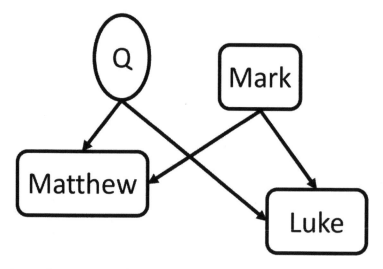

Fig. P.1. The Basic Q Hypothesis

This diagram shows the relative lengths and relationships of the various documents in question, as well as their relative dates (with the earliest at the top) and their order in the New Testament (from left to right). According to this theory, the now-lost Q is considered to have been the earliest written, with Mark coming soon after but written with no knowledge of Q. Similarly, Matthew was written before Luke, but Luke was not aware of its having been written. Thus, Matthew and Luke each combined Mark (which provided a narrative skeleton and the Triple Tradition material) with Q (which provided the Double Tradition material), along with their own unique material in their own ways to produce their respective Gospels. The Q solution is therefore

---

4. W. Marxsen, *Introduction to the New Testament: An Approach to Its Problems,* trans. G. Buswell (Philadelphia: Fortress Press, 1968), 118.

tidy and symmetrical and seems to account in a straightforward way for the various types of material found in the Gospels.

Variations on this theory often also include assorted additional hypothetical documents or different versions of existing documents in order to account for certain aspects of the Gospels, however, which suggests that the solution is perhaps not so tidy after all. For instance, Weisse suggested that Matthew and Luke did not use the version of Mark we now possess but a "Proto-Mark," which included some of the narrative passages now found only in the Double Tradition. Streeter's influential version of the theory, the Four-Source hypothesis, includes two additional written sources besides Q and Mark: "M," used exclusively by Matthew, and "L," used exclusively by Luke. Streeter also suggests that Luke was written in two stages, his "Proto-Luke," being a combination of Q and L, then the final edition adding in narrative material from Mark plus the birth narratives. Although few scholars now take Streeter's full theory seriously, the designations M and L are still often used to refer to the source or sources (whether written or oral) for the unique material of Matthew and Luke, respectively.

But since Q, if it did exist, has now been lost, it is impossible to know for certain what its contents were, and there has been considerable debate among scholars regarding this. Based on the work of the International Q Project, a group of scholars have recently produced the *Critical Edition of Q*, a proposed authoritative version of exactly what the contents of Q were in Greek, with translations into several other languages alongside. It also indicates parallels of Q's contents with the Gospel of Mark and the noncanonical so-called Gospel of Thomas. An edition of the identical text, but with only an English translation and less commentary, is also available: *The Sayings Gospel Q in Greek and English.*[5] For purposes of comparison and for consistency, the *Critical Edition of Q* will be used in this book as the definition of the contents of Q, which correspond closely to the Double Tradition material found in Matthew and Luke.

The Q theory has not gone unchallenged, however, particularly by modern advocates of the alternative "Farrer" hypothesis, which contends that Luke used Matthew's Gospel directly as a source alongside Mark, eliminating any need for the hypothetical Q. The main propo-

---

5. James M. Robinson et al., eds., *The Critical Edition of Q: Synopsis Including the Gospels of Matthew and Luke, Mark and Thomas, with English, German, and French Translations of Q and Thomas* (Minneapolis: Fortress Press, 2000); James M. Robinson et al., eds., *The Sayings Gospel Q in Greek and English: With Parallels from the Gospels of Mark and Thomas* (Minneapolis: Fortress Press, 2002).

nents of the Farrer school (Austin Farrer himself, Michael Goulder, and Mark Goodacre) have launched formidable attacks on the Q theory,[6] demonstrating that the Farrer hypothesis is a serious contender for solving the Synoptic Problem. The Farrer theory may be illustrated as follows:

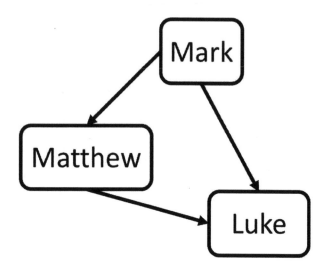

Fig. P.2. The Farrer Hypothesis

The Farrer theory is, in essence, not unlike the Q theory. Both assert that the Synoptics were written in the order Mark, Matthew, Luke, and both assert that Matthew and Luke each used Mark as a source. Where they differ is on the important point of whether Luke knew of Matthew's Gospel and used it as a source. If he did (as the Farrer school contends), there is no need for the hypothetical Q, since Luke could have drawn his Double Tradition material directly from Matthew. This simple difference, however, carries with it tremendous implications regarding the life of the early church: whether, for instance, there were two "alternate" forms of Christianity existing from the beginning, one represented by Q and one represented by Mark.

Other theories regarding the relationships of the Synoptics also exist, however. In addition to the Q and Farrer solutions, the most

---

6. Austin Farrer, "On Dispensing with Q," in *Studies in the Gospels: Essays in Memory of R. H. Lightfoot*, ed. D. E. Nineham (Oxford: Blackwell, 1955), 55–88; Michael Goulder, *Luke: A New Paradigm*, Journal for the Study of the New Testament: Supplement Series 20 (Sheffield: JSOT Press, 1989); Mark Goodacre, *The Case against Q: Studies in Markan Priority and Synoptic Problem* (Harrisburg, PA: Trinity Press International, 2002).

prominent options with modern advocates are the "Augustine" theory and the "Griesbach" theory. The Augustine theory (first proposed by Saint Augustine around 400 CE and championed in the twentieth century by Theodor von Zahn, B. C. Butler, and John Wenham[7]) asserts that Matthew was the first Gospel to be written, that Mark followed as an abbreviation of Matthew, and that Luke was written last, drawing on both Matthew and Mark. If this description is compared to the above illustration of the Farrer theory it will be seen that the only difference between the two is the order of Matthew and Mark. Yet, since the questions to be addressed in this book are how and why *Luke's* Gospel came to be written, the Augustine theory may for our purposes here be practically equated with the Farrer theory, since both assert that Luke used Matthew and Mark directly as sources. Hence, whether Matthew or Mark was written first would not have mattered to Luke and so need not concern us here. Nearly everything said in this book regarding the Farrer theory, then, will equally apply to the Augustine theory.

The other option, proposed originally in 1783 by Johann Jakob Griesbach and defended more recently by William R. Farmer,[8] is not so similar. Griesbach asserted that the Synoptics were written in the order Matthew, Luke, Mark. So, according to this theory, although Luke used Matthew's Gospel directly as a source, Mark's Gospel was actually the *last* of the Synoptics to have been written, as a deliberate reconciliation and condensation of both Matthew and Luke. This theory is radically different from the Q theory, disagreeing with it on nearly every point. It is also significantly different from the Farrer theory, agreeing with it only in that Luke used Matthew directly. Thus, although the Griesbach theory will not be one of the main theories considered in this book, it will be addressed when necessary regarding Luke's relationship to the other Synoptics.

By comparing the three non-Q solutions described here, we may also now see that they represent the three possible "reliance" theories, in which each successive Gospel writer drew directly from the Gospels already written—but all agree that Luke used Matthew as a source. The

---

7. Theodor Zahn, *Introduction to the New Testament,* trans. John Moore Trout et al. (Edinburgh: T&T Clark, 1909; repr., Minneapolis: Klock & Klock, 1977); Butler, *Originality of St. Matthew*; John Wenham, *Redating Matthew, Mark and Luke: A Fresh Assault on the Synoptic Problem* (Downers Grove, IL: InterVarsity Press, 1992).

8. Johann Jakob Griesbach, "A Demonstration That Mark Was Written after Matthew" (1789), trans. Bernard Orchard, in *J. J. Griesbach: Synoptic and Text-Critical Studies, 1776-1976,* ed. Bernard Orchard and Thomas R. W. Longstaff, Society for New Testament Studies Monograph Series 34 (Cambridge: Cambridge University Press, 1978); William R. Farmer, *The Synoptic Problem: A Critical Analysis* (New York: Macmillan, 1964).

differences lie simply in where Mark is placed as the "middle term," either first (Farrer), second (Augustine), or third (Griesbach).

The Q and Farrer theories, however, will provide the two main options to be considered in this book. This is not only because of their similarities but also because advocates of these two theories have more readily engaged each other in the debate over the issues surrounding what sources Luke may have used and what his procedures may have been than have advocates of the other theories. We will have reason to consider the arguments of the Q and Farrer theories in detail throughout this book.

Having thus outlined the Synoptic Problem and briefly described some possible solutions to it, we may now begin the task of looking specifically at Luke's Gospel and why and how it was written.

# 1

———

# Reading Luke

It has long been recognized that the Gospel of Luke may be divided into three main sections. The first and third of these sections follow the same basic outline as the Gospels of Mark and Matthew, feature similar stories, and indeed put those stories in much the same order. In all three Gospels, the story of Jesus's Galilean ministry is told in a similar fashion up to the climactic event of the transfiguration. In Matthew and Mark, this event leads almost immediately into an account of Jesus's passion and resurrection in Jerusalem. In Luke, however, the transfiguration comes only about one-third of the way through his Gospel (in chapter 9), and it is not until the *final* third (beginning partway through chapter 19) that Luke links back up with Matthew and Mark to proceed to recount the passion. Between these events, Luke presents a long, rambling string of stories, parables, and teachings of Jesus in a seemingly random and arbitrary order as Jesus slowly makes his way to Jerusalem.

It is this puzzling middle section of Luke that gives this Gospel much of its unique character but also presents some of the thorniest issues of the Synoptic Problem. In many ways, therefore, understanding how we should read this passage may be the key to unlocking not only Luke's own Gospel but also its relationship to the others. Any Synoptic theory that does not give an adequate account of the middle third of Luke ultimately fails to explain how and why the Gospels were written as they were and so cannot really answer the Synoptic Problem. In light of this, the exploration to be carried out here will seek to address afresh the writing of Luke's Gospel by focusing initially on what may be the single most important question regarding Luke in respect to the Synoptic Problem: Why is the middle part of Luke's Gospel organized as it is?

Instead of beginning by comparing Luke's Gospel directly to the others, or by asking what source or sources provided the material Luke used in this section of his Gospel, perhaps we ought to ask first how and why Luke arranged the material in this section as he did regardless of where the stories came from or how the section relates to the other Gospels. Only then will we be able to understand the choices the evangelist made concerning what material to include in his Gospel and, hence, where to pull that material from. Before we can focus on Luke's intentions for the middle section of his Gospel, however, we ought to ask what were his overall intentions for writing his entire Gospel in the first place.

## Luke's Prologue

One of the key indicators to Luke's intentions will be found in his own prologue to his Gospel, in which he sets out his understanding of his task. Because the words he used to describe this task are important, specific words in this passage are highlighted below, for which the roots of the original Greek words are then given, followed by the various meanings for these words according to Frederick W. Danker in his revision of Walter Bauer's *Greek-English Lexicon of the New Testament and Other Early Christian Literature*, ending with the page reference for the definition in that *Lexicon*.[1]

Luke begins his Gospel in this way (1:1–4):

> Since *many* [πολλοί {polloi}, many, a great number, 847]
> have *undertaken* [ἐπιχειρέω {epicheireō}, set one's hand to, endeavor, try, 386]
> to *draw up* [ἀνατάσσομαι {anatassomai}, arrange in proper order, to organize in a series, draw up, compose, compile, 73]
> a *narrative* [διήγησις {diēgēsis}, an orderly description of facts, events, actions, or words; narrative, account, 245]

---

1. Frederick W. Danker, rev. and ed., *A Greek-English Lexicon of the New Testament and Other Early Christian Literature,* 3rd ed. (Chicago: University of Chicago Press, 2000); based on Walter Bauer's *Griechisch-deutsches Wörterbuch zu den Schriften des Neuen Testaments und der übrigen urchristlichen Literatur,* and on previous English editions by W. F. Arndt and F. W. Gingrich.

of the things that have *been accomplished* [πληροφορέω {plērophoreō}, fill (completely), fulfill, accomplish, 827]

among us, just as they were *entrusted* [παραδίδωμι {para-didōmi}, hand over, give (over), deliver, entrust, 761]

to us by those who from the first became eyewitnesses and *servants* [ὑπηρέτης {hypēretēs}, helper, assistant, 1035]

of the Word, therefore it seemed good also to me, since I myself have *carefully* [ἀκριβῶς {akribōs}, accurately, carefully, well, 39]

*investigated* [παρακολουθέω {parakoloutheō}, follow a thing, follow a course of events, take note of, 767]

everything *from the beginning*, [ἄνωθεν {anōthen}, from the beginning, for a long time, 92]

to write an *orderly account* [καθεξῆς {kathexēs}, being in sequence in time, space, or logic; in order, one after the other, 490]

for you, *Your Excellency,* [κράτιστος {kratistos}, most noble, most excellent, 565]

Theophilus, so that you may know the *certainty* [ἀσφάλεια {asphaleia}, certainty, truth, 147]

of the things about which you have been *informed* [κατηχέω {katēcheō}, to share a communication that one receives, report, inform, 534].

Several words here especially require more clarification: παραδίδωμι, καθεξῆς, κράτιστος, and κατηχέω. The first two of these will affect our understanding of Luke himself, while the last two will affect our understanding of Luke's audience, specifically the enigmatic Theophilus.

The first word, παραδίδωμι, is sometimes used to refer to traditions being "handed down" from the past, and Luke's use of it here is often understood to mean that he is writing more than a generation after the "eyewitnesses" who had handed these traditions down to younger generations. Yet Luke's own use of παραδίδωμι throughout his Gospel and Acts does not warrant such a conclusion. Luke employs this word often, usually when referring to the "handing over" of a person charged with a crime into the care or authority of another, in particular Jesus himself being "handed over" or "entrusted" or "delivered" into the "hands of sinful men" (23:25; 24:7). Such a "handing over" implies the responsibility of keeping safe that which has been handed over or entrusted.

Luke uses the word once to refer to "the customs that Moses *delivered* to us" (Acts 6:14 ESV), customs that Stephen is accused of violating, and this is the only place where a long period of transmission would possibly be indicated. But it certainly need not mean this in Luke's Prologue. Rather, the implication seems to be that Luke (and others) have been entrusted personally by the eyewitnesses with the accounts of Jesus (just as Jesus was entrusted personally into the "care" of those who made sure he was crucified). That entrusting carried with it the responsibility that Luke would be true to those accounts and be faithful in recording them accurately. Regardless of how much time has transpired, therefore, between the events seen by the eyewitnesses and Luke's writing, Luke is clearly claiming to be relating a completely faithful version of what has been entrusted to him personally.

Another important word in this passage is καθεξῆς, which has here been translated as an "orderly account." This word is also used by Luke elsewhere, and in each case it refers to something happening in a specific sequence, whether chronologically ("all the prophets from Samuel *in sequence*" [Acts 3:24] and "Peter began and explained everything to them *in precise order*" [Acts 11:4]) or geographically ("Paul departed and traveled *successively* to each place" [Acts 18:23]). In each case there is a specific sequential order that must be maintained, but the type of order depends on the context, whether an order in time, or a sequence of logical steps, or a series of specific places to be visited one at a time. The key word for understanding the implications of καθεξῆς is, therefore, *sequence*. What Luke is claiming by using this word, then, is that he has carefully arranged his material in a specific and meaningful sequence.

## Luke's Audience

For what audience is he arranging this material? It is often suggested that Theophilus must have been a wealthy or otherwise prominent Christian who was Luke's patron, financing the publication of his Gospel. This would be consistent with the respect Luke shows Theophilus in the Prologue, calling him (as it is often translated) "Most excellent" (κράτιστος, a "strongly affirmative honorary form of address").[2] Ancient authors used this title when dedicating their works to their patrons. Such an understanding of this term would also explain why Luke tells Theophilus that he has written his Gospel (as the ending of his Prologue is often translated) "that you may have certainty con-

---

2. Danker, *Lexicon*, 565.

cerning the things you have been taught" (Luke 1:4 ESV). The Greek verb commonly translated as "taught" is κατηχέω (the fourth of the important words listed above) and its meaning is critical. The word κατηχέω is the word from which "catechism" is derived, often used to describe the instruction given to a new Christian. Theophilus is, there-fore, often thought to have been a fairly new Christian, eager to learn, for whom Luke wrote his Gospel and later the book of Acts.

Danker gives two slightly different meanings for the verb κατηχέω, the second being to "teach" or "instruct." The first, more general meaning, however, is to "report" or "inform," "to share a communi-cation that one receives."[3] Therefore, if Luke is using the word in this second sense, we might deduce something quite different about the identity of Theophilus. Luke would be writing "so that you may know the certainty of the things about which you have *been informed.*" In this case, there would be no reason to suppose that Theophilus was a Chris-tian receiving instruction; perhaps instead he was a *non*-Christian who had been informed *about* Christianity. How are we to know in what sense Luke is using this word here? Some English translations have chosen the sense of "instruct," while others have opted for "inform."

As with the other terms dealt with above, the best way to determine the meaning of the word in this context is to see how the author has used the same word elsewhere. Luke uses the word κατηχέω four times in his writings. The first is here in his Prologue to Theophilus. Later, the word appears in Acts 18, when Luke is describing Apollos as "a learned man, with a thorough knowledge of the Scriptures. He had *been instructed* in the way of the Lord, and he spoke with great fer-vor and taught about Jesus accurately, though he knew only the bap-tism of John. He began to speak boldly in the synagogue. When Priscilla and Aquila heard him, they invited him to their home and explained to him the way of God more adequately" (Acts 18:24–26 NIV). But had Apollos actually been *instructed* in the "way of the Lord" (Christian-ity), or had he simply been *informed* about it, and thus did not under-stand it adequately? The impression we are given is certainly not one of someone who had received an in-depth education in Christianity, but rather of someone who may have heard certain reports and had drawn his own conclusions about their meaning. Here, then, although either meaning is possible, the context would seem to make much more sense if the word carries the meaning of being "informed" rather

3. Ibid., 534.

than "instructed," since Apollos's understanding of Christianity was obviously limited and needed correction.

The other two times Luke puts the word κατηχέω to use are both in the same passage, Acts 21. Paul has arrived in Jerusalem and is told that many Jews "have *been informed* that you teach all the Jews who live among the Gentiles to turn away from Moses" and then Paul is encouraged to go to the temple, so that "everybody will know there is no truth in these *reports* about you" (Acts 21:21, 24 NIV). Here the meaning is clear. The unfounded rumors about Paul could hardly be classified as educational "instructions," but only as *information* that has been *reported*, and certainly not *taught*. The connotation of Christian instruction would be impossible in this passage. Therefore, it seems logical that, if we have two cases where the meaning is clear, one case where the meaning probably makes more sense when interpreted in this same way, and one case where the meaning is unknown, it is most likely that the word is intended by Luke in all four of these cases to convey the same meaning, that of "being informed."

So, if Theophilus is not a Christian who has been instructed but is a non-Christian who has received information about Christianity that has come to his attention through some sort of report or communication, Luke might have had a very different motive for composing his Gospel than is sometimes supposed. Do we have any other clues that might help us in establishing Theophilus's identity to help point our way? Perhaps we do. Theophilus is a Greek name meaning "Friend of God." Some scholars have suggested that Theophilus was not an actual person at all but simply a literary device used by Luke. Instead of being addressed to a person named Theophilus, his Gospel would simply be addressed generally to "you friend of God," hence to any Christian.

But the title κράτιστος ("noblest" or "most powerful" or "most excellent") speaks against this interpretation. It clearly points to a specific individual whom Luke is addressing with the respect due his position. The key here is to discover what that position is. The usual interpretation that he was a wealthy or prominent Christian now seems unlikely in light of Luke's use of κατηχέω. Just as we considered how Luke used *that* word, therefore, perhaps we can learn something by examining Luke's usage of the title κράτιστος elsewhere. Again, this word appears four times in Luke's writings, the first being here in his Prologue. Each of the other three times this word appears, it is used in addressing the Roman governor of Caesarea in the book of Acts. The first case is in a letter from the commander of the army informing Felix the governor that he is sending Paul to him: "Claudius Lysias to his *Excellency* the governor Felix, greetings" (Acts 23:26 NRSV). Then, a few paragraphs later, when Paul first appears before Felix, the lawyer Tertullus presents the case against Paul and begins his initial address by saying, "*Your Excellency*, because of you we have long enjoyed peace" (Acts 24:3 NRSV). Felix is later succeeded by Porcius Festus, and when Paul appears before him and claims that Jesus has been resurrected, Festus exclaims, "You are out of your mind, Paul. . . . Your great learning is driving you insane," to which Paul responds, "I am not insane, *most excellent* Festus" (Acts 26:24–25 NIV).

In each of these cases, the appellation κράτιστος appears to be not merely a general complimentary address to a superior but the specific, proper way in which to address a person in this particular office, an office of governance and the administration of justice. John Mauck confirms that, not only in the New Testament but for Greek and Roman writers in general, the term "'Most Excellent,' as a form of address, was used primarily as a title for rulers or government officials."[4] Perhaps, then, a better way of rendering this word in English in all these contexts (as it is commonly translated in the letter to Felix) would be to use the phrase "Your Excellency." If we apply all this to Luke's Prologue, it conveys a somewhat different sense than we are used to hearing when we read it: "It seemed good also to me to write an orderly account for you, Your Excellency Theophilus, so that you may know the certainty of the things that have been reported to you" or "about which you have been informed." Instead of a dedication to a patron, this Prologue actually sounds like the introduction to a testimony being provided to a high-ranking government official, perhaps even in a *legal* context.

### Luke's Task

So what is Luke telling us in his entire Prologue? First, he is telling us that at least some other Christians (but how many are "many"?) have already written narrative accounts of what Jesus has done (the things he "accomplished" or "fulfilled"). These existing accounts were based on actual eyewitness reports from the original disciples, and these reports were entrusted by the disciples personally to those who wrote these accounts down.

Second, Luke is telling us that this has inspired him also to "have a

---

4. John W. Mauck, *Paul on Trial: The Book of Acts as a Defense of Christianity* (Nashville: Thomas Nelson, 2001), vii.

go" at producing such an account himself. But he is not specifically saying that this is because he thinks the earlier attempts were somehow inadequate, although that may be the case. If he does believe them to be somehow lacking, the rest of the Prologue probably gives the reason: They are less accurate or less "well ordered" than his own account.

Third, Luke takes great pains to use words that emphasize his meticulousness in producing his Gospel: He has followed and investigated everything about Jesus's life carefully and exactly. He has either spent a long time himself carrying out this investigation, or he has investigated everything "from top to bottom" in painstaking detail. And he has now put together his own account in the exact sequence and order. Again, this sounds very much like Luke is preparing to give a precise testimony about the "goings on" of the Christian community, almost as though he were presenting a legal case.

But can we trust Luke in this? Or is he just "talking himself up?" He is most certainly trying to *persuade* Theophilus of the reliability of his account. But is he pulling the wool over Theophilus's eyes? As indicated earlier, the language Luke uses implies strongly that Theophilus is definitely *not* already a Christian. Rather, Theophilus has heard *reports* about Christianity or has been *informed* about Christians, but he has not been instructed as a Christian himself.

Luke is therefore actively trying to convince Theophilus of the truth of Christianity and is doing so with the conviction of someone giving legal testimony. Now, if we once again take a look elsewhere in Luke's Gospel and the book of Acts, we will find that, when Luke himself refers to Christians giving testimony in a legal setting, there seem to be two complementary aspects of such testimony. The first is the simple point of arguing the "truth" of the legal case itself (that the one being charged is innocent). The second is a presentation of the "truth" of the gospel as the Gospel, with the goal of possibly convincing the authority before whom one is appearing to become a Christian himself. We see this especially in the exchange between Paul and Agrippa in Acts 26:27–29, where Paul is obviously both trying to plead his own innocence and trying to convert King Agrippa to "become such as I am—except for these chains" (Acts 26:29 NRSV). Indeed, this dual purpose in Christian testimony before non-Christian authorities is implied in Jesus's own words to his disciples: "You will be brought before kings and governors because of my name. This will give you an opportunity to testify" (Luke 21:12–13 NRSV). Surely, in such circumstances, then, the early Christians would have wanted to be exonerated themselves and, at the same time, would have sought to "evangelize" the authorities as well.

Luke seems, therefore, in his Prologue to be trying to persuade Theophilus that regardless of whatever reports he may have heard about Christians, they should be exonerated of any crimes. He is equally trying to persuade Theophilus himself to become a Christian, and so he is telling him (and us) that all his meticulous care in putting together this Gospel is so that Theophilus will know with complete *certainty* that the reports he has heard are true (assuming they were positive reports—if not, then he is surely trying to set the record straight). Yes, Luke is using strong terms to convince Theophilus, but if it were to turn out that his account was not accurate, he would have completely defeated himself in what he was trying to do. Luke is therefore staking everything on the accuracy and veracity of his work and is almost inviting Theophilus to test this out so that he can feel personally assured of Luke's honesty. With this understanding, then, we certainly should be able to take Luke at his word and assume that his intentions and his research are honest to the best of his ability (which, of course, does not guarantee the accuracy of the things he reports, but it seems clear that he at least believed that his account was as accurate as possible).

And what of those earlier accounts? Luke does not specifically say that he has used all of the "many" accounts mentioned when drawing up his own, but if he has "carefully investigated everything," it would be logical to assume that he has at least read most of these accounts as part of such a careful investigation. Now, either he would have judged that all of these accounts were completely useless or untrue, or else we can also logically assume that they had some sort of influence on him, whether or not he relied directly on them when writing.

Further, it may well be that he was at least partially dissatisfied with these earlier accounts, since he says that many had "attempted" (with the possible implication that they had not fully succeeded), and that he himself wanted to write an "orderly account," again with the possible implication that he did not find the other accounts to be ordered to his own taste, or at least not ordered in a way that would be beneficial to Theophilus. In addition, his claim that he had carefully investigated everything may imply that these earlier attempts were not, in his view, completely accurate or reliable. But these are all inferences and may not carry as much weight as they are sometimes believed to do. It may simply be that Luke was inspired by such earlier efforts and likewise wanted to try his hand at producing his own Gospel. Regardless, his goal in doing so was certainly to convince Theophilus of the truth as Luke understood it.

We may note at this point that the hypothetical document Q could not have been one of the "many" accounts Luke mentions here. As Q is normally depicted, it is not an "account" or "narrative" at all, and certainly not an account of anything that might be described as having "been fulfilled (or completed or accomplished) among us." (This does not mean that Luke could not have used such a source, but if he did, that source does not seem to be one of those mentioned here.) Indeed, some of Paul's letters (such as Galatians) might better qualify as an account of what has "been fulfilled" (in the prophetic sense of that term) than would Q.

Both Matthew and Mark, however, certainly qualify as such accounts. Both provide narratives of what had "been fulfilled," and both seem likely candidates for containing the traditions that had been "entrusted to us by eyewitnesses." In addition, the similarities among all three Synoptics suggest strongly that Matthew and Mark could have been used by Luke as direct sources for his own work. Unless there are compelling reasons to think otherwise (such as proof that one or the other was written after Luke), it seems most plausible that both Matthew and Mark were among the "many" accounts Luke refers to, and that they may have been used as sources to which Luke added other material based on his "careful investigations." Luke's Prologue therefore suggests that Luke's was the last of the Synoptic Gospels to be written, and it would require compelling evidence to prove otherwise.

One of the basic foundations of the Q theory, however, is the assertion that Luke did not use Matthew directly as a source. As John Kloppenborg notes, "The case for Q rests on the implausibility of Luke's direct use of Matthew or Matthew's direct use of Luke."[5] It is precisely this assertion that makes Q itself a necessary element for the theory, in order to explain where material common to Matthew and Luke (but not Mark) has come from. The arguments against Luke's use of Matthew will therefore need to be taken seriously, as they may indeed provide the "compelling evidence" to reject Matthew as one of Luke's "many" accounts, which would then require us to look elsewhere (to "proto-

---

5. John S. Kloppenborg, "On Dispensing with Q? Goodacre on the Relation of Luke to Matthew," *New Testament Studies* 49 (2003): 210–36, here 211–12.

Gospels," other lost documents, or perhaps Gnostic Gospels) in order to make up Luke's "many."

Luke also says that it "seemed good to me" to write his Gospel, indicating that the initiative was his own, not that he had been asked by Theophilus to write it. It is possible, however, that he was asked by Theophilus to provide him with an account, and Luke found the available alternatives to be unsatisfactory for this purpose. This might also account for his having written his Prologue at all. Why tell Theophilus all this to begin with? The answer could be that he is explaining why he has written such an account afresh, rather than simply giving Theophilus an existing one.

But if Luke was partially dissatisfied with earlier attempts to write Christian narratives, he certainly does not seem to be condemning them outright. It is these other accounts, after all, that he says contain the truth that had been "entrusted to us by eyewitnesses." He is not saying that they had all made everything up and it was all nonsense. If he *is* criticizing these earlier attempts, it is either because he considers them to be somewhat less accurate or complete than his own research, or they are not orderly enough for his taste.

Here we reach the crux of the matter. If the key question regarding Luke is "Why is the middle part of Luke's Gospel organized the way it is?" and Luke is telling us that he has deliberately written an "orderly account" in a logical sequence, then why is it not self-evident to us just how Luke has organized his material?

## The Q Approach

The organization of Luke's material is a particularly interesting aspect of the Synoptic Problem, because it is precisely the perceived *lack* of order in Luke's Gospel that has prevented many scholars from believing that Luke could have used Matthew as one of his sources. For example, R. H. Fuller says, "Matthew has tidily collected the Q material into great blocks. Luke, we must then suppose, has broken up this tidy arrangement and scattered the Q material without rhyme or reason all over his gospel—a case of unscrambling the egg with a vengeance!"[6] Similarly, G. M. Styler observes, "If Matthew is Luke's source, there seems to be no commonsense explanation for his order and procedure."[7] (A more measured statement of this view is offered by Kloppenborg, who states that Luke's use of Matthew would "require one to

6. Reginald H. Fuller, *The New Testament in Current Study* (London: SCM, 1963), 87.

suppose that Luke rather aggressively dislocated sayings from the context in which he found them in Matthew, often transporting them to contexts in which their function and significance is far less clear than it was in Matthew."[8]) These evaluations, that this material is arranged in Luke's Gospel *"without rhyme or reason"* or with *"no commonsense explanation"* are directly in contradiction to Luke's own stated goal of presenting the material as an "orderly" account!

Indeed, it is this very perception that Luke's Gospel *lacks* order that leads most Q scholars to the conclusion that the order of this material in Luke is the original order of it in Q as well, and that Luke simply "cut and pasted" it into his Gospel based on whatever order he found it in to begin with. But if Luke is claiming in his Prologue that his own account is even more orderly than others, he is telling us exactly the opposite, that he did not simply leave the material in whatever order he found it but arranged it *deliberately* for his own purposes. How is it possible, then, that Luke and his modern critics have such conflicting ideas about the orderliness of his Gospel? Was Luke simply so stupid that he *thought* that he was doing a good job of arranging his material, when in reality he was making a mess of the whole business?

B. H. Streeter, one of the "founding fathers" of the Q theory, seemed to think so. He states:

> If then Luke derived this material from Matthew, he must have gone through both Matthew and Mark so as to discriminate with meticulous precision between Marcan and non-Marcan material; he must then have proceeded with the utmost care to tear every little piece of non-Marcan material he desired to use from the context of Mark in which it appeared in Matthew—in spite of the fact that contexts in Matthew are always exceedingly appropriate—in order to re-insert it into a different context of Mark having no special appropriateness. A theory which would make an author capable of such a proceeding would only be tenable if, on other grounds, we had reason to believe he was a crank.[9]

This same view has been reiterated more recently by Martin Hengel:

> Luke's "Sermon on the Plain" is itself a mere "shadow" of the Sermon on the Mount. Therefore it is utterly improbable that, for example, Luke reshaped a Matthaean original. He would not have torn apart discourses

7. G. M. Styler, "Synoptic Problem," in *The Oxford Companion to the Bible*, ed. Bruce M. Metzger and Michael D. Coogan (Oxford: Oxford University Press, 1993), 726.
8. John S. Kloppenborg Verbin, *Excavating Q: The History and Setting of the Sayings Gospel* (Minneapolis: Fortress Press, 2000), 39.
9. Streeter, *Four Gospels*, 183.

which have been worked out so masterfully, but integrated them into his work. One could make a Sermon on the Mount out of the Sermon on the Plain, but not vice versa. Therefore Luke cannot be dependent on Matthew, as is constantly asserted. . . . In no way may he be made the destroyer of such a grandiose work as that of Matthew, by claiming that he copied out Matthew and in so doing—in overweening vanity—destroyed the grandiose architecture of the work along with its impressive theology. Others may attribute that to Luke, I do not.[10]

In the view of Streeter and Hengel (as with the others already quoted), the *only* theory that seems to make sense of the (inferior) order of Double Tradition material in Luke's Gospel is that Luke himself did not create that order but simply took it from where he had found it and pasted it into his own work with little or no thought as he went along. Matthew arranged his material carefully, but if Luke actually chose himself to put this material in this order, he is a crank, without common sense, acting without rhyme or reason in overweening vanity!

Yet even those who adhere to the Q theory must face the fact that, even if Luke kept the "Q" material in its original order, he also inserted other material into it in the middle section of his Gospel, adding apparently arbitrary pericopes into arbitrary points of an already arbitrary order. No adequate explanation has ever been offered for why he would have done so, and so Styler's accusation is just as applicable to the Q theory that "there seems to be no commonsense explanation for his order and procedure." After all, the argument that Luke's material is not arranged in an orderly fashion does not only apply if Luke had used Matthew as a source. It cannot be the case that Luke's order makes logical sense if he constructed it from Q, but not if he constructed it from some other source. Either Luke's order makes sense in and of itself, or it does not.[11] This, therefore, represents a major failure on the part of the Q theory, since it cannot account adequately for the evidence that Luke considered his Gospel to be well ordered.

---

10. Martin Hengel, *The Four Gospels and the One Gospel of Jesus Christ: An Investigation of the Collection and Origin of the Canonical Gospels*, trans. John Bowden (London: SCM, 2000), 176–77.

11. A "Q" response to this might be that Luke would have been content to follow Q's order if this was the only order he had ever known, but once he had been exposed to Matthew's order, he would have immediately recognized its superiority and then would have followed it. But, as has already been noted, such an argument fails to account for why Luke would have inserted his own material at apparently arbitrary points in the Q order instead of (for instance) presenting all of the Q material in a single block, then all of his own new material in another. So the objection stands that the Q theory has simply *never* given an adequate explanation for the order of Luke's Gospel.

## The Farrer Approach

Unfortunately, Q critics have not fared much better in understanding Luke than have the Q advocates. Austin Farrer, in his seminal article "On Dispensing with Q," writes:

> It may well be that we shall have to accuse St. Luke of pulling well-arranged Matthaean discourses to pieces and re-arranging them in an order less coherent or at least less perspicuous. St. Luke would not be either the first planner or the last to prefer a plan of his own to a plan of a predecessor's, and to make a less skilful thing of it. We are not bound to show that what St. Luke did to St. Matthew turned out to be a literary improvement on St. Matthew. All we have to show is that St. Luke's plan was capable of attracting St. Luke.[12]

In commenting specifically on the middle section of Luke, the Journey to Jerusalem, Farrer even admits that "St. Luke's teaching section is not so complete a literary success as St. Matthew's great discourses."[13] He goes on to propose that Luke's plan was to mirror the structure of the Torah (as has often been suggested regarding Matthew), placing the bulk of Jesus's teaching in the "great Deuteronomic superstructure,"[14] as Farrer calls the Journey to Jerusalem. And why would Luke have chosen to do this? Farrer's answer is that "we are not bound to find certain answers to such a question, probable answers will do. If there are still more probable answers than those we find, why, so much the better."[15]

Farrer as much as admits here that he does not really have a clue as to why Luke organized his material as he did, only that somehow it must have made sense to Luke, even though it never has to anyone else. Surely this is an extraordinary evaluation of an author whose self-proclaimed *goal* was to produce an "orderly account"! But Farrer also admits that his own theory of Luke's intentions might be wrong and that "still more probable answers" would be welcome. In the meantime, Farrer's claim that what is important is to show that his plan "was capable of attracting St. Luke" is epitomized in his term "Luke-pleasingness"[16] to describe what was attractive to Luke.

Farrer's successor, Michael Goulder, has expanded on Farrer's

---

12. Farrer, "On Dispensing with Q," 65.
13. Ibid., 67.
14. Ibid., 81.
15. Ibid., 77.
16. Ibid., 57.

thought, producing a detailed account of what he believes Luke intended, but Goulder's picture of Luke bears little resemblance to Luke's own description in his Prologue. First, Goulder suggests that Luke used Matthew and Mark as his sources, but *only* Matthew and Mark, using his own imagination and creativity to expound on what he found in these Gospels. Mark Goodacre describes Goulder's theory, "Goulder makes the picture simpler than does Farrer and dispenses not only with Q, M, L and any other lost document but also with 'oral material.'"[17] This leaves no room for the eyewitness reports Luke himself refers to, reducing Luke's Gospel to being simply a commentary on Mark and Matthew, or else a literary fiction (which would hardly have provided Luke with an adequate means of proving to Theophilus that what he was presenting to him was highly accurate).

Second, Goulder takes Farrer's idea that Luke is echoing the structure of the Torah (or more precisely, the "Hexateuch," adding the book of Joshua to the Torah[18]) a step further, claiming that Luke's Gospel is structured around yearly lectionary readings for use in the early church. Again, Goodacre summarizes: "Goulder proposes that not only the Passion narratives but also the whole of Matthew, Mark, and Luke are designed to be read as lectionary books, fulfilling, in order, the relevant feasts and fasts in a Jewish-Christian year."[19] Such a plan on Luke's part, however, seems to make his Gospel simply redundant, if Matthew and Mark were already written for this purpose, and gives no plausible reason why Luke would have rearranged so radically what he found in Matthew, which was already fit for such a purpose, all of which reinforces the arguments of the Q advocates. Thus, although many of Goulder's specific criticisms of the Q theory (such as those regarding the Minor Agreements) are effective, he has still failed to offer a satisfactory alternative for understanding Luke's plan.

Other followers of Farrer, such as Mark Goodacre and Mark Matson, have attempted to define further the elusive quality of "Luke-pleasingness," but in doing so they have still not yet effectively addressed the issue of Luke's overall plan. They have looked at specific examples (particularly in comparing Matthew's Sermon on the Mount with Luke's Sermon on the Plain) and demonstrated that within small, isolated portions of Luke, the rearrangement of some of this material does seem to

---

17. Goodacre, *Goulder and the Gospels*, 18.
18. The idea of the Hexateuch as a grouping of books, however, is a construct of modern scholars, and there is no evidence that such a concept would or could have existed in the mind of Luke or of his audience.
19. Goodacre, *Goulder and the Gospels*, 298.

make good sense, but the best overall solution so far seems to be that, in order to tell his story effectively, Luke tends to prefer shorter discourses to longer ones and so breaks up longer speeches, whether they come from Mark or from Matthew.[20] Goodacre writes, "Luke's narrative is constructed on the principle of creating a plausible, biographical account in which special attention is paid to movement and sequence. There would be little place in such a narrative for the kind of excessively long monologue that is Matthew's speciality."[21]

Francis Watson also has made a start in examining the redactional procedures required by Luke according to the Q theory compared to the Farrer theory in certain specific cases (again with a focus on how Luke may have dealt with the Sermon on the Mount).[22] But none of these efforts has yet addressed the larger and more fundamental issue of why Luke arranged his whole Gospel as he did. This still remains a mystery.

In this regard, the work of the Farrer school may be described as analogous to a description of how the heart and circulatory system work to move blood around the body. Such a description is absolutely vital in understanding animal life, but it does not address the issue of why blood *needs* to be circulated in the first place. To say that it is "body-pleasing" to have blood circulating is not sufficient. We need an understanding of how that blood feeds and warms the body, removes wastes, fights off disease, and so on. Without a holistic understanding of how the body is alive, the circulation of blood remains something of a mystery. This is not to diminish the work the Farrer school has done, however. The understanding of how blood circulates may be a vital step in understanding how the body is alive as a single, whole, integrated being, but it is not in itself sufficient for such an understanding. So the steps already taken in explaining how certain aspects of Matthew's material might prove to be "Luke-pleasing" provide an indispensable aid for coming to understand Luke's overall intentions, but more work needs to be done as well.

Regardless, therefore, of whether such material came from Matthew, from Q, from some other source, or from Luke's own imagination, Luke obviously believed that he was producing an orderly account, and possibly one even more orderly than had been produced before. No Syn-

---

20. Goodacre, *Case against Q,* 92–93.
21. Mark Goodacre, "A Monopoly on Marcan Priority? Fallacies at the Heart of Q," *Society of Biblical Literature Seminar Papers, 2000* (Atlanta: Society of Biblical Literature, 2000), 538–622.
22. Francis Watson, "Q as Hypothesis: A Study in Methodology," *New Testament Studies* 55 (2009): 397–415.

optic theory can be considered adequate unless and until it comes to terms with this. Until a theory is able to say, "this is why Luke considered his Gospel to be well ordered" (or else explains how Luke, who in other ways is recognized as meticulous and careful, could be such an inept bungler when it came to organizing his material), it cannot legitimately claim to have a proper understanding of what Luke's sources might have been and why he chose to use them in the way he did. This is why the most critical question regarding Luke when approaching the Synoptic Problem is to understand why Luke's Gospel, and specifically its middle section, is organized the way it is.

## A Holistic Approach

Why, then, have past attempts to understand Luke been so inadequate? There are a number of interrelated factors that have contributed to a lack of understanding, and these factors seem to be closely related to the philosophical approach that has dominated biblical scholarship in modern times, based largely on the Enlightenment philosophy of religion and a belief in the gradual development of the Gospel traditions.

One of the basic assumptions of this approach is that each of the Gospels (or at least the traditions behind them) developed over time in its relatively isolated Christian community. The Synoptics (Matthew and Luke especially) are seen as encapsulating these developing traditions and so are viewed as having been written in virtually the same way and for the same purpose as each other, their differences reflecting simply the differences between their communities' perspectives and traditions.

In this view, the common purpose of the authors of Matthew and Luke might be described as giving expression to their communities' beliefs and providing handbooks for Christian instruction. The second aspect of this is reinforced in Matthew's Gospel by its arrangement of Jesus's teachings topically into five major discourses, each of which provides a good reference point for instruction on one particular aspect of Christian faith and life. The same aspect would appear to be reinforced in Luke's Gospel by Luke's use of the word κατηχέω in his Prologue, which has typically been read as confirming that Luke's motive was to promote catechesis (Christian instruction) within his community.

This theme has been reinforced by the church's own use of the Gospels liturgically for two thousand years. The Gospels have always been read in churches in small bits, short individual pericopes that each have something to say to the church. It is therefore assumed that the Gospels of Matthew and Luke are both best approached as collections or compendia of small pericopes placed for convenience within the basic framework of a history of Jesus's life. Thus, any attempts to understand (particularly the middle section of) Luke imply that we should break it down into such short pericopes and treat each as a short topical sketch.

This appears to be what is at the heart of the Q scholars' objections to Luke having drawn his material directly from Matthew. Matthew has already organized his material in a logical way for the purpose of topical instruction. But if Luke thinks that he also has done so, he is a crank! The response of the Farrer school has not been to call into question this assumption about Luke's intentions but to accept it just as heartily, yet claiming that Luke *did* think he was arranging his material logically for such instruction. Their attempts to explain what might be a "Luke-pleasing" order have for the most part still focused on breaking Luke down into bite-sized pericopes, each appropriate for liturgical use within the Lukan community's worship. Goulder writes that Luke "regularly likes teaching pericopes of about twelve to twenty verses, which he regards as the amount a congregation (or reader) can assimilate at one time."[23]

This tendency to chop Luke's Gospel into bits in order to try to understand it is then reinforced by the nature of the Synoptic Problem itself. Luke, of all the Gospels, is most certainly based on material that has come from more than one source (as Luke himself says nearly outright in his Prologue). The study of the Synoptic Problem has therefore focused so much on what those individual sources are, and how Luke has altered this material, that it has ignored how Luke's Gospel is put together as an integral whole regardless of the possible sources of individual bits.

One additional assumption related to this last point that is made by Q scholars, but *not* by the Farrer school, is that Luke would have used all of his sources in the same way. If his purpose was to create a Christian handbook out of all the diverse material he had at his disposal, it would be logical to assume that, when he found appropriate material in one source, he would incorporate it into his document in a fashion to similar to the way he treated material taken from another source.

---

23. Goulder, *Luke: A New Paradigm*, 41.

Let us take a look one by one at each of these assumptions:

Did the Gospel traditions develop slowly over time in specific geographical locations? Based on what we know from the New Testament itself, this seems highly unlikely. Paul's letters and the book of Acts abound in references to frequent travel among the centers of Christianity throughout the Roman Empire: Jerusalem, Antioch, Ephesus, Corinth, and Rome. Paul is even able in his letter to the Romans to greet by name more than two dozen members of a church he had never personally visited (Rom 16:1–15).[24] In such a context it would be surprising if Gospels that were written in one major location remained unknown in others for any amount of time at all.

Michael B. Thompson, in his article "The Holy Internet: Communication between Churches in the First Christian Generation," analyzes the evidence for frequent and rapid communication within the early church, noting that Roman roads and especially the shipping lanes throughout the Aegean and eastern Mediterranean Seas made travel and communication relatively swift and safe. The time it would take to travel from Rome to Jerusalem (the two farthest poles of the early Christian world) would have been two to three months, with considerably less time required to travel to the other main Christian centers. Then from these centers "many churches were less than a week's travel from a main hub in the Christian network,"[25] so any Christian work of literature could easily have spread throughout the entire Christian community in much less than a year's time. Thompson therefore concludes that "the burden of proof lies on the shoulders of any who would claim that evangelists wrote *many* years apart *and* in ignorance of their predecessors."[26]

---

24. It has been suggested that Romans 16 was not a part of the original letter but was added by Paul to an additional copy sent not to Rome but to Ephesus, since the last chapter of Romans is missing from some manuscripts of the letter (see Bruce M. Metzger, *A Textual Commentary on the Greek New Testament: A Companion Volume to the United Bible Societies' Greek New Testament*, 3rd ed. [New York: United Bible Societies, 1971], 533–36). This seems extremely unlikely, however, since the situation in the Roman church that Paul is addressing (the division between rival Jewish and gentile factions of the church) would not have been relevant to the Ephesian church, so there seems to be no reason why Paul would have spent a considerable amount of money to send an irrelevant letter to the Ephesian church. E. Randolph Richards estimates that it would have cost Paul the equivalent of over two thousand dollars in early twenty-first-century money to produce and send his letter to the Romans (*Paul and First-Century Letter Writing: Secretaries, Composition, and Collection* [Downers Grove, IL: InterVarsity Press, 2004], 165). It seems far more likely that later copyists of Romans would have left out the tedious list of greetings in chapter 16, since these would have been unnecessary for later readers of the letter.
25. Michael B. Thompson, "The Holy Internet: Communication between Churches in the First Christian Generation," in *The Gospels for All Christians: Rethinking the Gospel Audiences*, ed. Richard Bauckham (Grand Rapids: Eerdmans, 1998), 68.
26. Ibid., 69.

But there is an additional factor related to the writing of the Synoptics that also argues against their having "grown up" within specific communities. If there is any possibility that the Mark and Luke mentioned in the New Testament were actually the authors of the Gospels that bear their names (or even that the traditions that developed regarding their authorship had some basis in reality), these two Gospels at least were not the work of authors who were settled members of particular communities but were written by travelers, missionaries who had contact with a large number of diverse Christian communities.

Even if we cannot prove specifically who wrote these Gospels, there is no reason to suppose that they were written by permanent residents of specific geographical communities rather than by itinerant Christian evangelists. Such travelers would have been in a far better position both to collect Christian traditions and then to publish and transmit those traditions to a broad audience. This possibility opens up a dynamic view of how the Gospels came to be written that is very different from what has previously been assumed, but this possibility seems to fit the history and life of the primitive church (and Luke's own Prologue) very well.

Next, can we safely assume that the motivation and conditions in which Matthew and Luke wrote their Gospels were similar? Or is it instead possible that they were actually written for entirely different purposes altogether? While it is possible that Matthew's Gospel was written largely as a handbook for Christian instruction, the previous examination of Luke's Prologue seems to point in a different direction for that Gospel. Even if the identity of Theophilus is unknown, it is still the case that Luke's Gospel is addressed to an individual, not to a community. Luke is clearly concerned with addressing Theophilus's personal understanding of Christianity. And as we have already explored, that understanding appears to be one of an outsider, a non-Christian, rather than a current member of the Christian community.

Luke's use of the word κατηχέω has likewise already been discussed, but it is worth reemphasizing that Luke never elsewhere uses this word to mean "instruction," but only information that has been reported to someone. Luke is therefore concerned not with Theophilus's catechesis but with confirming the truth of the information in the reports that Theophilus has received regarding Christianity. This means that Luke, unlike Matthew, is not addressing a Christian community in order to give instruction but is addressing a non-Christian individual in order to persuade, convince, and possibly convert him to Christianity. Hence, the motivation and conditions behind Matthew and Luke are very different, and therefore we need to approach these two Gospels in quite different ways in order to understand them properly.

First and foremost, this means that Luke's Gospel was not intended to be read a little bit at a time in short bursts in the context of communal worship. It was intended (probably more than any of the other Gospels) to be read from start to finish, preferably in a single session (a task that takes only about two or three hours to accomplish). Theophilus may well have gone back after his first reading to mull over individual episodes in Luke's Gospel, but he would have initially read it as one continuous narrative. This means, then, that to understand Luke properly we need to do the same and to look at his Gospel as one continuous story.

This does not invalidate its use liturgically by the church in small portions, of course. In the context of Christian worship, a three-hour reading of Luke's entire Gospel would hardly be appropriate (although we may note that even the relatively lengthy letter to the Hebrews and Paul's letter to the Romans would almost certainly have initially been read publicly in churches in their entirety). But the applicability of portions of Luke's Gospel to be used as individual pericopes liturgically does not mean that this is the purpose for which Luke wrote them down to begin with. Nor does Luke's goal of producing a convincing story for the purpose of evangelization mean that earlier liturgical sources could not have contributed some of the material Luke chose to incorporate (such as the canticles in his first two chapters). But Luke has shaped his material for a specific purpose. Neither the original source of Luke's material nor its later use by the church sheds much light on how Luke chose to organize his own work.

For this reason, the conventional approach to the Synoptic Problem actually often seems to get in the way of resolving it. By focusing on each of the Gospels as being made up of material that is either Triple Tradition, Double Tradition, or unique, it encourages us to view all the Synoptics as simply collections of material patched together. This discourages us from looking at any one of the Gospels as different in structure or purpose from the others or to look at each Gospel's unique overall shape. Hence, it is easy to assume that each of the Synoptic authors set about his task in a similar way.

But Luke hints in his Prologue that this is not the case. He does not say that other Gospels exist but that this one is better *for our particular community.* He implies, rather, that the other Gospels are not appropriate *for the very specific purpose he has in mind,* the purpose of convincing Theophilus of the truth of Christianity. He also seems to imply that what makes his Gospel unique (and hence more fit for his purpose) is that it is more accurate (perhaps). More importantly, however, it is set out in a better sequence, more logically ordered than the others, at least for Luke's intentions.

This brings us to the last of the assumptions of the Q scholars, that Luke would have used all of his sources in the same way. Surely this would have to depend on the nature of his sources and on the nature of the material he was drawing from each of them. Specifically, we may note an important difference in this regard between the contents of Mark when compared to Matthew, and so, if Luke did use both of them, there are some good reasons why he may not have used them both in the same way.

In general, all the material in the Gospels may be placed into one of two broad categories: stories about Jesus and Jesus's own teachings. These are not absolute categories, of course, because often an event (such as a healing on the Sabbath) is used as a means of illustrating a teaching point or as a launching pad for further discourses. In general, however, there tends to be a perceivable difference between these two types. Yet Mark and Matthew are quite different in respect to these categories. Mark predominantly records the events of Jesus's life, with only a few cases of teaching included. Matthew, on the other hand, includes far more parables and other sayings of Jesus mixed in with stories about Jesus.

If Luke did use both Mark and Matthew as sources, he would have found that, for the most part, the stories about Jesus are nearly the same in both of these Gospels and are usually found in a similar order. Hence, if Luke wanted to focus on Jesus's life, it would have been logical for him to have followed Mark in most cases when relating these events (without the extra "clutter" of Matthew's added teachings). The main exception to this would have been the few stories about Jesus not present in Mark but present in Matthew. So if we removed all the "teaching" category of material from all three of these Gospels we would find that, indeed, Luke did tend to use Matthew in the same way he used Mark regarding events. He included Matthew's stories in about the same order he found them in Matthew, just as he included the stories from Mark in approximately the same order he found them there. All three Synoptics therefore tell pretty much the same stories about Jesus in pretty much the same order. This is logical and understandable, especially if the events in Jesus's life did actually occur in the basic order the Synoptics tell us.

But would Luke have used Matthew's teaching material in the same way as his narrative material? There is not the same type of inherent order to sayings and parables as there is when we consider the various events of Jesus's life. It would have been quite impossible for anyone to remember exactly in what order Jesus had told every parable throughout the course of his ministry. Therefore, it makes sense to arrange this sort of material in a different way than the events, in a logical sequence rather than a chronological one. Matthew's order in his Gospel is logical and fit for his purpose of Christian instruction, distributing the teaching material in his five major discourses, alternating with the stories of Jesus's life. But if Luke did not consider this order to be fit for his *own* purpose (perhaps because he felt it to be too static and lacking in dramatic effect), there is no reason to suppose that he would have needed to use whatever material he did choose to include from Matthew in the same order it appeared in Matthew's Gospel. He might, for instance, have chosen to concentrate most of it into a single lengthy passage as Jesus journeyed toward Jerusalem.

And so we come back once more to this puzzling middle section of Luke's Gospel and the question of why Luke organized it as he did. But we now have something more to go on in attempting to understand it. We know that Luke's purpose in writing his Gospel was to convince a non-Christian of the truth of Christianity, and we know that it was intended to be read straight through from start to finish. It is therefore not a collection of short pericopes intended for individual consumption (even if it is also able to be used in this way). Primarily it is a narrative, a history, a story, with a beginning, a middle, and an end. Like every other story, it therefore has a specific overall shape, plot, and objective, and that objective (as with any story) is to bring its readers to its climax and conclusion. But how we get there and what we discover along the way are vitally important to what we are expected to find once we get to the climax, and to how we are then to understand the significance of that climax and conclusion (with the ultimate goal, in the case of Luke's Gospel, of thereby coming to Christian faith). Luke's Gospel must be approached, therefore, as an integrated whole, a literary composition that is a work of art.

Perhaps in order to understand and read Luke's Gospel, then, we need to approach Luke not just as a theologian or as a historian but as an artistic *composer*. After all, the objection that Luke's ordering of his material is less satisfactory than Matthew's is an aesthetic argument, not a theological one. This is especially evident when we notice the tone of those scholars who dismiss the idea that Luke could have intentionally rearranged Matthew, especially Hengel, who offers no justification (other than his own aesthetic sense) for his assessment that Matthew's arrangement of material was "worked out so masterfully" in a "grandiose architecture," so that if Luke had presumed to reorder it he would have done so in "overweening vanity" (or, in Streeter's opinion, he would have simply been a "crank"). Given such aesthetic judgments, we should therefore seek an aesthetic answer to this puzzle rather than a theological one. Hence, a holistic approach to Luke, one that seeks to appreciate his Gospel as a unified whole, seems essential.

# 2

## Luke's Sonata

Attempts to understand Luke as an alternate version of Matthew have not proved fruitful, as the previous discussion demonstrates. Luke's Gospel does not appear to be an effective handbook for Christian catechesis, nor should we expect it to be. Attempts to analyze Luke's middle section in a short topical pericope framework very quickly begin to break down. Patterns that appear to be present at first suddenly disappear. It seems impossible realistically to assign specific topics to different passages, and even the lengths of such passages vary tremendously. If this was indeed Luke's intention here, perhaps he really *was* a "crank," as Streeter suggested! Yet rather than letting this evaluation lead us to the conclusion that he therefore did not have any plan in mind but instead merely pasted bits and pieces together from his sources with no "rhyme or reason," or that his plan was ultimately a poor one, perhaps this ought to set alarm bells ringing in our collective brains. Maybe this simply means that Luke was actually up to something quite different, and it would make far more sense for us to discover what this was rather than pointing fingers at Luke and calling him a "crank" with "overweening vanity."

Perhaps treating Luke's Gospel not as a "manual" but as a literary composition, a *story*, makes far more sense and seems far more consistent with Luke's own statement of his intentions in his Prologue.

If we were to do so, and were to seek to appreciate his Journey to Jerusalem as a literary device and not merely a dumping ground for material that Luke did not know what else to do with, some new possibilities of understanding may be opened to us. It therefore seems best to approach this portion of his Gospel not as a string of individual pericopes but as a specific, purposeful segment within a specific, literary composition.

If we approach Luke's Gospel as a composed work of art, we may discover that its shape is similar to the shape of other works of art that are experienced *through time.* Unlike paintings or sculptures, which are static, a story changes as we read and experience it. It is, indeed, not unlike music in this respect, which we also experience through time. An understanding of the temporal shape of music may therefore also help our understanding of Luke's Gospel. A piece of music, like any story, also has a beginning, a middle, and an end, and a well-written one brings us skillfully to its climax and conclusion and, in the process, may change us profoundly.

One of the most sophisticated forms of music, and one that has a carefully crafted beginning, middle, and end, is the classical sonata form, used extensively by composers such as Haydn, Mozart, and Beethoven for the first movements of nearly all their symphonies and other works. A comparison between Luke's Gospel and a piece of music written in Sonata Form may therefore provide a potential means for us to understand Luke the composer and his intentions and craftsmanship in constructing his work.

## Sonata Form

Sonata form, like Luke's Gospel, has three parts, and it is this structure that may be enlightening for an understanding of the shape and composition of Luke's Gospel as a whole. This is not merely because these structures happen to be somewhat analogous in form, but rather because the structure of Luke and the structure of sonata form turn out to be similar in that they both provide similar solutions to a similar problem within their respective artistic media. Sonata form is an *aesthetic* solution to an *aesthetic* problem,[1] and Luke is facing the identical aesthetic problem: how to hold the interest of his audience and how

---

1. It is interesting that Mark Goodacre also turns to aesthetics in order to gain insight into Luke's composition technique, but in his case it is the medium of film. See Goodacre, *Case against Q,* 121–32.

40

to bring them with him to the climactic point of his work while potentially affecting them deeply in the process. Luke's is not a theological
problem but an artistic one. He has a considerable amount of material
he wants to present to his audience, much of it consisting of short parables and sayings. How is he to arrange this in such a way as to keep his
audience interested and to keep his plotline moving? Again, this is an
artistic problem, and his solution must therefore likewise be artistic.
But he will also use that solution as a vehicle for expressing profound
theological insights (just as the classical composers used sonata form as
a vehicle for expressing profound emotional insights). To understand
how and why, let us take a look at sonata form as an aesthetic structure
to see how it solves the problem of holding interest and building to a
satisfactory climax.[2]

Even a short piece of music needs some sort of structure in order to
carry its audience along. This prevents it from ending up at one of two
extremes: If a piece of music remains the same, simply repeating the
same phrases over and over with no variation, it quickly becomes bor-
ing and we lose interest. But if, at the other extreme, it varies too much,
with no common elements whatsoever as it continues, there ceases to
be any aspect of it for us to "hold on to," and we likewise lose interest.
A balance must be struck between repetition and variation.

One of the most basic structures in music to maintain this balance is
the "ABA" form. The first part (A) presents a specific theme. Then the
middle part (B) presents a contrasting theme, providing the interesting
variation. But then the original theme is repeated (A again), rounding
out the piece and reminding us of where we started. Not only do we
have some repetition and some variation here, but in a skillful composition the very contrast of the B section can prepare us emotionally for
the climactic and powerful return of the familiar A theme, now heard
in a more potent context.

Sonata form is a sophisticated version of this ABA form:[3] The first
part, the Exposition section, presents a series of themes in sequence.
The first part of this series (often referred to as the "First Theme
Group") is in the "home" key of the piece; then the second part (the
"Second Theme Group") is in a contrasting key. Then the series usually

---

2. See Roger Kamien, *Music: An Appreciation,* 11th ed. (New York: McGraw-Hill, 2015), 191–94. Descriptions of sonata form may be found in many music appreciation or music theory textbooks. For
instance, Kamien includes a set of CDs with musical examples.
3. Interestingly, the Gospel of Mark also sometimes uses such an ABA form on a small scale, since
the author sometimes begins a story, then interrupts it with a different event, then returns again
to the original story, but now with added insight gained from the interrupting event.

ends with a "little tail," a "Codetta," still in the contrasting key, which brings the series to a close. In shorter works in sonata form, the entire Exposition is usually repeated, but this has no specific relevance for our analogy.

The second part, the Development section, utilizes the themes that were presented in the Exposition but alters them in various ways (by shortening or lengthening them, juxtaposing them against each other, or by other techniques) and, in addition, explores many different keys. The Development section therefore provides a great deal of variation, but still with some familiarity, since the themes being developed have mostly been heard by us in their original form in the Exposition. This middle Development section does much more than simply add variation and interest, however. By exploring and subtly altering the various themes individually and in relation to each other, we come to understand them better emotionally and they come to carry more and more significance for us. These variations, along with the many key changes, help to prepare us for the ultimate climactic realization of the themes in the final part of Sonata form, the Recapitulation. The last portion of the Development section (known as the Retransition) serves a specific purpose, preparing us for the return to the "home" key and the restatement of the primary themes that will follow in the final part. The Development section does not typically advance in one continuous crescendo to this climax. Instead, it usually builds up tension to a certain point, then relieves that tension in order to build back up to an even higher point in several "waves," preparing for the ultimate climax, which usually comes at the beginning of the Recapitulation.

The final part of sonata form, the Recapitulation, returns to the basic structure of the Exposition, with the themes being presented once again in their original order but with the important difference that now there is no change of key, and so the piece ends as it began in the "home" key. Additionally, longer pieces written using sonata form (especially the first movements of symphonies) often begin with a "Slow Introduction" before the main themes of the piece are presented, and the often end with a "Coda," a "tail," which (like the shorter "Codetta" at the end of the Exposition section) is designed to bring the entire work to a completely satisfactory conclusion.

The entire sonata form structure may be illustrated in table 2.1.

Table 2.1. Sonata Form

|  | Optional Introduction | Preparatory Key |
|---|---|---|
| **Exposition:** | 1st Theme Group | Home Key |
|  | 2nd Theme Group | Contrasting Key |
|  | Codetta | Contrasting Key |
| [if repeated] | 1st Themes repeated | Home Key |
|  | 2nd Themes repeated | Contrasting Key |
|  | Codetta | Contrasting Key |
| **Development:** | 1st and 2nd Themes |  |
|  | developed and altered | Many Keys |
|  | Retransition | back to: |
| **Recapitulation:** | 1st Theme Group | Home Key |
|  | 2nd Theme Group | Home Key |
|  | Codetta | Home Key |
|  | Optional Coda | Ending in Home Key |

The first and final major sections (the Exposition and Recapitulation) are therefore highly structured in a specific way, requiring certain themes and key changes to occur at particular points. The middle section, however, the Development, is unstructured, freely using themes (or bits of themes) from the Exposition, mixing them around, revealing new relationships between them and building up to their final Recapitulation, which occurs once more in a structured way. It is therefore impossible to "outline" or map the Development section of a sonata in the way that the beginning and ending can be mapped, and yet it is a vitally important element in the overall structure. No one would suggest that the first movement of Beethoven's Fifth Symphony is chaotic or has "no rhyme or reason," and yet any attempt to formulate a sequential plan of its Development section in some sort of an outline based on its themes would be hopelessly inadequate and would ultimately fail. One of the most sophisticated and rigidly structured of all forms of music, therefore, requires its middle section to be formally unstructured!

It is also clear that, although we can break a symphonic movement down and analyze it in detail, such a piece of music is intended to be listened to as one continuous piece. We do not listen to a few bars today, then another selection from it tomorrow. We certainly *could* do that in order to focus on what the composer was doing at one particular point in the piece, so that we might gain a better understanding of his skill or of how he has handled one specific aspect of a theme, but even such a systematic analysis would surely be for the purpose of enhancing our appreciation for the whole piece. Such a procedure would be useless if we never listened to the entire work again straight through from start to finish.

What I suggest here, then, is that, faced with the same aesthetic problem (how to hold his audience's interest throughout a fairly long, continuous piece, while at the same time preparing for the climactic moment of his work), Luke the composer hit upon a solution that shares many of the same characteristics as the sonata-form solution. Like a musical piece composed using sonata form, Luke's Gospel is structured in a similar three-part way, with the first and final parts displaying a logical, chronological sequence, but the middle part being a much more "freewheeling" section that explores recurring themes in a manner similar to the Development section of the classical sonata form. This solution was not only "Luke-pleasing" but also hopefully "Theophilus-pleasing"—ultimately "church-pleasing." With a proper analysis it should even be "scholar-pleasing" as well.

It would be absurd, of course, to suggest that Luke was somehow familiar with a musical form that would not be invented until more than a millennium and a half after his death, but if we were to examine the aesthetic senses of many human cultures throughout history we would find that there are certain common threads throughout, such as a desire for symmetry, yet with a corresponding need for contrast, which most human cultures have found aesthetically pleasing. Sonata form is specifically designed to exploit the concepts of symmetry and contrast to their fullest (with symmetry between the Exposition and Recapitualation and contrast both in the two Theme Groups of the Exposition and, to an even greater extent, in the Development section). But the classical composers who employed sonata form did not consider it to be a rigid and confining form, but rather one that flowed naturally, almost inevitably, from their own aesthetic sensibility. If we were to examine other human art forms, we might find yet more examples that resemble sonata form in certain aspects. (For example, it would not be a difficult exercise to compare the structure of a Gothic cathedral to sonata form, with the façade corresponding to the Introduction, the nave to the Exposition, the transept to the Development—with themes from the nave being explored in different directions—the quire to the Recapitulation—similar to but shorter than the nave—and the apse to the Coda.)

We should not be surprised, then, if Luke's own sense of aesthetic symmetry and his desire to construct an engaging literary work led him to compose his Gospel using a "natural" structure similar to sonata form, or that he employed dramatic effects similar to those used by the classical composers. But we need to be careful not to carry this analogy too far. This comparison does not suggest that there should necessarily be a specific correlation between the structure of the first and final parts of Luke's Gospel and the Exposition and Recapitulation portions of sonata form. They are both carefully structured in their own ways, but we should not consciously look for anything analogous to the different theme groups or key changes in sonata form reflected in Luke. As we shall see, Luke certainly does present his basic themes in a logical order in his own "Exposition" (up to 9:50), and these will reach their culmination in his "Recapitulation" (beginning with 19:28) after being explored in his "Development" (the passage between these two verses, the Journey to Jerusalem or Travel Narrative), but we need not look for any closer similarities in his overall structure. It is the techniques he uses to develop his themes in the middle part of his Gospel that makes the comparison most valid, and this is where our analysis will need to focus.

There are a number of ways we might approach Luke's Development section in this light, which are not mutually exclusive. Just as a classical composer uses melody, harmony, and rhythm in different ways in order to create the entire effect of his Development section, so Luke displays an equal depth of ability in using various methods in constructing his. We might say that the analysis offered in this book is primarily a "melodic" one, emphasizing the various themes Luke is developing and how they relate to each other. This is comparable to identifying the motifs in one of Beethoven's symphonies (whose Development sections tended to be longer and more involved than those of Haydn or Mozart) and exploring how he has broken these motifs down and used them in relation to each other. This serves to give us one level of understanding, but other analyses might be equally fruitful.

For instance, such a thematic exploration would not necessarily touch on the subject of key changes, which are also critical in sonata form. In his Development sections, Beethoven frequently uses a significant chord as a means of making a transition from one key to another. Similarly, Mark Goodacre and Mark Matson have identified key words that Luke often uses in order to make a transition from one pericope to another, so the analysis already done by scholars of the Farrer school might be described as more of a "harmonic" analysis of Luke.[4] Such techniques employed by Luke may be just as important as the concept of thematic development and may be as crucial to Luke as are key changes to Beethoven. But we might also note that Beethoven (even more than other classical composers) often employed dramatic and sudden key changes, startling in their effect, and so we should not be surprised to find Luke also occasionally making sudden transitions in his own Development section in order to grab his audience's attention, both to hold interest and to make a specific point.

A "rhythmic" analysis of Luke might also be possible. One of the barriers to understanding Luke's purpose in his Journey to Jerusalem has been his seeming resistance to dividing it up into clear-cut topical sections of similar length. Sometimes he seems to spend a very short time on one theme; then next he will continue a similar theme for quite some time. Rather than indications that Luke is not purposeful, however, these changes are probably an indication that he is employing variations in "rhythm" in order to keep interest. Short pithy sayings are often juxtaposed against longer parables, or sometime strung in succession, and then Luke will deliberately present several longer parables in sequence, again varying the rhythm.

We would also not expect Beethoven to present all the variations of one particular theme at one point in his Development section and then move on to the next theme in a "topical" sequence. He might indeed focus on one particular theme for some time, exploring it in depth; at other times, however, he might present one short burst of such a theme and then immediately juxtapose another theme against it so that we hear the connections and the contrasts between them as well.

Such techniques enable a composer, and also an expert author such as Luke, to build tension and then relieve it in order to build it yet further. This is especially evident in Luke's handling of Jesus's conflicts with the Pharisees, which sometimes seem to be coming to a head, only

---

4. Mark Matson, "Luke's Rewriting of the Sermon on the Mount," in *Questioning Q: A Multidimensional Critique*, ed. Mark Goodacre and Nicholas Perrin (London: SPCK, 2004), 50–62.

to be left for a considerable time while Luke pursues other themes. This maintains the overall dramatic tension of the entire work and builds anticipation for the final conflict between Jesus and the Pharisees in Jerusalem in Luke's Recapitulation.

Such a use of material in Luke's Journey to Jerusalem therefore seems to be totally consistent with his methodical style and makes complete sense in the overall structure and dramatic effect of his Gospel. Rather than being evidence that Luke is behaving like a "crank" or merely pasting in material from other sources "without rhyme or reason," this handling of material demonstrates that Luke is deliberately crafting his presentation of Jesus's story with just as much skill as Mozart and Beethoven showed in crafting their symphonies.

## Luke's Development Section

If the Journey to Jerusalem is directly analogous to the Development section of sonata form, we will probably not be able to produce a viable outline of the structure of this section, but we ought to be able to plot the most important individual themes that are being developed, how they relate to one another, and how the whole passage works toward the climax in the final part of the Gospel. If such an analysis makes logical sense out of what has been described by others as "scrambled" or "without common sense," we will have gone a long way toward understanding Luke's purpose and artistry in composing his Gospel. Then and only then can the questions of what sources Luke may have used and how he may have used them be addressed seriously.

The whole Gospel of Luke, as a single composition, tells the story of Jesus's life, death, and resurrection. In the first third of the Gospel, up to 9:50, we hear of Jesus's birth, a bit of his childhood, then his baptism and a concise description of his ministry and teachings. The high point of this segment of Luke comes with the transfiguration, where we not only receive confirmation of Jesus's divine nature but are also directed to look forward to his passion, which will soon transpire in Jerusalem. This entire sequence, therefore, forms the Exposition section of Luke's Gospel, in which we are introduced to Jesus and his basic teachings. Luke could at this point have proceeded directly to Jesus's entry into Jerusalem, as in both Matthew and Mark. Instead, Luke chooses first to explore in much greater depth the significance of Jesus's teachings and of his life on earth. In 9:51, Jesus resolutely sets out toward Jerusalem, where his teachings and actions will ultimately be put to the test in the final Recapitulation segment of the Gospel (which will begin at 19:28 with the Triumphal Entry into Jerusalem).

But Jesus does not proceed to Jerusalem immediately, or on his own. Instead, he invites others to follow him and to follow his teachings as his disciples. The entire passage from Luke 9:51 to 19:27, the Development section of the Gospel, might therefore be said to deal with the matter of discipleship, and what better mechanism could Luke have employed to treat this subject than a journey narrative, a story literally about following Jesus? Jesus has "set his face to go to Jerusalem" (9:51 NRSV), where his own faithfulness toward God and discipleship will be tested. Who will be those who will follow him faithfully, and who will be those who oppose him? These questions have great bearing on the whole plot of the story, of course (awaiting their resolution in Jerusalem), but this also poses the personal question to Theophilus himself regarding his own personal choice either to embrace Christianity or to reject it. Presenting this choice, as we have seen, seems to be one of Luke's intentions in writing his Gospel. An exploration of what discipleship entails, therefore, has significance aesthetically, theologically, and personally, and it is literally at the center of Luke's whole Gospel.

In this light, then, throughout this whole passage Luke gives numerous alternating descriptions of those who are true disciples, true members of the coming kingdom of God, true children of God (characterized as giving and compassionate), as opposed to those who reject Jesus and the coming kingdom, whether out of greed or out of a desire for power. Over all this is the theme that God "sees all" and is ready to judge between the faithful and the unfaithful, to condemn those who think themselves righteous but are not, to care for those who are oppressed, and to call others to repentance. Those who are true disciples are encouraged to continue praying, to serve God faithfully (but not as the "greedy" do in order to receive a reward), to bear up under persecution from those who are not disciples, and to be patient when it appears that the kingdom will never come. Jesus, of course, is the epitome of the true disciple, and his own actions exemplify all these characteristics.

As noted before, these themes are not dealt with by Luke topically, in sequence one after another (and hence in isolation from one another), any more than we would expect Beethoven to give us each iteration of a given theme altogether at one point in one of his Development sections (even though that is precisely what happens in the Exposition and Recapitulation). Instead, we hear a bit of one theme juxtaposed against another, altered slightly each time it reappears, so that as we come to hear all of the different variations in context we come to understand the depth and interrelatedness of all of the themes. So Luke uses Jesus's teachings to illustrate all of his ideas in a continuous progression, playing them off each other, constantly reorganizing them (developing them) in new ways. In this skillful manner, Luke produces an ever-building tension, particularly between Jesus and his antagonists, the Pharisees, who are often used as illustrations of those who are not true disciples. Each pericope tends to relate to the one before it and to the one following it, either reillustrating a theme, offering a deliberate contrast, or sometimes moving on to a new aspect. The entire unified journey, therefore, seems to be far more effective for producing an integrated understanding of Christian life and discipleship than if Luke had dealt with his topics one by one.

The final contrast between true and false disciples comes in Luke's "Retransition" passage where the Rich Young Man, who thinks himself righteous but is unwilling to give up his wealth to follow Jesus, is contrasted with Zacchaeus, a rich man who knows he is not righteous but voluntarily redistributes his own wealth and does become a true disciple. This will lead to Jesus's final entry into Jerusalem, to the final confrontation between Jesus and the Pharisees, and ultimately to the demonstration of Jesus's own faithfulness in Luke's Recapitulation in the last portion of his Gospel.

Under the broad headings of the faithful, the unfaithful, and God's response to them both, then, we may identify the following themes:

1. The Faithful (True Disciples):

   a. Recognize and accept Jesus
   b. Give to God and others
   c. Pray to God
   d. Serve God faithfully with no thought of reward
   e. Persevere under persecution, waiting for God's deliverance

2. The Unfaithful (False Disciples):

   a. Reject Jesus
   b. Are greedy and selfish
   c. Ignore God
   d. Fail or refuse to serve God

    e. Hinder and persecute true disciples

3. God:

    a. Calls the lost to repentance and faith
    b. Cares for the weak and oppressed
    c. Answers those who pray
    d. Rewards faithful servants
    e. Punishes the unfaithful

In each case, the themes identified under one heading relate directly to the corresponding themes under the others. For instance, theme c in each case deals with the attitude of prayer and God's response to that attitude. But these are not "absolute" categories, of course. For instance, category 1b covers a multitude of subthemes—giving up everything for God, having compassion, caring for others, and so on—but all of these attitudes may be contrasted with the basic characteristic of the unfaithful: greed (category 2b).

Other schemes of categorizations are possible. Just as no two musicologists would give exactly the same explanation of how a particular Development section from a Beethoven symphony is constructed, so what is being suggested here is not intended as a definitive description. Indeed, one of the strengths of this type of development of themes is that it opens up the possibility for the listener or reader to discover new relationships and insights each time the passage is encountered.

Nor should we expect any given pericope to deal exclusively with only one of these themes, since they are all interconnected. But this is the whole point. Luke is building up a complete picture of what it means to follow Jesus (or to refuse to do so). Such an understanding of the scope of this entire sequence is the opposite of the "normal" approach, which sees this passage as a hodgepodge of mostly unrelated sayings. Instead, we will explore how these elements are all related. These (perhaps slightly arbitrary) categories will serve to give us some basic pointers to look out for and will help us to see some of the distinctions and contrasts Luke is making.

In the following tables, the entire passage has been broken down into its constituent pericopes (based on the divisions in Aland's *Synopsis Quattuor Evangeliorum*)[5] in order to examine the ebb and flow of

---

5. *Synopsis Quattuor Evangeliorum*, ed. Kurt Aland, 4th ed. (Stuttgart: Württembergische Bibelanstalt, 1967), 255–361.

the identified themes as they are developed in relation both to each other and to the dramatic buildup Luke is crafting in this segment of his Gospel. Although it is one continuous passage with no "outline" as such, I have divided it into a number of "waves" simply for convenience. This will allow us to pause periodically to see where we have come from and where we are going, as Luke builds and relieves tension in his story. These "waves" have not been defined based on an analysis of climactic points, however. Instead, the passage has simply been broken up at chapter divisions in such a way that each "wave" contains approximately the same number of pericopes. While chapter breaks may have originally been applied at specific points precisely because there seemed to be a logical pause at these points, such breaks are still somewhat arbitrary. The use of them here is simply intended to keep us from getting lost, not to imply any sort of actual underlying structure.

## First Wave (Luke 9–10)

Luke does not ease us into his topic but begins his Development section as forcefully as Beethoven at his most vehement. If Luke is trying to convince Theophilus to become a Christian, he is certainly not trying to seduce him by painting a rosy picture of what that might mean. Jesus has just come from the transfiguration, where he has discussed his "exodus," which he will achieve in Jerusalem through his death (9:28–31), and he is resolutely facing this as the most faithful follower of God (9:43–45). At the very start of his journey he asks for the same commitment from his own disciples (9:57–62). The entire Development section therefore begins (as it will end) with the stark choice given to all who encounter Jesus as to whether they will be faithful or unfaithful. Hence, the first few pericopes all deal with this choice.

**Table 2.2. The Beginning of Luke's Development Section (Luke 9–10)**

| Verse | Pericope | Theme |
|---|---|---|
| 9:51 | Decision to Go to Jerusalem | 1a—Accepting |
| | Jesus in his obedience and perseverance to his calling epitomizes the faithful disciple, accepting God's will. | |

| 9:52–56 | Jesus Is Rejected by Samaritans | 2a—Rejecting |
| | | 2e—Hindering |
| | | 3e—Punishing |

By refusing to welcome the disciples, the Samaritans show themselves to be among the "unfaithful." They both reject Jesus and hinder the faithful. James and John presume to take God's place in condemning and punishing the unfaithful, but Jesus rebukes them, since it is only God who may condemn them.

| 9:57–62 | On Following Jesus | 2d—Failing |

Other potential disciples are unwilling to commit themselves completely to Jesus. Thus, at the very beginning of the journey we encounter both those who openly oppose God and his faithful ones, and those who want to be faithful but who fail the test because they are unwilling to do what is required to be faithful.

| 10:1–12 | Commissioning the Seventy | 1a—Accepting |
| | | 1d—Serving |
| | | 2a—Rejecting |
| | | 2e—Hindering |
| | | 3e—Punishing |

In contrast to both of these groups are the Seventy, who are faithful to Jesus and are sent out to serve him by preparing his way. The encounters they have will not only test their own faithfulness but will also test those whom they encounter as to whether they receive them as true servants of Jesus. Those who do not, who reject and hinder them, will be subject to God's judgment and punishment (not James's and John's).

| 10:13–15 | Woes Pronounced on Galilean Cities | 3e—Punishing |

The preceding theme is continued, as Jesus pronounces woes against those cities that have already refused to accept him.

| 10:16 | He Who Hears You Hears Me | 1a—Accepting |
| | | 2a—Rejecting |

Jesus concludes his instructions to the Seventy by reiterating that the response given to the faithful is equivalent to the response given to Jesus himself, and to God. The choice is clear, and there is no middle ground. The faithful accept what comes from God, but the unfaithful do not.

10:17-20   The Return of the Seventy                          3d—Rewarding

    The Seventy return after their faithful service, and Jesus promises them that God will reward them for their faithfulness, just as he will punish the unfaithful.

10:21-22   Jesus's Thanksgiving to the Father                 1a—Accepting
                                                             2a—Rejecting

    Jesus's advice to the Seventy to rejoice leads into his own rejoicing, which once again involves a contrast between those (the children) who see the truth (and accept it), and those (the supposedly wise) who fail to see the truth (and so reject it). The truth in question, of course, includes the truth that Jesus is one with the Father, and the recognition of this is part of accepting Jesus.

10:23-24   The Blessedness of the Disciples                   1a—Accepting

    The disciples are (as we would hope) among the accepting ones, and the ones who recognize Jesus's true nature. We have now reached the "crest" of this first "wave" with this declaration of the blessedness of the faithful (in contrast to the impending doom of the unfaithful).

10:25-28   The Lawyer's Question                              1d—Serving

    Having made these contrasts, Luke is now ready to begin developing in more detail the characteristics of the faithful, but this is still very much in relation to what has preceded this pericope. The lawyer (like the potential disciples from 9:57) wants to be faithful but may be held back by his inability to commit himself fully. But he does know that faithfulness includes obedience to God's commands. What he may not be prepared for (nor may Luke's entire audience) is how uncompromising those commands really are.

10:29-37   The Parable of the Good Samaritan                  1b—Giving

    The parable of the Good Samaritan serves several purposes at this point. It signifies (with blazing trumpets perhaps) the entrance of the major theme that the most prominent characteristic of the faithful is uncompromising selfless giving. It also emphasizes, however, that such giving is not restricted to those whom one thinks are in the right "camp." The faithful one in the parable is, after all, a Samaritan, one of those who only a few verses back were the ones who had rejected Jesus. We must therefore not prejudge anyone or any group as "unfaithful." (This will apply also to the Pharisees later on.) We must be willing to give uncompromisingly, with no restrictions.

    This parable also gives the first faint echoes of the theme of God calling the lost to repentance. God gives not only to the faithful but also to the unfaithful, thus answering James's and John's impetuous desire to bring judgment too soon on those who reject God, instead of offering them a chance for repentance.

| 10:38–42 | Mary and Martha | 1a—Accepting |
| | | 1b—Giving |

Following immediately at this point, the story of Mary and Martha marks a transition (to a more serene key perhaps). Martha is certainly among the faithful and also serves as an example of selfless giving (although she is not entirely *self*-giving, since she asks that Mary be made to help her). Yet, like the lawyer, she is perhaps too quick to limit what such giving might entail. It is Mary, therefore, who is commended by Jesus for giving her complete attention to his wisdom and thus giving her acceptance and recognition of Jesus's connection to God. Her willingness to listen to Jesus and to God provides a transition to the theme of prayer, which will begin the next "wave."

## Second Wave (Luke 11)

Having thus begun by presenting the unavoidable choice Theophilus (and all of us) must eventually make, Luke now settles into exploring the themes of what choosing to be a true disciple will really involve. Lest readers become too discouraged by such a daunting task, however, Luke will now show us that God is with us to help us. But it will not be long before we find ourselves thrust into the inevitable conflict that will arise. To illustrate this, Luke will begin a series of digressions here (from prayer to the Holy Spirit to warnings against evil spirits to the importance of recognizing what is true), which he will then roll back in his third "wave."

Table 2.3. The "Second Wave" of Luke's Development (Luke 11)

| Verse | Pericope | Theme |
|---|---|---|
| 11:1–4 | The Lord's Prayer | 1c—Praying |

Perhaps inspired by Mary's example of undivided attention, the disciples now approach Jesus to learn about prayer. Luke's version of the Lord's Prayer provides the root for the life of the disciples, their connection to God, which will give them their needed strength.

| 11:5–8 | The Importunate Friend at Midnight | 1c—Praying |
| | | 1e—Persisting |

Jesus continues his instruction on prayer, emphasizing that we must keep on, even when it does not seem that God is listening. This marks the entrance of yet another theme regarding discipleship, that the faithful must persevere in spite of hardships (including the seeming silence of God).

| 11:9–13 | Encouragement to Pray | 1e—Persisting |
| | | 3c—Answering |

But such patience and persistence will be rewarded, and God will answer the prayers of the faithful, giving them good gifts. And the greatest gift of all is the Holy Spirit.

| 11:14–23 | The Beelzebub Controversy | 2a—Rejecting |

Here we appear to have a rather sudden transition, but it is a necessary one so that Luke can make yet another contrast between the faithful and the unfaithful. It is the Holy Spirit, given by God to those who pray, who is both the *source* of the recognition by Mary and the disciples of Jesus's true nature and the *object* of that recognition as well, since it is the presence of the Holy Spirit of God in and with Jesus that Mary and the others are recognizing.

In sharp contrast, the unfaithful here not only fail to recognize the Holy Spirit in Jesus but falsely accuse him of having an *evil* spirit, the exact opposite of the Holy Spirit. Verse 23 ("Whoever is not with me is against me") reemphasizes the stark choice before us all, with no middle ground available.

| 11:24–26 | The Return of the Evil Spirit | 2d—Failing |

This leads into a warning against complacency. Those who do turn to Jesus must continue in their faithfulness, or they will easily slip back into a state of unfaithfulness.

| 11:27–28 | True Blessedness | 1d —Serving |

Hence Jesus reemphasizes that it is those who *continue* to be faithful (through their obedience) who are truly blessed.

| 11:29–32 | The Sign of Jonah | 1a—Accepting |
| | | 2a—Rejecting |

And so we return again to the matter of recognizing and accepting Jesus and recognizing and accepting the Holy Spirit within him. The unfaithful want proof that Jesus is who he claims to be (and that he is not of Beelzebub), but such a demand is itself already a rejection. In contrast, the queen of Sheba and the Ninevites *did* accept God's presence with Solomon and Jonah and so are among the faithful.

| 11:33 | Concerning Light | 1a—Accepting |
|-------|------------------|--------------|

The theme of recognizing the truth (specifically the truth about Jesus) continues in the next two sayings, which both have to do with light and with seeing. As with the lamp on the stand, the truth about Jesus is there to be seen by anyone willing to look and accept it. It is not hidden away in secret.

| 11:34–36 | The Sound Eye | 1a—Accepting |
|----------|---------------|--------------|

Therefore, anyone who is truly able to see truth, who is not clouded by darkness, will recognize and accept Jesus. Only those who choose darkness, who choose the lie instead of the truth, fail to recognize him.

| 11:37–54 | Discourses against the Pharisees and Lawyers | 2c—Ignoring<br>2d—Failing<br>2e—Hindering<br>3e—Punishing |
|----------|-----------------------------------------------|-------------------------------------------------------------|

This is one of the most important points in Luke's whole development section. The continuing contrast between the faithful and the unfaithful comes to a head when the Pharisee here challenges Jesus about washing hands. It is a far subtler challenge than accusing him of being in league with Satan, but a challenge nonetheless. Jesus's response reiterates everything that has been said up to this point about the unfaithful. Indeed, we might include every subcategory under the "faithless" here, but especially that Jesus accuses the Pharisees and lawyers of ignoring and failing to serve God (by insisting on their own traditions instead of understanding what those traditions really mean), and of hindering the faithful (killing and approving the killing of the prophets). Therefore they will be held responsible, judged by God.

In terms of the plot of Luke's story, we are now at a critical point. After Jesus has delivered his "woes" we are told that the Pharisees now begin to "press him hard and to provoke him . . . lying in wait for him, to catch him" (11:53–54 ESV). They are not yet seeking to do him harm, but the plot has definitely begun to "thicken." Their opposition to Jesus will now continue as an undercurrent, ready to bubble up at any time to produce the conflicts necessary to a good story.

## Third Wave (Luke 12)

Luke has now spent a considerable amount of time building up to this crest. He has made numerous contrasts between the faithful and the unfaithful. Even the earlier reprieve, marked by the first teachings about prayer, was short-lived as we were plunged suddenly into the conflict between Jesus and his antagonists. Having now reached this point, however, Luke the expert storyteller is going to bring the level of tension down somewhat, but without dissipating it altogether. He will now concentrate for a time not so much on conflicts with the unfaithful as on the qualities of the faithful (although this will often be accomplished by examples of how *not* to behave). To achieve this, he will work his way out of his previous digressions and back (briefly) to the subject of prayer.

This new focus will produce its own sort of tension, however. Because Luke interrupted his earlier excursion into prayer so quickly, we now never know when such an interruption will come again. As listeners to the story we are now more attentive than we might have been if he had taken time earlier to explore the qualities of the faithful at a more leisurely pace.

**Table 2.4. The "Third Wave" of Luke's Development (Luke 12)**

| Verse | Pericope | Theme |
|---|---|---|
| 12:1 | The Leaven of the Pharisees | 2d – Failing |

The transition to teachings about how the faithful should live is gradual. Jesus first turns from talking *to* the Pharisees to talking to his disciples *about* the Pharisees. This will allow him to show the contrast between their deeds (of hypocrisy, failing to serve God whom they claim to serve) and the deeds of the faithful.

| Verse | Pericope | Theme |
|---|---|---|
| 12:2–9 | Exhortation to Fearless Confession | 1a – Accepting |
| | | 3b – Caring |
| | | 3d – Rewarding |
| | | 3e – Punishing |

But such hypocrisy does not go unnoticed by God, who sees everything the Pharisees do, though they might wish to keep their actions concealed. God also sees the worth of the weak and lowly and cares for them. Therefore, Jesus warns the people not to fear the Pharisees or to be afraid of the repercussions of not following them, but to consider what God thinks, who will reward the faithful (and the weak) but punish the unfaithful. It is important for the faithful themselves not to conceal anything—and specifically not to conceal their acceptance of Jesus, reemphasizing that they will be rewarded by God for this acceptance. So here we have once again returned to the theme of recognizing and accepting what is true.

| 12:10 | The Sin against the Holy Spirit | 2a – Rejecting |
| | | 3e – Punishing |

Luke finally returns at this point to the Holy Spirit, so that everything he has relayed to us from the Beelzebub controversy onward is seen in its proper context. Failing to recognize the Holy Spirit at work in Jesus is to sin against the Holy Spirit, and this sin brings down upon oneself the full weight of God's judgment as it has been described.

| 12:11–12 | The Assistance of the Holy Spirit | 1a – Accepting |
| | | 1c – Praying |
| | | 2e – Hindering |
| | | 3c – Answering |

Returning to sayings about the Holy Spirit at this point allows Luke to pick up where he left off regarding prayer, but now with the added meanings explored in the intermediate passages. God gives the Holy Spirit to those who pray, and it is this Holy Spirit who enables the faithful to proclaim publicly (and hence not in concealment) their acceptance of Jesus, especially when faced with the open opposition of the unfaithful.

| 12:13–15 | Warning against Avarice | 2b – Taking |

We now have another seemingly abrupt change of theme, as Luke begins to contrast the greed of the unfaithful with the selfless giving of the faithful. But even this shift has been prepared for, since Luke is now at long last returning to the themes introduced in the parable of the Good Samaritan, taking one further step back from his series of digressions about prayer, the Holy Spirit, and punishment of the unfaithful.

But Luke is also picking up on the warning Jesus had recently given against the Pharisees' hypocrisy. Now the warning is against greed, which is, for Luke, the most prominent characteristic of the unfaithful. The transition has thus been accomplished, and Luke will now focus on the theme of greed versus giving.

| 12:16–21 | The Parable of the Rich Fool | 2b – Taking |
| | | 3e – Punishing |

The parable of the Rich Fool shows that being greedy, taking everything for oneself, accomplishes nothing in the end. Once again, God sees all and judges all.

| 12:22–32 | Anxieties about Earthly Things | 3b – Caring |

Likewise, God sees the weak, the lowly, and the humble who are not greedy, and he cares for them.

| 12:33–34 | Treasures in Heaven | 1b – Giving |
| | | 3d – Rewarding |

Therefore the faithful should be giving, not greedy. God sees this as well and rewards it.

| 12:35–40 | Watchfulness | 1d – Serving |

Giving entails giving of oneself in service, not merely giving up material possessions. The faithful are not selfishly concerned with themselves, but are concerned with serving God.

| 12:41–48 | Faithfulness | 1d – Serving |
| | | 2d – Failing |
| | | 3d – Rewarding |
| | | 3e – Punishing |

Such service is also seen and rewarded. But failing or refusing to serve God will be punished. The stark choice is once again presented. There is no middle ground. One is either faithful or unfaithful.

| 12:49–53 | Division in Households | 1e – Persisting |
| | | 2e – Hindering |

Because there is no middle ground, each of us must make our own choice whether to be one of the faithful or one of the unfaithful. This will inevitably lead to tension and division between true disciples and false, with the false violently opposing the true. Jesus must face this opposition himself (his "baptism in fire"), but so must all the faithful.

| 12:54–56 | Interpreting the Times | 1a – Accepting |

Jesus also gives a warning here that the moment of making that choice is fast approaching for all who would be disciples. Jesus's own baptism of fire will require a timely response from the faithful.

| 12:57–59 | Agreement with One's Accuser | 3e – Punishing |

The importance of this moment of decision is reemphasized by the saying about being reconciled to one's accuser. Once again, the one to fear is the one who "has authority to cast into hell" (12:5 NASB). The only way to avoid such punishment is to accept Jesus and choose the good.

## Fourth Wave (Luke 13–15)

Throughout the entire third "wave" there has been no sign of opposition to Jesus himself, allowing us time to understand better what it means to be one of the faithful. Yet, interestingly, whenever Luke begins to focus on the theme of selfless giving, he follows it with the antagonism that such selflessness and faithfulness elicits from those who resist God (as illustrated by the saying about divisions in households). Luke has also made it clear that there is a stark choice before all of us to choose either good or evil, to be true disciples or false, and that there can be no middle ground.

Luke now betrays the fact that he is not simply telling a story, one that may be interesting but exists in and of itself apart from its audience. To be told the story of Jesus is to be presented with the inescapable choice of whether or not to follow him. If Luke has successfully drawn Theophilus (and us) into the story at this point, he (and we) cannot remain unaffected. The choice to follow Jesus or to reject him has been presented, and to fail to choose one way or the other is itself a choice *not* to follow. Luke will now begin to concentrate on how God is present to call readers to make the right choice and to help us to choose the good and reject evil.

**Table 2.5. The "Fourth Wave" of Luke's Development (Luke 13–15)**

| Verse | Pericope | Theme |
|---|---|---|
| 13:1–5 | Repentance or Destruction | 3a – Calling |

The warning that the time of choice is fast approaching does not mean that it is already too late, however. Those who have not been faithful in the past are called to repent and to choose good now, before the time of judgment fully arrives. Thus, Jesus's response to the reports of people being killed is both a warning and a sign of hope: "Unless you repent, you will all perish as they did" (13:3 NRSV), that is, you will perish without hope.

| 13:6–9 | The Parable of the Barren Fig Tree | 3a – Calling |

The parable of the Fig Tree repeats this warning and hope. God is patient, willing to give everyone a chance to repent and bear fruit (to be a true disciple), unlike those (such as James and John) who would call down judgment immediately. But the time for this choice is limited, and God will not wait forever.

| 13:10–17 | The Healing of the Crippled Woman on the Sabbath | 2c – Ignoring<br>2e – Hindering<br>3b – Caring |

This motif of time (which has been present ever since Jesus's saying about interpreting the times) carries over into the next story. God's time of deliverance has arrived for the crippled woman (after eighteen years), and, significantly, that time is the time of the Sabbath. This, however, enrages Jesus's opponents, who (also significantly) fail to recognize God's time of deliverance. So once again, goodness provokes the reaction of increased opposition from the unfaithful, and the eventual confrontation in Jerusalem draws a little closer.

This incident has therefore allowed Luke to remind us briefly of the growing opposition to Jesus (which must not simmer too long in the background for the sake of the plot), but notably at this point, the opposition comes specifically not from the Pharisees but from the synagogue ruler.

| 13:18–19 | The Parable of the Mustard Seed | 3a – Calling |

Undeterred, Luke—and Jesus—continue the motif of hope for those whom God is calling to be true disciples, calling them into his kingdom, which grows and flourishes as God gives it life.

| 13:20–21 | The Parable of the Leaven | 3a – Calling |

Likewise, the kingdom is permeated with God's Spirit and life just as bread is permeated with yeast.

| 13:22–24 | The Narrow Door | 1a – Accepting |

Not everyone will come into the kingdom, but only those who accept Jesus's message.

| 13:25–30 | Exclusion from the Kingdom | 3e – Punishing |

Once again, the time of the choice to accept Jesus's message is limited. Once that critical time has passed, God's judgment will stand. Thus, although God calls everyone to repentance, only those who respond in good time will be blessed.

| 13:31–33 | A Warning against Herod | 1e – Persisting |

Jesus, of course, is the epitome of the one who responds to God's call, and who perseveres regardless of the hardships involved. So Jesus continues unflinchingly toward Jerusalem, in spite of the warning that Herod (another representative of those who oppose God) wants to kill him.

What is particularly interesting in this and the next few pericopes, however, is that the Pharisees mentioned here are *not* among those opposed to Jesus. It is not all Pharisees by nature or by belief against whom Jesus has pronounced woes (and hence not Pharisaism itself as a movement or a sect), any more than he has pronounced judgment against the Samaritans as Samaritans, but only against those who fail or refuse to serve God. Thus, God's call to repentance and Jesus's call for all to follow him are extended just as willingly to the Pharisees as to the weak, the poor, and the oppressed.

| | | |
|---|---|---|
| 13:34–35 | The Lament over Jerusalem | 2e – Hindering |
| | | 3e – Punishing |

But Jesus knows that his true opposition, the real forces of evil, await him in Jerusalem. Like his woes against those Pharisees who ignore God, his lament over Jerusalem (the city that has so often rejected and hindered God's prophets) shows that those who reject him are poised for God's judgment. And the sentence of judgment against the city will be the departure from it of God's presence (as embodied in Jesus himself).

| | | |
|---|---|---|
| 14:1–6 | The Healing of the Man with Dropsy | 3a – Calling |
| | | 3b – Caring |

This series of pericopes, coming shortly after the Pharisees became enraged by Jesus's healing on the Sabbath, is just as important for Luke as the parable of the Good Samaritan, coming shortly after the Samaritan villages had rejected Jesus. Jesus continues to be invited to eat with the Pharisees, and he continues to accept doing so. This is just as significant as his eating with tax collectors and sinners. *All* are offered the choice to follow him; and although the Pharisees continue to watch what Jesus does, there is no indication here of any intensified opposition. But there *is* a reiteration of God's care for those in need as Jesus heals the man.

| | | |
|---|---|---|
| 14:7–14 | Teaching on Humility | 1b – Giving |
| | | 2b – Taking |

Jesus extends his teaching on selflessness versus greed, in this case greed for honor. The proper attitude ought to be to give honor to others, not to take it for oneself. Likewise, hospitality should be offered as a gift to those in need, not as a means of gaining something for oneself.

| 14:15–24 | The Parable of the Great Supper | 2d – Failing |
| | | 3a – Calling |

This last point is reemphasized by Luke's use of the parable of the Great Supper, as Jesus shows that God offers hospitality to everyone, although many refuse his call.

| 14:25–33 | The Conditions of Discipleship | 1b – Giving |
| | | 1d – Serving |

Accepting God's call is not an "easy ride." It demands a total commitment. It requires the willingness to give up everything and to serve God unconditionally, even to the point of death.

| 14:34–35 | The Parable of Salt | 1e – Persisting |
| | | 3e – Punishing |

If one *should* turn away after initially making such a commitment, then that one is like salt that has lost its flavor and cannot regain it. Hence, those who fail to persevere are also subject to God's judgment.

| 15:1–7 | The Parable of the Lost Sheep | 2a – Rejecting |
| | | 3a – Calling |

Now Luke is ready to let the antagonism between Jesus and the Pharisees grow, to build the tension and foreshadowing once again. Jesus has given the Pharisees their chance and showed them what true service to God entails. Yet, when he shows by his own example of eating with outcasts, that he is willing to accept *anyone*, the Pharisees can no longer accept *him*. They have failed to learn the lessons he has tried to teach, and their opposition will now increase steadily as he nears Jerusalem.

Jesus's response is to emphasize even more that God's call to repentance is open to everyone, and indeed that God actively seeks out those who will respond to his call, no matter how "lost" they may seem.

| 15:8–10 | The Parable of the Lost Coin | 3a – Calling |

This point is doubly emphasized by the parable of the Lost Coin.

| 15:11–32 | The Parable of the Prodigal Son | 3a – Calling |

The two previous brief parables pale in comparison to the parable of the Prodigal Son. Here the son is not only "lost" but has actively rejected his father. He comes to his senses, repents, and presents himself to his father to be his servant and no longer his son. Yet the father welcomes him back with open arms, just as God welcomes back *all* repentant sinners (including repentant Pharisees).

The older brother is, of course, critical to the point as well. He is rebuked for his attitude but not rejected, and one hopes that he accepts his father's rebuke (as James and John had accepted Jesus's rebuke earlier). Thus, the Pharisees are once again offered a chance to remain "always with God" by accepting God's acceptance of repentant sinners. But they will choose to reject God's grace, mercy, and calling to outcasts, which will prove to be their undoing.

## Fifth Wave (Luke 16–17)

Luke has covered a considerable amount of territory here, but all of it has been permeated with God's ever-present call to *everyone* to turn to him and become true disciples. Even the Pharisees have been included in this call, and it is only with the last few pericopes that it is becoming evident that they at least will not respond positively to God. This realization will now fuel a dramatic buildup of tension and conflict, reaching its final climax in Jerusalem.

In terms of the story, then, Luke has carefully orchestrated the emotional content of his Development section. The first two "waves" built up to their own "crest" in the conflicts between Jesus and his opponents. The middle two "waves" were then far more subdued, allowing Luke to explore the theological implications of discipleship and of God's calling, with the tensions of the plot only surfacing briefly in order to remind us of the overall story. But now that the conflicts have reappeared in earnest, they will continue to grow stronger again in the final two "waves."

Table 2.6. The "Fifth Wave" of Luke's Development (Luke 16–17)

| Verse | Pericope | Theme |
|---|---|---|
| 16:1–9 | The Parable of the Unjust Steward | 1b – Giving<br>1d – Serving |

This curious parable carries on the motif from the Prodigal Son of God's acceptance. In the former parable God had accepted the repentant sinner. Here he accepts one whose behavior is meant to illustrate not dishonesty (as it seems to do) but rather generosity. Although we may question the steward's faithfulness to his master, he does show himself to be faithful to his master's debtors, and so is an agent of God's forgiveness to them.

It may be an odd parable, even a problematic one, but it does serve Luke as a bridge (perhaps a slightly shaky bridge, however) between talking about God's acceptance and talking about faithfulness regarding material wealth.

| 16:10–12 | On Faithfulness in What Is Least | 1d – Serving |

It is such faithfulness that now becomes the focus. True disciples serve faithfully, no matter how insignificant the task and thus prove themselves faithful in all matters.

| 16:13 | On Serving Two Masters | 1a – Accepting |
| | | 1d – Serving |

It also matters whom one is faithful *to*. The steward in the previous parable was not faithful to his (perhaps greedy) master but was faithful to the lowly and the oppressed. True disciples must be faithful to God, not to their own selfish interests.

| 16:14–15 | The Pharisees Reproved | 2b – Taking |

This emphasis now allows Luke to resume with full force the conflict between Jesus and the Pharisees. Just as the Pharisees were not willing to accept God's acceptance of those *they* did not accept, now they are unwilling to give up their own greed. It is such greed that Luke identifies as the dominant characteristic of the unfaithful. Jesus delivers here a series of sayings showing how the Pharisees take what is not theirs with no concern for others, while in the process they attempt to justify themselves (thus also taking for themselves the name of "faithful" even though they are not worthy of that title).

| 16:16–17 | Concerning the Law | 2a – Rejecting |
| | | 2c – Ignoring |

They ignore what God requires in the Torah, as well as rejecting the gospel.

| 16:18 | Concerning Divorce | 2c – Ignoring |

Allowing divorce is just one small example of how the Pharisees ignore God's requirements (by allowing themselves to abandon their responsibilities to their wives).

| 16:19–31 | The Parable of the Rich Man and Lazarus | 2b – Taking |
| | | 3b – Caring |
| | | 3e – Punishing |

Much more serious, however, is their treatment of the poor and the needy. The parable of the Rich Man and Lazarus is clear in its condemnation of those who callously ignore those in need, even if there is no specific requirement that they must extend help (complementing the earlier parable of the Good Samaritan). But God, of course, sees all and will care for the weak and punish the unfaithful.

The final saying in the parable (that if the unfaithful are not moved by God's word in the Scriptures, they will not be convinced even if someone were to rise from the dead) provides ironic and tragic foreshadowing, displaying Luke's penchant for pathos and increasing the drama of his story.

| 17:1–2 | Warning against Offenses | 2e – Hindering |

Even worse than those who are selfishness and greedy are those who actively harm others in various ways. The Pharisees, by demanding that others comply with their requirements rather than God's, hinder and persecute those who want to be faithful to God, causing them to "stumble" and sin (by believing that they are *not* faithful or by thinking that they should follow the Pharisees' example of greed).

| 17:3–4 | On Forgiveness | 1b – Giving |

The opposite of causing someone to sin is forgiving someone's sins. Thus, the answer when someone stumbles is to help that person back to faithfulness and to forgive (no matter how difficult this may be).

| 17:5–6 | On Faith | 1a – Accepting |

In recognition of this difficulty, the disciples ask Jesus to "increase their faith," to help them to become more faithful (and thus more able to forgive). Jesus's response is to show the power inherent in even small acts of faith.

| 17:7–10 | We Are Unprofitable Servants | 1d – Serving |

A number of sayings have now been given by Jesus in rapid succession, and with each one the stakes seem to have been raised. The selfishness of the unfaithful (as represented by the Pharisees) has been condemned in ever-stronger terms, whereas the demands on the faithful have become more and more challenging. The high point of this escalation is seen here as Jesus says that the faithful must serve God unconditionally, with no thought at all for a reward, and even if none is ever given.

| 17:11-19 | The Cleansing of the Ten Lepers | 1a – Accepting |
| | | 1b – Giving |
| | | 1d – Serving |
| | | 3b – Caring |

This last requirement applies to Jesus himself, of course, as the epitome of the true disciple. So it is no accident that Luke tells us now that Jesus is nearing Jerusalem, where his unconditional discipleship will be proved. On a smaller scale, his discipleship is also proved by his willingness to help those in need (like the Good Samaritan, but in contrast to the rich man's treatment of Lazarus).

The response to Jesus's help is also telling. Although God extends his care to everyone, there is no guarantee that such care will elicit a response of faithfulness (just as a supernatural warning to the rich man's brothers is apt to be ignored). Here again, it is significant that it is a Samaritan who responds. The faithful are not always those we might expect.

| 17:20-21 | On the Coming of the Kingdom of God | 1a – Accepting |
| | | 2a – Rejecting |

With all of Jesus's talk about God's kingdom, judgment, and rewards, the Pharisees pose the question asked over and over in the Psalms: When? How long will it be before God finally delivers the faithful? Jesus's answer is that God's kingdom is already in their midst (in the presence of Jesus himself among them). The Pharisees have misunderstood God all along, and so it is no surprise that they fail to recognize or accept Jesus for who he is, the very presence of God among them.

| 17:22-37 | The Day of the Son of Man | 1e – Persisting |

This leads naturally into Jesus's discussion of his "exodus," his departure, already foretold at the transfiguration, when he will suffer and be rejected. At that time he will no longer be present among the people, but his ultimate presence and the ultimate coming of the kingdom will follow. This is not a contradiction of what he told the Pharisees but a confirmation, since the kingdom of God is present whenever and wherever Jesus is. But true disciples must continue to be faithful until the ultimate fulfillment of the kingdom does come.

## Sixth Wave (Luke 18–19)

As Luke nears the conclusion of the Journey to Jerusalem, the conflict grows stronger, as does the contrast between the faithful and the unfaithful in Jesus's sayings. Having laid out the stark choice facing Theophilus (and all of his readers), here in the last few pericopes in his Development section Luke will conclude (as he had begun) with examples of how actual people faced with this choice have responded. Unlike the beginning of the journey, however, when the Samaritans (and perhaps even the Seventy) faced that choice without understanding its full implications, now those implications are completely clear, and so the joy and the tragedy inherent in the right and wrong choices are greatly amplified. This last wave marks the Retransition passage in Luke's Development section, which prepares us for the Recapitulation, when Jesus will enter Jerusalem.

### Table 2.7. The "Sixth Wave" of Luke's Development (Luke 18–19)

| Verse | Pericope | Theme |
|---|---|---|
| 18:1–8 | The Parable of the Unjust Judge | 1c – Praying |
| | | 1e – Persisting |

The theme of perseverance is carried over from Jesus's previous sayings to the parable of the Unjust Judge, which Luke specifically tells us was told by Jesus to his disciples "to the effect that they ought always to pray and not lose heart" (18:1 ESV) (one of the few editorial comments Luke offers in his entire Gospel). Faced with hardships and the seemingly endless wait for God's justice and the coming of the kingdom, the faithful must not give up hope, or give up praying. Jesus ends with a challenge, asking whether anyone remain faithful to the end.

| Verse | Pericope | Theme |
|---|---|---|
| 18:9–14 | The Pharisee and the Publican | 1c – Praying |
| | | 2b – Taking |
| | | 2c – Ignoring |
| | | 3a – Calling |
| | | 3c – Answering |

Prayer provides a transition here, as Luke begins to concentrate on how different people react when faced with the choice between being a true disciple or a false one. The theme is familiar: the Pharisee who thinks himself to be righteous is really only concerned with himself, and so his greedy act of claiming and taking righteousness for himself is indeed a sign that he is *not* righteous and has ignored God's calling. The tax collector, on the other hand, is repentant even though he knows he is not righteous. Since God calls everyone to repentance and faith, it is this tax collector who is accepted by God, just as the repentant Prodigal Son had been accepted by his father.

This parable will now be acted out in real life in the following pericopes.

| | | |
|---|---|---|
| 18:15–17 | Jesus Blesses the Children | 3b – Caring |

God's acceptance of the humble is reemphasized by Jesus's blessing the children. Again, it is not those who think themselves righteous or faithful who are accepted but those who present themselves to God in humility.

| | | |
|---|---|---|
| 18:18–23 | The Rich Young Man | 2d – Failing |

The Rich Young Man is perhaps not as self-righteous as the Pharisee in the preceding parable, but nevertheless he relies on his own understanding of what God requires of him. Jesus does not challenge him on this but asks for the complete commitment that he has been describing throughout his journey. This is too much for the young man, who cannot bring himself to give up all that he has in order to serve God completely. Thus, he is one of the most tragic figures in all the Gospels, one who comes so close to being a true disciple but who fails in the end.

| | | |
|---|---|---|
| 18:24–27 | On Riches | 2b Taking |
| | | 3c Answering |

Jesus's response to the Rich Young Man is to point out how difficult it is for the rich to give up everything to be true disciples, but even this is not impossible with God's help.

| | | |
|---|---|---|
| 18:28–30 | The Rewards of Discipleship | 3d – Rewarding |

Those who have shown themselves to be true disciples will be rewarded for their faithfulness.

| | | |
|---|---|---|
| 18:31–34 | The Third Prediction of the Passion | 1d – Serving |

Once again, Jesus himself is shown by Luke to be the epitome of the true disciple, willing even as he approaches certain imminent death, to serve God unflinchingly.

| | | |
|---|---|---|
| 18:35–43 | The Healing of the Blind Man | 1a – Accepting |
| | | 3b – Caring |

As before with the lepers, Jesus shows his faithfulness and God's caring by healing the blind man who calls to him. And the blind man himself, like the children, shows that those who recognize and accept Jesus are themselves accepted by God as among the faithful.

| 19:1-10 | Zacchaeus | 3a – Calling |
| | | 1a – Accepting |
| | | 1b – Giving |

The final encounter on the Journey to Jerusalem is with Zacchaeus, the personification of the tax collector in the parable, who recognizes his own unworthiness and unrighteousness but responds to God's calling by repenting. His repentance and his faithfulness are shown by his giving of his wealth to the poor, and his repayment to those he has cheated, in contrast to the unwillingness of the tragic Rich Young Man to give up his wealth. Thus, Jesus's statement that the rich *can* be saved is proved true.

| 19:11-27 | The Parable of the Pounds | 1d – Serving |
| | | 2b – Taking |
| | | 3d – Rewarding |
| | | 3e – Punishing |

Jesus's final parable offers the choice to all those listening to act on everything he has taught and so to make their choice either to remain greedy and selfish (as the servant who buries his pound does) or to become faithful servants. But a very stern warning of God's judgment is promised to those who reject Jesus' message.

We have reached the point where Jesus's entry into Jerusalem has been prepared for, not only in terms of our understanding of who Jesus is and what he expects of his disciples but also in terms of understanding the opposition against him. He will now face that opposition head on and prove himself to be the epitome of the true disciple by giving himself completely to God's will.

Luke has accomplished all of this not by adding his own commentary to events (as John often does throughout his own Gospel) but simply by recording these events and teachings as accurately as possible (as he had claimed in his Prologue), and in *this* specific order. It is this very order (which is therefore not random or arbitrary or without rhyme or reason) that itself produces the desired effect. It generates the necessary tension (and occasional relief of that tension) for the story to remain lively and interesting, with the proper conflicts and foreshadowing needed for such a tale. It also gives a clear picture to Theophilus (and to all other readers) of the nature of true Christian discipleship and the implications of refusing such discipleship, thus (it is hoped) convincing Theophilus that he ought to become a Christian himself.

It is one of the main assertions of the present work, then, that the middle section of Luke's Gospel makes perfect aesthetic sense exactly the way it has been composed in the context of the whole Gospel. It is not the case that Luke has simply taken material from his sources and pasted it into this segment of his Gospel in whatever order he happened to find it. He has deliberately organized the material in the way he has, in a manner consistent with his purpose, in a carefully crafted progression that leads brilliantly into the final portion of his Gospel. In other words, Luke's work is precisely what he claimed it to be in his Prologue, "an orderly account for . . . Theophilus, so that you may know the certainty of the things about which you had been informed." (1:4). To gain an even better understanding of this remarkable Development section, however, we must also look at it in the full context of Luke's whole Gospel.

## The Complete Sonata

We have already observed that Luke's Gospel displays a recognized three-part structure, which we have compared to sonata form as typically employed in classical symphonies. Let us therefore now take a look at Luke's Gospel as a complete work, using the structure of sonata form (Exposition, Development, and Recapitulation) as a guide.

As noted earlier, when sonata form is used for the first movement of a symphony, it is often augmented with a Slow Introduction before the Exposition proper and often ends with a distinct Coda (its "tail") after the Recapitulation. Luke's Gospel also seems to follow this pattern—and, again, for the same aesthetic reasons. The Introduction (in Luke's case, the narratives in chapters 1 and 2) sets the scene and prepares for the more dramatic entrance of the Exposition. The Coda (the resurrection appearances) serves to round out the whole movement, bringing it to a satisfactory conclusion.

Luke begins his Gospel in the temple and indeed continues to focus on temple worship throughout his Introduction. This may appear to be an odd topic on which to expend so much effort in a work written with the goal of explaining Christianity to non-Christians—and probably *gentile* non-Christians.[6] Yet there may be several reasons why Luke has chosen this path.

One reason has to do with the specific identity of Theophilus. It has been suggested earlier that Luke's intention seems to be to give a con-

6. The common assumption that Luke is writing to a gentile audience does seem to be valid for a number of reasons, including the likely identity of Theophilus, Luke's tracing of Jesus's genealogy back to Adam rather than to Abraham, his lack of emphasis on the Jewish Torah, and his indications that salvation is available to gentiles as well as to Jews (such as in 2:29–32 and 4:23–27).

vincing testimony regarding Christianity, almost as if he were giving witness in a legal context. This is reinforced by his use of the title "Your Excellency" when addressing Theophilus, a title also used by Luke in Acts when individuals are addressing a Roman official in a legal context. If Theophilus were such an official to whom Luke is appealing (whether or not in an official context) on behalf of the Christian community, there may be a good reason why Luke concentrates so much on the temple.

One of the charges commonly brought against Christians in the Roman Empire was "atheism," a failure to offer the proper sacrifices either to Caesar or on behalf of Caesar. In his book *The Trial of St. Paul*, H. W. Tajra discusses the implications of this crime and the special status that Judaism (sometimes) enjoyed in the Roman Empire:

> Augustus renewed and confirmed the considerable and indeed exceptionable privileges historically enjoyed by the Jews throughout the Empire .... The Jews also had the right to use special forms of service insofar as Emperor-worship was concerned. They did not offer sacrifices to the Emperor himself: rather they offered prayers and sacrifices to God (Deo aeterno) for the sovereign's welfare....
> In reality, a Roman could practise a foreign cult so long as its usages did not violate Roman law or constitute a threat to the Roman political or social structure. . . . We have to note here that there was no specific crime of apostasy to Judaism. "The sole crime," writes A. M. Rabello, "was atheism which meant the failure to perform certain ceremonies, refusal to worship the gods and so forth."[7]

This situation had important implications for all Christians in the empire. The earliest Christians were clearly still a small sect within Judaism and, as such, enjoyed the special privileges accorded to the Jews; they were not required to offer sacrifices to Caesar. As Christianity began to spread, however, and especially once gentiles began to be accepted within the church in great numbers, this situation was threatened. If such Christians were no longer considered Jews, they *would* be required to sacrifice to Caesar or face the consequences for refusing. Refusal would be tantamount to treason, since such sacrifices were as much political as they were religious.

If Christianity, however, were a valid sect *within* Judaism (particularly one that continued to participate in the sacrifices of the temple),

---

7. H. W. Tajra, *The Trial of St. Paul: A Juridical Exegesis of the Second Half of the Acts of the Apostles*, Wissenschaftlicht Untersuchungen zum Neuen Testament 2/35 (Tübingen: Mohr Siebeck, 1989), 15–16, 22–23.

the charge of treason could not be brought against Christians in the empire. Thus, Luke seems keen throughout his Gospel (and Acts) to show Theophilus the continued participation of Christians in worship at the temple. If Theophilus *was* a Roman official, especially one involved in administering justice, this emphasis by Luke would have been an understandable way of defending the Christian movement within the Roman Empire. Although Luke's general "Roman-friendly" proclivity makes sense in this context, it would be appropriate if he were simply attempting to appeal to a gentile non-Christian audience in order to convert his readers. His emphasis on the temple, however, seems to point directly to Luke having written the Gospel partly to defend Christianity as a valid Jewish sect (either in principle or within an actual legal context).

Luke's Introduction (in the first two chapters of his Gospel) centers on worship in the temple. This liturgical focus is all the more evident because of the four canticles that dominate this portion of Luke: the songs of Mary and Zechariah in chapter 1, and of the angels and Simeon in chapter 2. So memorable are these canticles that they continue to this day to feature prominently in the Christian liturgical tradition: the songs of Zechariah, Mary, and Simeon being the high points respectively of Morning, Evening, and Night Prayer, and the song of the angels (expanded as the *Gloria in Excelsis*) being sung at the beginning of the Eucharist (and in the Lutheran tradition, the song of Simeon also being sung at the end of the Eucharist). These canticles are reminiscent of canticles from the Old Testament, which is significant for what Luke is trying to achieve in his Introduction. Mary's song specifically contains echoes of Hannah's song in 1 Samuel 2, and this link is worth exploring (although we will find that the parallels will be much closer between Hannah and Elizabeth than between Hannah and Mary).

There are only three lifelong Nazirites mentioned in the Bible, children dedicated to God from before their birth: Samson, Samuel, and John the Baptist. All three of these figures were born to previously barren mothers, and their births were all promised by God. Here the similarities between Samson and the others seem to end (unless one counts his appetite for wild honey), but the parallels between Samuel and John are striking. Samuel becomes the one to anoint the first kings of Israel, Saul and, far more importantly, David. John the Baptist, in exact parallel, is to become the one to anoint Jesus as David's successor through his baptism. Thus, the similarities in the stories of Samuel's birth and John's birth cannot have been an accident. Luke appears to be deliberately making this connection for anyone familiar with the story of Samuel.

Gentile non-Christians would hardly be familiar with the story of Samuel, and this too is significant. Matthew draws a clear connection between Jesus and David in the very first verse of his Gospel, claiming blatantly that Jesus is the Messiah, the successor of David. This claim invites Herod's wrath toward the infant Jesus as a possible rival. Luke, on the other hand, if he *is* writing his Gospel partly to defend Christianity in the Roman Empire, would not want to draw too much attention to Jesus being the Messiah, that infamous Jewish political threat to Rome whom countless insurrectionists claimed to be. Indeed, Luke seems careful throughout his Gospel to circumvent, wherever possible, any implications that Christianity is a threat to Rome. Hence, he takes care to cast even the "kingdom of God" in terms that are "Roman-friendly," showing that it is *not* a political kingdom whenever it is discussed.

Luke does not, however, avoid the term *Messiah* (using it twelve times in his Gospel, compared to Mark's eight times and Matthew's more enthusiastic seventeen times), nor does he deny that Jesus is the heir of David (as Gabriel's announcement to Mary in Luke 1:32–33 indicates). But Luke does here (and elsewhere) play down the link between Jesus and David, forgoing any of the political implications in the birth narratives that Matthew seems eager to draw. Hence, in Luke's Gospel, it is not in order to avoid contact with Herod's successor that Joseph and Mary move to Nazareth (as it is in Matt 2:19–23), but it is simply because this was their original home. Similarly, it is not the lofty and prominent who recognize Jesus's birth but the poor and lowly shepherds (the first of Luke's many references to the poor as those whom God favors).

For Christians, however, who are already familiar with the story of Samuel, the parallels between Samuel and John the Baptist, and hence also between David and Jesus, would have been recognizable. For "those who have ears to hear," then, Luke is affirming just as strongly as Matthew that Jesus is the Messiah, but without overstating it in a confrontational way. This is consistent with what we have already seen of Luke's technique in his Development section. He achieves his purpose not by giving his own running commentary but simply by the way in which presents the facts (both in terms of which facts he includes and in how he arranges them sequentially), allowing readers to draw their own conclusions.

Yet there *is* something in this Introduction that would appeal directly to a gentile audience. The "oracles" spoken over John and Jesus before and after their births have parallels not only in prophecies in the Old Testament but in Greek and Roman myths as well. Important figures in these myths typically would have had destinies proclaimed about them at birth, and so gentile readers of Luke would have understood that the canticles and the prophecies of Simeon and Anna marked John and Jesus as being special people indeed.

By means of his Introduction, then, Luke has set the scene for the life of Jesus, telling everyone in his audience that Jesus is unique and emphasizing the significance for all those associated with Jesus of maintaining proper temple worship. The story of the boy Jesus in the temple (at the end of chapter 2) reinforces this as Jesus himself refers to the temple as his "Father's house," linking Jesus himself personally to the temple, its liturgy, and to God himself.

## Luke's Exposition Section

The scene having thus been set, the story proper begins (as in all the other Gospels) with John the Baptist's preaching and Jesus's baptism (chapter 3), followed (as in the other Synoptics) by Jesus's temptation and his return to Galilee. These events mark the beginning of Luke's Exposition, in which he will set out the main themes of his Gospel. Jesus's baptism by John not only inaugurates Jesus's ministry but also (for those with ears to hear) is his anointing as Messiah by Samuel's successor. The temptation (chapter 4) tests Jesus at this critical point as to whether he will be the true, faithful servant of God, and Jesus passes this test, remaining faithful no matter how severe the conditions.

Luke chooses at this point, rather than giving an account of Jesus's ministry in Capernaum and around Galilee (as do Matthew and Mark), to bring Jesus first of all to his home synagogue in Nazareth. Here Jesus proclaims that he himself is the fulfillment of Isaiah's prophecy of God's promise to bless his people. Again, for those with ears to hear, Jesus is clearly claiming here to be the Messiah, and the reaction is violent. The people of his own hometown try to kill him. Thus, at the very beginning of Jesus's ministry, Luke presents the theme of rejection, hindering, and persecution of the faithful servant, which, as we have seen, will become increasingly prominent throughout Luke's Development section, pointing ultimately to Jesus's final rejection in Jerusalem.

Those in Jesus's hometown cannot recognize or accept who he truly is, nor can they accept his message of salvation to the gentiles (4:23–27).

This incident is followed by the first series of events in Jesus's ministry in which he heals the sick, performs his first miracles, and calls his first disciples (chapter 5). It also includes the first indications of opposition by the Pharisees, provoked by Jesus's acts of healing on the Sabbath and of eating with outcasts. Nearly all of these themes will be developed later in the Gospel.

In chapter 6, Jesus delivers his Sermon on the Plain, setting out for the first time the themes of his teaching on how the faithful are to live. The sermon begins with a series of blessings on the lowly and on those who are persecuted for their acceptance of Jesus; it then continues with a series of "woes" on those who are greedy and who are the persecutors. Jesus then focuses on selfless giving as the central characteristic of good servants of God. The faithful are even to give unselfishly to their enemies, since God himself cares for all. Thus, the faithful must also leave it up to God to be the judge as to who is righteous and who is not. It is the responsibility of the faithful simply to serve diligently, bearing good fruit. The brief sermon ends with a warning that, although rewards await those who are faithful, the unfaithful will be punished and lost.

A review of the categories of themes in the earlier analysis of Luke's Development section will show that a majority of these themes have been laid out in basic form in this very succinct sermon. This is precisely what we would expect in an Exposition, and the technique of introducing these themes briefly, one by one, works just as well in this story as it does in a Beethoven symphony. We have thus been introduced to the main themes, which we will later be able to follow and understand better as they are developed. The sermon is followed by more miracle stories (chapter 7), this time more dramatic ones, including the "long distance" healing of the son of the centurion of Capernaum (a Roman-friendly miracle) and the raising of a dead boy to life in the town of Nain.

This leads into a section that sets out the choice that must ultimately be made by all of us (and by Theophilus in particular) as to how to respond to Jesus. John the Baptist's question serves to pose the choice, and different responses are given by the woman with the ointment (who loves much because God has forgiven her much), by the Pharisees (who ignore and reject God's calling), and then by the disciples (who accept Jesus, even if they have not yet recognized fully who he is).

All of this is then reemphasised by the parable of the Sower (chapter 8), which shows that God calls everyone but not everyone responds equally well. The parable of the Lamp on the Stand and Jesus's response to his mother and brothers show that those who choose to accept Jesus will be rewarded. Thus, nearly all of the themes to be developed in the middle portion of the Gospel have now been introduced in brief and basic form. One more section of miracles ensues, including the Stilling of the Storm, more dramatic healings, and the Feeding of the Five Thousand. Jesus also briefly sends out the twelve disciples on their own (chapter 9) to act as true servants of God.

We are now at a critical point in Luke's Gospel. All of his basic themes have been set out in sequence, with very little repetition (as we would expect in the Exposition section of a work as described above). Jesus has begun to be recognized and accepted for who he truly is, and there has also been some opposition (the inevitable conflict between good and evil at the heart of any good story, and especially this one). Now Luke is ready to introduce the most important theme of all: Jesus as the perfect servant of God who will give everything, his very life, in service to God.

The final portion of the Exposition in sonata form is referred to as the "Codetta" (the "little tail"), which brings the whole section to its conclusion. Luke's Codetta begins with Peter's declaration that Jesus is the Messiah (in 9:18–21, where Luke is careful to associate this term more with Jesus's suffering than with kingship, which helps Luke to maintain his Roman-friendly posture). This declaration leads directly to Jesus's first prediction of his passion (9:22), and then to the transfiguration (9:28–36). The transfiguration, for Luke, is not merely a revelation of Jesus's glory, but directly links that glory to the "exodus" (departure) that Jesus will accomplish in Jerusalem—in other words, his death. Jesus's true glory is in his selfless giving as the perfect servant of God.

The link between Jesus's glory and his impending death is strengthened by the healing miracle that follows (9:37–43a), when the resulting praise leads Jesus again to predict his death (9:43b–45). The Exposition ends with Jesus's rebuke of the disciples for wanting to be great (9:46–48) and his first rebuke of James and John for arrogating to themselves God's position of judgment (9:49–50). Jesus is thus showing that the faithful are to serve and to give and must not be greedy and take for themselves (including taking power for themselves).

Luke's entire Exposition has therefore proceeded methodically and precisely in order to present in a carefully building sequence and, with virtually no repetition, the main themes of his Gospel. We are now ready for the development of all these themes, as they will be repeated, expanded, and juxtaposed during the Journey to Jerusalem. As Luke the expert storyteller works with these themes, he builds, then relieves, then again builds tension in his story with the growing opposition of the Pharisees and the occasional foreshadowing of what will occur once he reaches Jerusalem. Theologically, Luke uses his Development section to place before Theophilus, and the rest of his audience, the stark choice that must inevitably be made either to follow or to fail to follow Jesus.

The Development section begins, then, near the end of chapter 9 with Jesus resolutely heading for Jerusalem and the choice being presented as to who will be willing to follow him and who will oppose him. In chapter 10, the opportunity to follow is made available to many through the sending out of the seventy disciples and through various encounters with Jesus, culminating in the story of Mary and Martha, who both receive Jesus faithfully but in contrasting ways. This leads to a discussion of how the faithful ought to live (chapter 11), through prayer and recognizing the Holy Spirit. These teachings provoke a confrontation with the Pharisees, who, through their actions, are in danger of being unfaithful to God. In contrast to the behavior of the Pharisees, Jesus urges the faithful to seek spiritual treasures rather than earthly ones (chapter 12). This is followed by warnings (chapter 13) that the time is short to choose the right way, urgings (chapter 14) to make the right choice, and parables (chapter 15) about God's desire for those who are lost to choose the right way, illustrated especially in the parable of the Prodigal Son. In chapter 16, Jesus warns that one must not vacillate between faithfulness and unfaithfulness, and, in chapter 17, the difficulties of remaining faithful are faced. In chapter 18, Luke gives examples of those who have chosen to be faithful (with the promise that they will be rewarded) and of those who have failed to be faithful. At the end of the Development section (at the beginning of chapter 19), the tax collector Zacchaeus is presented as an example of one who has chosen to cease his unfaithfulness, and the final parable of the Development section, the parable of the Pounds, presents the choice between faithfulness and unfaithfulness in no uncertain terms.

## Luke's Recapitulation Section

We reach Jerusalem with heightened expectations and intrigue, ready for the final outcome of the story in Luke's Recapitulation. Here the themes Luke has presented and developed will be given their ultimate restatement. Not every theme will need to be recapitulated, but, because of Luke's conclusion, we will still be able to understand all of them in their fullness.

The Recapitulation begins with Jesus's Triumphal Entry into Jerusalem (in the second half of chapter 19) to the cheerful acceptance of the people but to the dismay of the Pharisees. Jesus pauses to lament over Jerusalem and to predict its desolation "because you did not recognize the time of your visitation from God" (19:14 NRSV). Again, these are all familiar themes: acceptance versus rejection of Jesus within the critical time available, and God's judgment. Jesus proceeds to cleanse the temple (19:45–46). This is a purification, not a rejection. As he will later do in Acts, Luke is careful to make a distinction between the temple itself and those who currently control it. This is key to his contention that Christianity is not only *one* valid sect within Judaism but is indeed the *true* form of Judaism. Hence, there is no judgment against the temple itself, only against the city of Jerusalem and against the current Jewish leaders.

After Jesus's arrival in Jerusalem, the final confrontation with his opponents, the Pharisees (now joined by the Sadducees), takes place (chapter 20). Jesus's authority to teach is finally challenged outright, showing that the Pharisees do not recognize or accept Jesus or the Holy Spirit within him. Jesus's answer is also telling. He transfers the question of his own authority to the authority of John the Baptist to baptize. This is not merely a trick to avoid answering the question; it points to the actual foundation for his own authority, which came through his being anointed as the Messiah at his own baptism by John. Again, this is clear only to those who have ears to hear. Jesus goes on to tell the parable of the Wicked Husbandmen, who kill the owner's son (foreshadowing Jesus's own death) but who are then killed themselves in punishment and are crushed by the "stone that the builders rejected [which] has become the cornerstone" (20:17 NRSV). This parable is Jesus's final proclamation of judgment against the Pharisees, and it is clear that the conflict has now become a matter of life and death.

Luke presents other challenges (but no longer openly by the Pharisees themselves), all of which Jesus answers (including the Roman-friendly response that one should "render to Caesar the things that are Caesar's" [20:25 ESV] when asked about paying taxes). Then Jesus points out the injustice of the widow's having to pay all that she had to live on as a temple tax (chapter 21), illustrating again God's (and Luke's) care for the poor (and the Jewish leaders' failure to care).

This entire confrontation in Jerusalem has been a testing not of Jesus but of Jerusalem itself and of its leaders as to whether they will recognize and accept Jesus. The leaders fail this test and prove themselves to be opposed to God and hindering God's servant. Jesus now proclaims the ultimate judgment against Jerusalem in Luke's version of Jesus's discourse that is often referred to as the "Mini-Apocalypse." Although this passage begins in Luke as it does in the corresponding versions in Matthew and Mark, with Jesus saying that the temple will not remain with one stone on top of another, Luke deflects the predicted punishment from the temple itself onto the city of Jerusalem. Significantly, Luke's Jesus makes no mention of the "abomination of desolation" in the temple but instead speaks of armies surrounding Jerusalem, thus maintaining a more "Roman-friendly" stance, since the gentile armies are accused not of desecrating the temple (where Christians will continue to worship legally) but of carrying out God's judgment against the current Jewish leaders.

With the pronunciation of this judgment, the second phase of the Recapitulation, the passion, begins (chapter 22), in which Jesus proves himself to be the perfect servant of God, giving up his life. Along the way, Luke includes many interesting variations on Matthew's and Mark's versions of the passion that highlight his own concerns. Luke is the only Gospel in which Jesus specifically refers to the Passover *during* the Last Supper (22:7-14, 15); in addition, he gives more details about this ritual (including two different cups of wine [22:17, 20]), again highlighting his liturgical interests and showing that Christianity continues the practice of true Jewish worship. The Last Supper also provides Luke with the opportunity to have Jesus discuss the coming kingdom of God with his disciples. Although he speaks of the disciples sitting on thrones and judging the tribes of Israel, he also takes pains once again to show that this is not a political kingdom. Jesus says, "I confer on you a kingdom, just as my Father conferred one on me" (22:29 NIV), thus showing (as he had done earlier when he said that the kingdom of God was already in their midst) that the kingdom was already present wherever Jesus himself was present—hence it was not a kingdom that threatened Rome. Luke is also careful when Jesus appears before the

Sanhedrin not to include the charge that he had claimed that he would destroy the temple.

Luke also shows emphatically that Rome's representatives (both Pilate and Herod) did not find any reason to believe that Jesus was a threat to Rome (chapter 23). Pilate especially is portrayed by Luke not so much as a weak, indecisive figure caught in the middle of things and frantically attempting to avoid any responsibility (as in Matthew), but as a prudent, thoughtful governor. His decision to send Jesus to Herod was in order to follow the proper protocol, not in order to avoid responsibility. His final decision to "grant their demand" to have Jesus crucified was again a prudent choice in the situation, not a desperate act of resignation (as it seems to be in Matthew). Pilate is not portrayed as one of Jesus's opponents, nor as a dupe; hence, there is no need for him to "wash his hands" of the matter, as he does in Matthew's Gospel. Luke seems careful here not to include Pilate among those who must make a choice about Jesus, so that he remains perhaps the only neutral figure in the passion, if not in the whole Gospel. Thus, Pilate is neither condemned nor exonerated, and Luke has managed to walk a *very* thin line. By not including some of the material he could have done, Luke has given his readers the impression that Pilate was acting appropriately, as a Roman governor should do; Luke thereby avoids the possibility of offending a Roman audience, particularly a *legal* Roman audience.

In the same vein, there is no mention in Luke's account of Roman soldiers mistreating Jesus. Moreover, Jesus asks God to forgive the soldiers who crucify him (if 23:34 is genuine, since it does not appear in all of the earliest manuscripts—nevertheless, it is certainly in the spirit of Jesus as he is portrayed by Luke).

Luke is also unique in his treatment of the two criminals crucified with Jesus (23:39–43). Here again are two representatives of the choice between accepting or rejecting Jesus. Just like the Rich Young Man and Zacchaeus, one individual makes the correct choice and one does not. There is then one other final hint of this theme in the person of Joseph of Arimathea, who, although he was himself a member of the Sanhedrin (probably a Pharisee), had not rejected Jesus but, in contrast, showed his own faithfulness by personally burying Jesus (23:50–56). Once again, God calls everyone, and (regardless of their position or loyalties) anyone may respond faithfully. Thus, Luke's Recapitulation ends with Jesus having proven himself to be the perfect servant by giving up everything in service to God, and various other characters have made their own choices to follow him or not.

But this is not the end of the story, and Luke's Coda explores some of his themes once again, this time in light of the resurrection (chapter 24). Like his Introduction, Luke's Coda is steeped in liturgical references, particularly Jesus's "opening the Scriptures" and being known in the "breaking of bread" in his appearance to the disciples on the road to Emmaus (which, of course, has obvious links forward to the Christian celebration of the Eucharist, but which also has links back to Jewish Sabbath rituals, thus again emphasizing the continuity between Jewish and Christian liturgical practices). Luke once again links Jesus's messiahship to his suffering, with his resurrection showing that he is not the typical anti-Roman insurgent who might use this title but has been proved to be truly the Son of God. Hence, the disciples accept him (as Luke implies that Theophilus is also called to do), and as true disciples they are charged with the responsibility of serving God by preaching "repentance and forgiveness of sins to all nations." Thus, once again, God is calling the lost to repentance and faith, now with the disciples as his agents.

Very significantly, Luke ends as he began, *in the temple*, with the disciples continually "praising God" there. Christianity is shown to be the true form of Judaism and the ultimate truth for all nations. Luke has done his best to achieve his purpose, hoping that Theophilus will have understood and responded appropriately. When we look at Luke's entire Gospel as an artistic literary composition through which Luke has made profound theological statements, we can see not only has the material that Luke has chosen to include worked effectively to communicate his intentions but also that the order in which that material has been arranged is crucial for conveying Luke's meanings.

We may therefore now partially answer Luke's critics and not only fulfill Farrer's challenge to show "that St. Luke's plan was capable of attracting St. Luke,"[8] (whether or not it ever satisfied anyone else), but also go much further and assert that, if Luke did use Matthew as one of his sources, then what Luke did to Matthew turned out to be not necessarily a literary *improvement* on Matthew but certainly the literary *equal* of Matthew.

This analysis has shown Luke's Gospel to be a carefully crafted work of art, and one that actually relies on the specific sequence of much of its material in order to achieve its full effect. If Matthew *was* one of his sources, we can see that Luke has rearranged Matthew's material not

8. Farrer, "On Dispensing with Q," 65.

just in a way that is somehow secretly "Luke-pleasing" but in an artistically understandable way. Matthew had arranged his material in a manner suitable for teaching, especially for teaching Jewish Christians. Luke has arranged similar material in a manner conducive to effective and persuasive storytelling, especially for telling his story to gentile non-Christians.

## The Second Movement

It is noteworthy that Luke's sequel to his Gospel, the Acts of the Apostles, also reveals a nearly identical three-part structure to his Gospel but with a much shorter Introduction and no Coda. Interestingly, this is also consistent with sonata form when used for the *second* movement of a symphony. Hence, the two-part work often referred to as "Luke-Acts" reveals a consistent approach, one that corresponds structurally and aesthetically to the first two movements of a classical symphony (in this case, perhaps Luke's compositions could be compared to Schubert's *Unfinished Symphony*, of which only the first two movements were ever completed).

In both Luke and Acts, the first of the three main sections is the longest and the last is the shortest, and these sections correspond precisely in both books. This parallel structure appears to be intentional. Luke seems to be telling us (among other things) that the ministry of the early church as described in Acts echoes the ministry of Jesus himself as described in Luke's Gospel. Thus, the early church has, like Jesus, become a faithful servant of God. If we chart out the structure of both books, we see how Luke seems to be drawing a comparison between specific events in Jesus's life and events in the life of the early church:

Table 2.8. Events in Jesus's Life (Luke) and
in the Life of the Early Church (Acts)

| Luke | Acts |
|---|---|
| **Introduction:** Jesus's Infancy (1:1–2:52) | **Introduction:** The Infant Church (1:1–26) |
| **Exposition:** Jesus's Early Ministry (3:1–9:50) | **Exposition:** The Church's Early Ministry (2:1–12:25) |
| Jesus's Baptism and Temptation (3:1–4:13) | Pentecost (2:1–13) |
| Jesus's Preaching in Nazareth (4:14–30) | Peter's Preaching in Jerusalem (2:14–41) |
| Ministry and Miracles (4:31–6:16) | Ministry and Miracles (2:42–6:7) |
| The Sermon on the Plain (6:17–49) | Stephen's Speech (6:8–8:1) |
| Expanded Ministry (7:1–8:3) | Expanded Ministry (8:2–9:43) |
| Parables of the Kingdom (8:4–9:17) | Peter's Vision allowing Gentiles into the Kingdom (10:1–11:30) |
| Peter's Confession and the Transfiguration (9:18–50) | Peter's Release from Prison (12:1–25) |
| **Development:** Jesus's Journey to Jerusalem (9:51–19:27) | **Development:** Paul's Missionary Journeys (13:1–21:14) |
| **Recapitulation:** Jesus's Trials (19:28–23:56) | **Recapitulation:** Paul's Trials (21:15–28:31) |
| The Triumphal Entry into Jerusalem (19:28–44) | Paul's Arrival in Jerusalem (21:15–19) |
| Jesus in the Temple (19:45–21:38) | Paul in the Temple (21:20–26) |
| Jesus's Last Supper and Arrest (22:1–53) | Paul's Arrest (21:27–22:29) |
| Jesus before the Sanhedrin (22:54–71) | Paul before the Sanhedrin (22:30–23:22) |
| Jesus before Pilate, Herod, and Pilate again (23:1–25) | Paul before Felix, Festus, and Agrippa (23:23–26:32) |
| Jesus's Crucifixion and Burial (23:26–56) | Paul's Shipwreck and Arrival in Rome (27:1–28:31) |
| **Coda:** Jesus's Resurrection (24:1–53) | |

As the second movement of Luke's symphony, Acts begins with a brief Introduction (chapter 1), which describes the fledgling church in the days just after Jesus's resurrection. Interestingly, Luke identifies Mary the mother of Jesus as one of the founding members of the church (1:14), so that she is present at the inception of the church, just as she had been (of course) at the conception of Jesus.

With the dramatic events of Pentecost (chapter 2), the ministry of the church begins in earnest, as does the Exposition section of Acts. The Holy Spirit descends on the church in visible form just as she had done on Jesus at his baptism. It is clear that Luke intends this to be a parallel, especially since Jesus had been referred to by John at his baptism as the one who would baptize in the Holy Spirit, just as John had baptized in water. Thus, Pentecost, coming after the resurrection and the ascension, represents the anointing of the church for its ministry, just as Jesus had been anointed for his ministry at his own baptism.

After this anointing in Acts, Peter initiates the public ministry of the church with his sermon in Jerusalem at Pentecost, just as in Luke's Gospel Jesus initiated his own public ministry with his teaching in the synagogue at Nazareth. Both sermons focus on the fulfillment of prophecies from the Old Testament and proclaim that, in Jesus, God is present with his people. Following these sermons, Luke describes in both cases the earliest events in the ministries of Jesus and the church. These events include miracles (especially healing miracles, such as the healing of the lame beggar in Acts 3), teaching in the synagogues (by Jesus) and in the temple (by Peter and John), and questions of authority (with Jesus having been challenged by the Pharisees, and Peter and John being challenged by the Sanhedrin in Acts 4). Indeed, Luke gives even greater details about the early life and authority of the primitive church (including the dramatic story of Ananias and Sapphira in Acts 5, and the appointment of the first deacons in Acts 6) than he had written about Jesus in his Gospel. Both ministries are limited in their geographical scope: Jesus in Galilee, and the church in Jerusalem.

This initial phase culminates in two of the longest discourses in Luke's works: Jesus's Sermon on the Plain in the Gospel and Stephen's speech before the Sanhedrin in Acts 7. As discussed above, Jesus's sermon served to introduce his basic teaching regarding discipleship, that the faithful are to be giving of themselves. Stephen's speech also serves to relate a basic concept for Luke, the proper relationship of the Christian community to the temple. This speech is often thought of as a rejection of the temple, since Stephen says that "the Most High does not live in houses made by men; as the prophet says, 'Heaven is my throne, and the earth is my footstool. What kind of house will you build for me? says the Lord'" (Acts 7:48–49 NIV). We need to realize that Stephen is not only quoting Isaiah here but is also quoting Solomon at the dedication of the temple: "Even heaven and the highest heaven cannot contain you, how much less this house that I have built!"

(2 Chr 6:18 NRSV). If Stephen were here rejecting the temple, we would be forced to conclude that Solomon himself had also rejected the temple! Since this would be absurd, it is evident that Stephen is saying something different here, not that God is not present with his people in the temple but that God is present in an even more profound way through Jesus himself.

In both Luke and Acts, these critical speeches inaugurate an expanded phase of ministry. In Luke, Jesus told the parable of the Sower, indicating that God is calling all people, who must choose how to respond. This was followed by Jesus's touring some of the areas surrounding Galilee, even ministering to gentiles. In Acts, the martyrdom of Stephen drives the disciples out of Jerusalem, and the church expands into Samaria and even Ethiopia (via the Ethiopian eunuch in chapter 8), into Syria and into all of Judea and Galilee (chapter 9, which also tells of Paul's conversion). The church ultimately begins to accept gentiles, based on Peter's vision in chapter 10. This is reported to the Jerusalem church in chapter 11, and following this the Jewish-gentile church of Antioch is founded and led by Barnabas and Paul.

The Exposition section of Luke's Gospel culminated in Peter's confession that Jesus is the Messiah, followed by the glorious revelation of the transfiguration. The Exposition of Acts also culminates in a glorious event, in which Peter is a central figure, this time in his release from prison by an angel (chapter 12). In Luke's Gospel, the climactic event prepared for Jesus's Journey to Jerusalem. In Acts, it prepares for a vastly expanded ministry of the church beyond Palestine, a ministry that will be totally dominated by the activities of Paul.

The Development section of Luke's Gospel explored the nature of discipleship and filled out Jesus's teachings. The Development section of Acts now gives us a detailed description of Paul's missionary journeys. It reveals Paul as a true disciple and servant of God (not the perfect one that Jesus had been, however). It not only tells about the expansion of Christianity within the Roman Empire under Paul, but it also reveals Paul's character. Like Jesus, he is frequently hindered by opponents, usually Jewish leaders, but Paul perseveres as a faithful servant ought to do. By recounting Paul's various legal encounters, Luke shows in great detail how Paul was never the one to instigate trouble but was a faithful Jew and Christian and at every occasion spoke the truth.

We read in Acts 13 of Paul and Barnabas setting out on the First Missionary Journey to Cyprus and southern Asia Minor, including the southern cities of the Roman province of Galatia: Pisidian Antioch, Iconium, Lystra, and Derbe (chapter 14). This is followed by the Council of Jerusalem in Acts 15, at which it is decided that gentiles may become Christians without first needing to become Jewish. Then, in chapter 16, Paul (with Silas and then Timothy) returns to Asia Minor on the Second Missionary Journey, on which he brings the gospel to Europe (to Philippi in Macedonia and then to Thessalonica and Athens (chapter 17) and to Corinth (chapter 18), after which Paul returns to Antioch for the last time. In chapter 19, Paul makes Ephesus (on the west coast of Asia Minor) his base of operations for the Third Missionary Journey, which includes another visit to Corinth (chapter 20) and then a return past Ephesus on the way back to Jerusalem, during which Paul is pursued by his opponents who seek to kill him.

Thus, just as in Luke's Gospel, the Development section of Acts serves to prepare for the climax of the work, in this case the final confrontation between Paul and his antagonists in Jerusalem, and then Paul's legal hearings. But whereas Luke had organized the Journey to Jerusalem in his Gospel as a *logical* sequence of interwoven themes, in Acts Luke organizes his Development section as a *chronological* sequence. This allows him to interweave his various themes progressively in an expert way, themes such as Paul's relationships with Jewish leaders, his unwitting involvement in riots, and the true relationship of the Christian sect with the rest of Judaism. What this analysis does, then, is to allow us to read this portion of Acts not merely as a sequence of isolated and unrelated incidents but as the purposeful actions of Paul (or, more accurately in Luke's retelling, of the Holy Spirit *through* Paul) to build up the new worldwide Christian community in a consistent manner, even though he is frequently hindered by those who oppose God. In both books, such hindrance throughout the Development sections produces increased tension and foreshadows the imprisonment and possible death that await the faithful servant in Jerusalem.

The final segment of Acts also has many parallels with the Recapitulation in Luke's Gospel. Both Jesus and Paul arrive in Jerusalem after predictions of their impending death or imprisonment, and both concentrate their activities there in the temple. Jesus cleansed the temple, whereas Paul cleanses *himself* in the temple (Acts 21), offering the sacrifice of a temporary Nazirite. In both cases, then, the sanctity of the temple is confirmed and emphasized. Both Jesus and Paul are arrested after having observed Jewish rituals: Jesus after the Passover, and Paul after his sacrifice.

One parallel that Luke does *not* draw, however, but which he might have done, is that both are accused of desecrating the temple, Paul for supposedly bringing gentiles into it, and Jesus for claiming that he would destroy it and raise it back up. Luke avoids this accusation against Jesus, which is given in the other Gospels, precisely because he does not want to suggest that Jesus either rejected or replaced the temple. Instead, Luke emphasizes to the end that Christians continued to worship there, nearly thirty years after the resurrection. It is highly significant that the last glimpse that Luke gives us of the temple is one of Paul the Christian making a sacrifice there, followed by Paul's initial defense of himself (Acts 22).

There follows a series of trials for both Jesus and Paul, beginning before the Sanhedrin and followed by hearings before various Roman officials. Here again, there is *almost* a parallel. In John's Gospel, but not in Luke's, when Jesus appears before the Sanhedrin, he is struck in the face for insulting the high priest, to which he responds, "If I have spoken wrongly, testify to the wrong. But if I have spoken rightly, why do you strike me?" (John 18:23 NRSV). In Acts 23, Paul is likewise struck on the mouth for insulting the high priest, to which *he* responds, "God will strike you, you whitewashed wall!" (Acts 23:3 NIV). He thinks better of it and apologizes, however. Paul is a *faithful* servant, but he is never portrayed as a *perfect* servant (as his earlier argument with Barnabas in Acts 15 had also shown).

In both cases, the Sanhedrin condemns their prisoner, but also in both cases the leaders are forced to hand their prisoner over to the Romans, who in both cases find no evidence for a guilty verdict and attempt to release the prisoner. Again, Luke is being Roman-friendly here. But here the two stories go their separate ways. Although the Sanhedrin had convinced Pilate to execute Jesus, after several hearings before Roman rulers in Caesarea (Felix in Acts 24, Festus in Acts 25, and Agrippa in Acts 26), Paul appeals to Caesar and so must be sent to Rome. While both antagonists suffer as a result (Jesus being crucified and Paul being shipwrecked)—hence, both suffer as servants of God—no greater comparison may be drawn. Yet Jesus's crucifixion and Paul's shipwreck (Acts 27) do, from a *storytelling* point of view, provide the most dramatic points in their respective books. At the end of the Recapitulations, Luke finds Jesus locked in a tomb and Acts finds Paul locked in a house in Rome (chapter 28). The Coda of Luke's Gospel, telling of Jesus's resurrection, makes all the difference in the world (since there is no corresponding Coda in Acts), and therefore any attempt by a reader to elevate Paul to the level of Jesus would be impossible.

This brief comparison shows that the significant number of precise parallels between the two volumes of Luke's grand work simply cannot be coincidence. It is evident that Luke composed these two books in a deliberate manner so as to complement each other, both structurally and thematically. The comparisons made above also confirm the validity of the proposed interpretation of Luke's intentions, since this interpretation makes perfect sense consistently across both volumes of Luke's work.

# 3

---

# Luke's Sources

Having finished our analysis of the content of Luke, and having found a plausible answer to the question "Why is the middle part of Luke's Gospel organized the way it is?" we may now explore the effect that answer has on the Synoptic Problem. We may now address the question of Luke's sources, including the "many" he mentioned in his Prologue, and how he employed them in order to achieve the ultimate form of his Gospel discussed above.

## Mark?

Was Mark one of Luke's sources? Nearly every serious Synoptic theory holds that it was, but we should not simply take this for granted. We need to consider the evidence carefully, especially since there is *one* prominent Synoptic theory, the Griesbach hypothesis, that suggests that Mark was written later than Luke (produced partly as a harmony of Matthew and Luke).

In favor of Mark being one of Luke's sources, there is internal and external evidence.

## Internal Evidence for Mark as a Source

Luke's own Prologue refers to "many" other accounts that have pre-ceded Luke's own. This suggests that Mark may have been one of the "many," since otherwise we are left with few choices available to us to place in that category. The textual evidence also suggests that Mark could have been one of Luke's sources. The similarity between the two, both in content and especially in the order of their common peri-copes, points strongly to one of the two being directly dependent on the other. But in which direction does this dependence lie?

If one looks at their content, it seems logical that Luke would have drawn on material from the shorter, more concise Mark, adding new material to it (especially expanding on Jesus's teaching) and improving Mark's rougher Greek style. The alternative seems somewhat less likely, that Mark would have condensed Luke and, in the process, elim-inated the majority of Jesus's teaching, including virtually all of his ethical teaching. This is particularly the case if we consider the impli-cations of the Griesbach theory. This theory contends that Mark was written at least partly as a deliberate condensation and reconciliation of Matthew and Luke. If such was Mark's intention, however, why did he not include any of what we know as the Double Tradition material (which from Mark's point of view might simply have been part of the material common to both Matthew and Luke)? Why would all of *these* pericopes simply have been eliminated rather than reconciled (espe-cially the Double Tradition narrative pericopes, such as the Centurion of Capernaum)? If a harmony of the two other Gospels was Mark's goal, why would he have rejected so many of their common pericopes, even though he did include some material present in Luke but not in Matthew, plus even more material present in Matthew but not in Luke? And why, after making these choices and rejecting so much that is common to Matthew and Luke, would Mark then have added the few odd pericopes unique to his Gospel: the parable of the Seed Grow-ing Secretly (4:26–29), a blind man who is not fully healed on Jesus's first attempt (8:22–26), an account of Jesus's family thinking that he is insane (3:19b–21), and the strange account of the young man fleeing naked when Jesus is arrested (14:50–52)? It seems more likely that both Matthew and Luke would have eliminated these slightly problematic pericopes (if Mark was one of their sources) than that Mark would have added them after eliminating so much else from Matthew and Luke (if they were *his* sources). Based on this criterion, then, the Griesbach theory already seems somewhat less plausible than the alternatives.

Yet we should not dismiss this theory quite so easily on these grounds. According to Griesbach scholars, the reconciliation of Matthew and Luke was not so much Mark's *goal* as it was his *method* for achieving his goal. Mark's ultimate reason for writing his Gospel would not have been just to produce a harmony of Matthew and Luke, but to tell his own version of the story of Jesus, whom he depicts as the miracle-working savior, with more emphasis on his actions and less on his teachings than one finds in either Matthew or Luke. This does indeed make good sense of Mark's potential motives for creating the Gospel he did, if he used Matthew and Luke as his sources. (Again, our exploration above of Luke's reasons for organizing his own Gospel in the way that he did should warn us against presuming that any of the Gospel writers were merely editors or compilers.) Combining material from two different source scrolls, which contained no breaks between sentences or even words, would not have been an easy task in the first century. Mark's solution to this difficulty, according to this theory, was that the easiest way to combine material from Matthew and Luke was to work through both scrolls at the same time, following their *common* order whenever possible, while adding in some new material that enhanced the portrait of Jesus that Mark wished to paint.

The main argument in favor of the Griesbach hypothesis, therefore, is the argument from order, which speaks to Mark's *procedure* rather than his aim. Mark generally serves as the "middle term" between Matthew and Luke when we compare the order of their pericopes. When Matthew disagrees with Mark's order, Luke almost always agrees with Mark, but when Luke disagrees with Mark, Matthew agrees with Mark. William R. Farmer, the most prominent twentieth-century Griesbach advocate, claims that the discrepancies in the order of material in the Synoptics are best explained if Mark was written so as to harmonize the orders of Matthew and Luke. Farmer adopted the Griesbach theory because of "the rediscovery of its central and essential strength—viz. that it offers a credible explanation for the order of the episodes in the synoptic gospels . . . lacking in the alternative accounts. . . . Mark on this view can only be third and must have known Matthew and Luke. There seems to be no other satisfactory solution."[1]

According to this theory, as further described by Bernard Orchard

---

1. William R. Farmer, "Modern Developments of Griesbach's Hypothesis," *New Testament Studies* 23 (1977) 280–93.

and Harold Riley, "When we draw the inevitable conclusion that Mark used Matthew and Luke, there is an illuminating corollary. In choosing the episodes with which he continues his narrative, Mark never turns back: he always goes forward with the text either of Matthew or of Luke."[2] Yet this claim is not entirely true. There are a number of individual verses in Mark (including Mark 9:50, 10:11–12, and 10:38) that do not correspond to their contexts in either Matthew or Luke. In addition, there is one major case—Mark 13:9–13, Jesus's warning to his disciples of coming persecutions, part of Mark's version of the "Mini-Apocalypse"—where the corresponding passages in Matthew and Luke come much earlier in their Gospels (Matt 10:17–22 and Luke 12:11–12), so that Mark would have needed to "turn back" his source scrolls in order to find those pericopes. This passage, therefore, is highly problematic for Griesbach advocates, since it challenges the basic intention and procedure of Mark, which is the cornerstone of the whole theory.

So we may question whether the argument from order is sufficiently strong to suggest that the Griesbach theory is more plausible than the alternatives. As we have seen in the analysis of the middle portion of Luke's Gospel, Luke certainly had good reasons for organizing and ordering his chosen pericopes as he did. It is therefore highly likely that, when we look at those cases where Luke does not agree with Mark's order, we will find credible explanations as to why Luke may have chosen such deviations. A similar analysis of Matthew would also probably reveal a reasonable explanation for why he may have wished to depart at times from Mark's order. Indeed, Matthew's basic structure seems to consist of a series of sections, each of which recounts a number of events that are similar thematically, followed by a related major discourse by Jesus. The section of Matthew that follows directly after the Sermon on the Mount consists of just such a group of similar stories (in Matthew 8–9), all of which relate important miracles of Jesus but which have been drawn seemingly from different parts of Mark in order to create this sequence. This one section accounts for nearly all of Matthew's deviations from Mark's order.

There is one condition, however, under which the argument from order might bear some weight. If Matthew and Luke were each following Mark but were working independently, it would be a coincidence that each chose to depart from Mark's order at different points but never at the same point. The Griesbach solution eliminates such a

---

2. Bernard Orchard and Harold Riley, *The Order of the Synoptics: Why Three Synoptic Gospels* (Macon, GA: Mercer University Press, 1987), 11.

coincidence by claiming that Mark deliberately reconciled the orders of Matthew and Luke. But this argument has validity only if it is given in answer to the Q theory, which insists that Matthew and Luke worked without knowledge of each other. If, on the other hand, Luke had both Matthew and Mark available to him, he would have already known that Matthew had departed from Mark's order at certain points. There would therefore have been no coincidences regarding Luke's choices, and Farmer's assertion that Mark "can only be third" would bear no weight at all.

We may conclude, then, that the argument from order does not demonstrate that Mark *must* have been written after Luke, or even that it is likely that Mark was written later. Instead, when we combine all the internal evidence, including Luke's Prologue and the content and style of both Gospels, we may conclude that the more likely scenario is that Luke used Mark as a source rather than that Mark used Luke.

## External Evidence for Mark as a Source

The preponderance of external evidence also points to Mark having been written prior to Luke. The testimony of nearly all the early church fathers is that the four Gospels were written in the order in which they now appear in the New Testament. In the fragments still extant of Papias's writings, there is no specific mention of Luke, but Papias does tell us that Mark wrote his Gospel based on the preaching of Peter, which suggests that Luke was not a source for Mark. Similarly, Justin Martyr refers to Mark as the "Memoirs of Peter,"[3] indicating the same. Irenaeus seems to imply the order Matthew, Mark, Luke, John in his brief statement about the Gospels, and, from the time of Origen on, this order is affirmed explicitly by various writers.

There is one church father, however, Clement of Alexandria, who appears to contradict this order. As Clement is normally translated, Eusebius quotes him as saying that "the Gospels containing the genealogies were written first."[4] This in turn is normally interpreted to mean that Clement is claiming that Matthew and Luke were written before Mark and John. This would provide some external evidence that Mark was written after Luke and, in particular, seems to support the Griesbach theory that the Synoptics were written in the order Matthew, Luke, Mark. Indeed, after the argument from order, this quo-

---

3. Justin Martyr, *Dialogue with Trypho* 106.3 (*Ante-Nicene Fathers*).
4. Eusebius, *Ecclesiastical History* 6.14.5 (*Nicene and Post-Nicene Fathers*).

tation from Clement is the next most important piece of evidence on which the Griesbach theory is based. Yet even if this *is* what Clement claims, he appears to stand alone, and so the preponderance of external evidence is still in favor of Luke having used Mark as a source.[5]

When we look at the quotation from Clement in its original Greek, it is not at all certain that the traditional translation is correct. In analyzing the text itself, and the history of how it has been interpreted, Stephen C. Carlson suggests that the word προγράφω should be translated not as "written first" but as "openly published." Carlson writes:

> Just as the preposition προ has a locative sense in addition to a temporal sense, so too does προγράφειν have another sense, "to write before the public," i.e., "to set forth publicly" or "proclaim in public." In particular, J. B. Lightfoot, in connection with Galatians 3:1, commented that this verb "is capable of two meanings, (1) 'To write beforehand,' [and] (2) 'To write up in public, to placard.' It is the common word to describe all public notices or proclamations."[6]

Based on this double meaning, and on the only other usage of this verb by Clement (in which the temporal meaning is not possible), Carlson concludes that here Clement is not claiming that Matthew and Luke were *written* before the other Gospels but that they were *published*, put before the public or, in other words, circulated widely, whereas Mark (as Clement goes on to say) "shared his with whoever wanted it."[7] Carlson continues:

> If προγεγράφθαι is taken in the sense of writing publicly, Clement's statement would mean: "He said that those gospels having the genealogies were published openly," with an implication that their publication was official. In contrast with the standard chronological interpretation, this sense provides a better fit with its literary context and poses no difficulty for Origen's ordering of the gospels."[8]

Clearly the contrast between being "published" and being "shared with whoever wanted it" (presumably by Mark giving personal copies to

---

5. It also seems to be the case that Augustine may have eventually become convinced that Mark was written after Matthew and Luke, but, if so, this was based on his own analysis, not on external evidence. See Watson, "Q as Hypothesis," 397n2.
6. Stephen C. Carlson, "Clement of Alexandria on the 'Order' of the Gospels," *New Testament Studies* 47 (2001): 118–25, doi: 10.1017/S0028688501000091.
7. Eusebius, *Ecclesiastical History* 6.14.6, trans. Stephen C. Carlson.
8. Carlson, "Clement of Alexandria."

those who asked) makes far more sense than a contrast between being "written first" and being "shared with whoever wanted it."

In further support of this interpretation Carlson notes that Origen was Clement's student and that Origen claims that he received the order Matthew, Mark, Luke, John "as having learnt by tradition."[9] Origen does not say that he knew this order apart from his teacher; from whom, therefore, would he have learned this tradition if not from that very teacher? Thus, Clement does not support the Griesbach theory at all, and hence there seems to be no evidence, either internal or external, that favors the Griesbach solution. Unless the other alternatives prove to be untenable for other reasons, then, there appears to be no reason to consider it further.

The implications of this interpretation of Clement are extremely interesting: Luke's Gospel, although written originally for Theophilus, was subsequently published openly. Although Mark's Gospel may have been *written* before Luke's, it was at first available only privately and not published and circulated until a later date. If that is the case, this has important repercussions for the entire Synoptic Problem. If this quotation from Clement of Alexandria is no longer a weak piece of evidence outweighed by other witnesses (or the sole external evidence that Mark may have been written after Luke), but instead is based on a valid tradition consistent with other testimony (and when Eusebius quotes it, he tells us that "Clement presented a tradition of the original elders about the disposition of the gospels"[10]), then perhaps it provides us with some real clues about the history of the Synoptic Gospels.

Further, we have available to us firsthand evidence of a situation not too different from the one Clement is describing here, in the case of the famous physician Galen of Pergamon, who died around 200 CE. Galen wrote and published many medical treatises, but he also gave lectures to students and apparently sometimes gave copies of his lecture notes to them to help them remember what he had said. In a letter to one Bassus, he complains that certain unscrupulous parties had published some of these notes as their own works:

> So for this very reason, and because many people have mistreated my books in many different ways (for they have read them as their own among one nation or another, after taking things out, adding things and changing things), I think it best to demonstrate first the reason for this

9. Eusebius, *Ecclesiastical History* 6.25.4, trans. Lake, Lawlor, and Oulton.
10. Eusebius, *Ecclesiastical History* 6.14.5, trans. Stephen C. Carlson.

maltreatment, then to set out which were really written by me and what their contents are. As for the reason why many read my books as their own, this you know yourself, most excellent Bassus; for they were given to friends or pupils without an inscription [*chōris epigraphēs*], simply because they were not for publication but were done for those very people as they requested memoranda of what they had heard. . . . I just used to give them to my students without any inscription [*chōris epigraphēs*], and thus later as they came into the hands of others, one gave them one title, one another.[11]

In making a comparison between Galen and Mark here, I do not imply that any type of unscrupulous misappropriation of Mark's Gospel was ever attempted, but it is interesting that, just as Galen gave private copies of his notes (not intended for publication) to students who requested them, so Clement is claiming that Mark gave private copies of his Gospel (also apparently not originally intended for publication) to those who requested it.

If there is some truth in Clement's statement, and Mark's Gospel was written before Luke's but was not circulated publicly, how could Luke have obtained a copy in order to use it as a source for his own Gospel? If it had not yet been published, he could not have had a published copy; the only possibility would be that he obtained a *private* copy. This scenario implies that the authors of these two Gospels may have actually known each other (or had at least met) and that the author of Mark had personally given a copy of his Gospel to the author of Luke. Given what was said earlier—that it is distinctly possible that these Gospels were written not by members of isolated Christian communities but by itinerant preachers—there is certainly a possibility that two such preachers might have met and exchanged Gospels.

If we go one step further and accept the possibility that the traditionally named authors may have actually been the authors of the Gospels that bear their names, is there any clue available to us to indicate that Luke might have obtained a private copy of Mark's Gospel before he began writing his own? The answer to this question is a resounding yes! Paul's letter to Philemon (and his letter to the Colossians if genuine) would have been written either during Paul's imprisonment in Caesarea (from 57 to 59 CE) or during the early portion of his house arrest in Rome (beginning in 60 CE). In both Philemon and Colos-

11. Galen, *De libris propriis* proem, quoted in Loveday Alexander, "Ancient Book Production and the Circulation of the Gospels," in *The Gospels for All Christians: Rethinking the Gospel Audiences* (Grand Rapids: Eerdmans, 1998), 96–97, Alexander's translation.

sians, Paul mentions that, among those with him at the time are both Luke and Mark! (Philemon 24, Col 4:10–14). Hence, we actually have documentary evidence that these two potential Gospel writers knew each other and were together on at least one occasion, so at this or some subsequent time Mark could have provided Luke with a copy of his Gospel (depending on when it was actually written). But regardless of whether we take these claims of authorship seriously, there is certainly the possibility that two other itinerant preachers in the early church could have met and exchanged their writings.

If there is even a shred of truth in the traditions regarding the authorship of the Gospels (that they were written by travelers) and in the statement of Clement of Alexandria (that Matthew and Luke were circulated publicly but Mark was only circulated privately), we are faced with the following plausible and intriguing scenario: Although the Gospels of Matthew and Luke were both immediately put into circulation after their writing, the Gospel of Mark initially had an extremely limited circulation, probably dependent on personal contact with its author. If so, then Luke may not have obtained a copy of Mark (even if it was the first Gospel written) until shortly before he began work on his own Gospel and so may not have been as familiar with Mark as with his other sources, the very opposite of what is usually assumed.

## Q?

We have provisionally found one of Luke's sources, the Gospel of Mark. But there must have been others as well, particularly if we are to believe that he knew of (and had at least read) "many" accounts. There must have been at least one other source (whether oral or written) for the material in Luke that does not parallel Mark. Unless we propose that Luke invented all his other material himself (in which case we must give valid reasons for proposing this, and for explaining Luke's claims to have carefully researched everything, to have had these stories entrusted to him by eyewitnesses, and to have known of other accounts), there must be at least one, and possibly two other sources from which Luke extracted material.

Mark may be sufficient to account for the Triple Tradition material in Luke, but when we consider the Double Tradition material, there are three possibilities: Either Luke used some unknown source and then was himself a direct source for Matthew (which virtually every Synoptic theory has rejected[12]), or Matthew was a direct source for Luke (as the Farrer theory proposes[13]), or both Luke and Matthew used the same or at least a similar source (as the Q theory contends).

Even more so than for Mark, the evidence for the possibility that Matthew came later than Luke is extremely weak. The external evidence all points to Matthew being the earlier of the two: the evidence of the church fathers that Matthew's was the first Gospel written, and the evidence from quotations and allusions in early noncanonical Christian writings, in which parallels to Matthew are far more frequent than parallels to Luke. Again, Luke's Prologue itself is strong evidence that other accounts already existed, so that his was most likely the last of the Synoptics to be written. Indeed, even if Matthew's Gospel was not a direct source for Luke, it might still be possible that his was one of the "many" accounts Luke at least knew existed, even if he had not actually read it.

This leaves two possibilities: Either Luke used Matthew as a source, or both Matthew and Luke used a similar source. It is the belief that Luke could not have used Matthew directly that is the foundation for the Q theory. The Q theory is therefore a negative theory, not a positive one. It is based not on direct evidence but on the conclusion that Luke could not have used Matthew. If Luke did use Matthew as a source for Double Tradition material, there is no point whatsoever in proposing the existence of Q. Hence, if the objections to Luke having used Matthew as a source can be overcome, the raison d'être for Q disappears, allowing us to discard it.

We have already noted that, even if Luke had used Q as a source, Q could still not have qualified as one of the "many" narratives of what had "been accomplished" mentioned in Luke's Prologue, since Q contains no narrative of "accomplishments."[14] The possibility that Q was one of Luke's sources is therefore already weak, resting solely on the conclusion that it would have been impossible for Matthew to have been one of Luke's sources. But the unsuitability of Q as a source, based on Luke's own description, also casts doubt on the validity of the Q theory.

12. One notable exception to this is Martin Hengel, who suggests that Matthew used Mark, Luke, and some form of Q as sources (*Four Gospels*, 169–207).
13. Anything said about the Farrer theory in regard to Luke's Gospel applies equally to the alternate Augustine theory (that Matthew was written first, then Mark abbreviated Matthew, then Luke used both Matthew and Mark), since the exact relationship between Matthew and Mark has no bearing on how Luke would have later chosen to use them both as sources.
14. This would not necessarily be the case if we were to propose that Q included a passion narrative, but proponents of Q have not typically taken this possibility seriously.

We have also seen that if Luke had used Q, then, based on our analysis of Luke's Development section, the assumption is not valid that he must have used it by pasting its contents into his own Gospel in the order in which he found them. The order of the Q material in Luke is not arbitrary or somehow mysteriously "Luke-pleasing" but appears to be logical and deliberate and makes perfect sense in terms of Luke's intentions. Hence, it would seem to be an incredible coincidence for Luke simply to have happened to find the Q material in the order in which he wanted to develop it, and to be able to weave in his other sources around it in the way he would have needed to do if the Q theory is correct.

We may also now question the assumption that if Luke used Q he must have used virtually *all* of Q. Luke's Development section is concerned with a specific sort of information and deals with specific areas of Jesus's teaching. It is not simply a hodgepodge of random pericopes thrown together "without rhyme or reason." There is strong evidence, therefore, to believe that Luke may have been quite selective in terms of what material he chose to use. He was, after all, extremely limited in the amount of material he could use, since the evidence suggests that he included as much as he could physically fit onto one scroll, thus probably leaving out much material he might have incorporated had he had unlimited space.

The largest scroll that could be produced in the first century would theoretically be about thirty-two feet long, possibly as long as thirty-five feet. In reality, however, the longest scroll yet discovered, the Temple Scroll from Qumran, was about twenty-nine feet long.[15] The Gospel of Luke would have required about a thirty-foot scroll, and the books of Acts and Matthew each a scroll only slightly shorter.[16] Although we do not have direct evidence whether the Gospels were originally written as scrolls or codices, it would seem quite a coincidence if they had been written as codices (which offered much more space), since the three longest books in the New Testament are all very close to the practical limit for a document written on a single papyrus scroll. It seems to be a safe conclusion, therefore, that at least these three documents were probably written originally on scrolls, and that their authors were therefore limited to the amount of content that

15. Michael E. Stone, ed., *Jewish Writings of the Second Temple Period: Apocrypha, Pseudepigrapha, Qumran Sectarian Writings, Philo, Josephus,* Compendia rerum Iudaicarum ad Novum Testamentum, section 2 (Philadelphia: Fortress Press, 1984), 527.
16. Bruce M. Metzger, *The Text of the New Testament: Its Transmission, Corruption, and Restoration,* 2nd ed. (Oxford: Oxford University Press, 1968), 12.

could be included on one scroll, with especially Luke requiring very careful planning in order not to run out of space.

Therefore, if Q was one of Luke's sources, it may be necessary for us to rethink our idea of Q in order to fit the evidence. There are ways that we might rethink Q—such as with a passion narrative (which would then allow it to be one of Luke's "many accounts")—but is there any point? The only basis for proposing Q in the first place is the idea that Luke and Matthew both worked independently of each other. If, in light of the above analysis of the middle portion of Luke's Gospel, we find sufficient reason to believe that Luke could have used Matthew directly, there would be no reason left for Q (for *any* sort of Q whatsoever, rethought or not). Unless we rule out Matthew as one of Luke's sources, there is simply no reason to continue speculating at this point about Q.

## Matthew?

Is it possible, then, that Luke used Matthew directly as one of his sources? There are a number of reasons to conclude that he did. The tradition of all the church fathers is that Matthew's was the first Gospel to have been written, and even if this should turn out to be inaccurate, the evidence is still very strong that Matthew was written prior to Luke. (Even most Q scholars would agree. They would simply argue that Luke had not seen Matthew's Gospel by the time he wrote his own.) Matthew is initially an obvious candidate for one of Luke's "many" previous accounts. In addition, Matthew and Luke both contain a large amount of similar material. The simplest explanation for this is that one of them took this material directly from the other. It seems extremely unlikely that Matthew took this material from Luke, so the most obvious alternative is that Luke took it from Matthew.

Beyond their similarity in material, there is also a certain similarity in structure between Matthew and Luke that is not shared by either Mark or John (or any other document). Mark Goodacre observes:

> Even the most casual reader of the Gospels cannot help noticing that Matthew and Luke have a remarkably similar literary plan. On the assumption that both Matthew and Luke knew Mark's Gospel, it is interesting that both decided to write a similar book at around the same time . . . in which Mark's perceived shortcomings are overcome by major improvements in Greek style, the addition of a prologue dealing with

Jesus' infancy, an epilogue providing resurrection appearances, and a great deal of new teaching in between.[17]

It is far easier to explain such similarities if Luke was already familiar with Matthew than to assume that both of them decided completely independently of each other to augment Mark in such parallel ways.

## Objections

Nevertheless, there are reasons to doubt the idea that Luke used Matthew, and it is these reasons that have led many scholars to believe that it is impossible that Luke could have had Matthew's Gospel available to him as a source. Objections to Luke having used Matthew include the following:

1. Luke's "inferior" arrangement of the Double Tradition material. As discussed already, many scholars consider Matthew's topical arrangement of material to be more logical than Luke's, which has "no commonsense explanation." If Luke had known Matthew's Gospel, he would not have "scrambled" Matthew's superior arrangement of material.
2. The physical difficulty of rearranging Matthew's material. Even if Luke had wanted to "scramble" Matthew's material, the logistics involved for a first-century author to have scanned back and forth through a physically awkward scroll with no spaces between words or sentences in order to find the desired passages would have been virtually impossible to achieve.
3. The inconsistent use of sources. If Luke did use Matthew, he must have used it in a way very different from the way he used Mark, whose order he did follow fairly faithfully. Such inconsistency would also have been illogical.
4. Luke's lack of use of Matthean material *outside* of Triple Tradition contexts. Luke's birth narrative, genealogy, and resurrection narratives seem not only to be uninfluenced by Matthew but in some aspects to be directly contradictory.
5. Luke's lack of use of Matthean material *within* Triple Tradition contexts. Luke appears to be ignorant of any of Matthew's changes to Mark's material. If Luke was familiar with Matthew, we would expect him to include more of Matthew's versions of Triple

17. Goodacre, *Case against Q*, 47–48.

Tradition pericopes. This is especially true in the passion narratives, where, if Luke knew Matthew, we would expect him to include (for example) Pilate's wife's dream and Pilate washing his hands (Matt 27:19, 24–25).

6. Luke's lack of use of Markan material within Double Tradition contexts. When he uses material where Matthew has expanded on Mark's version, Luke appears to omit passages that Matthew and Mark have in common. This suggests that Matthew's version is a conflation of Mark with another source and that Luke is using that other source prior to its conflation with Mark.

7. Mutual primitivity. Sometimes Matthew's version of a Double Tradition pericope seems to be more primitive, while sometimes Luke's version seems to be. If Luke were copying Matthew, we would expect Matthew's versions always to be the more primitive.

8. The occurrence of doublets in Matthew and Luke. Repeated verses or pericopes within a single Gospel are more easily explained if one occurrence came from Mark and the other occurrence came from a common source.

9. Q's distinct theology. When Q is examined as a separate document, it seems to display its own characteristic theology, somewhat distinct from either Matthew or Luke. This suggests that Q did exist and was a common source for Matthew and Luke.

All but the first two of these objections to Luke having used Matthew have to do with *how* Luke used his sources. Since this is a matter that has not yet been discussed, it is premature to attempt to address any of these issues at this point. Since we cannot deal with how Luke used his sources until we have some idea about what those sources were, we must first at least provisionally suggest what his sources may have been before attempting to answer how he used them. Based on other evidence, then, if we determine that Luke *may* have used Matthew as a source, we will be able to analyze *how* he might have used it. Only thereafter may we return to the question of whether such usage addresses these objections.

Toward this goal I have already given some preliminary reasons to suspect that Luke did use Matthew. Further, the detailed analysis of Luke's Journey to Jerusalem has adequately answered the first objection listed above. Luke's arrangement of material is just as artistic, just as logical, and just as appropriate and effective for his purpose as Matthew's arrangement is for his. This is therefore not a valid objection to Luke having used Matthew as a source. There is a perfectly rational reason why Luke would have chosen to rearrange Matthew's material in this way for his own specific purpose.

## Logistics

The second objection is a serious one (perhaps the most serious). If it were to turn out that it was impossible, or even extremely difficult, for Luke to have physically made such a rearrangement of the Matthean material, we might have to abandon the idea that Luke used Matthew and reconsider Q instead. Rather than an argument from content, then, this is an argument based on logistics: The physical operations required to relocate Matthean material would simply have been too daunting.

Before addressing the specifics of how Luke would have needed to rearrange Matthew's material, however, we should note that someone at some point certainly did rearrange this material in order for it to appear in Matthew and in Luke in such different orders. According to the Q theory, it was Matthew who rearranged Q; and according to the Farrer theory, it was Luke who rearranged Matthew. Neither of these tasks would have been easy, so regardless of which theory is adopted, a plausible account must be given as to how a first-century writer could have reordered so much material so dramatically.

To address this problem, Michael Goulder has suggested a rather complicated process by which Luke relied partly on his memory from having read Matthew, then first scanned forward through Matthew's Gospel to find desired pericopes, then rescanned backward.[18] While awkward, such a process would not have been impossible. Yet, because of its complexity, Goulder's theory remains somewhat unconvincing, and if a simpler answer could be found for Luke's procedures, this would be preferable to Goulder's.

John Wenham has argued that even if Luke knew of Matthew's Gospel and consulted it in a minor way, many of the pericopes that appear to be common between them actually seem to represent two different traditions, especially since their sense often appears to be different. For example, the parable of the Great Supper has a very different emphasis in Matthew 22 from what it does in Luke 14. In Matthew's

---

18. Michael D. Goulder, "The Order of a Crank," in *Synoptic Studies: The Ampleforth Conferences of 1982 and 1983*, ed. C. M. Tuckett, Journal for the Study of the New Testament: Supplement series 7 (Sheffield: JSOT Press, 1984), 111–30.

Gospel it is used to illustrate the Pharisees' opposition to God, whereas in Luke it is used to encourage hospitality to those who cannot reciprocate. Wenham points to such differences to suggest that Luke was relying almost entirely on a separate *oral* tradition for the supposed Double Tradition material, and probably not on Matthew (or Q) at all. Wenham writes:

> Attempts to find a common order of Q-material in Luke and Matthew have failed to convince. Equally, no argument can be based on the wording. Luke cannot have got his main Q-material from Matthew, since this would have entailed changing the sense of his source in a manner belied by his known fidelity to Mark. However . . . a modest use of Matthew by Luke would seem likely on this supposition; and where Luke seems to be following Matthew, he is found to follow him closely. . . . The picture which is emerging would suggest that Luke had two documents which are known to us which he used quite differently but equally scrupulously. He took Mark as his guide to the basic framework of the gospel, following the order and main substance of Mark's pericopes in the first third and final third of his book, though seldom following his actual wording. Matthew he seems to have used in a minor way to provide some supplementary information in the early part of the book.[19]

Wenham concludes that the only actual Double Tradition material is limited primarily to the narrative sequences that Matthew and Luke share that are not paralleled in Mark, such as the accounts of Jesus's baptism and temptation and the centurion of Capernaum. The vast majority of parables and other teachings that *seem* to be parallel come not from Matthew at all, or from a common source (and thus Q as a source is also precluded), but from separate oral traditions.

Wenham's argument does have some merit. As we have seen, Luke's technique seems to have been the careful juxtaposing of pericopes and the equally careful editing of what he wants to include, but *not* commenting on or apparently altering the material he did choose to include. Thus, he did not change what was said at Jesus's trials before the Sanhedrin or Pilate but simply left out statements that did not suit his purpose. Likewise, in his Journey to Jerusalem, he did not alter the rather difficult parable of the Unjust Steward but used it as it stood, in spite of its difficulties, as a transitional piece. This is completely consistent with his own stated goal of giving an accurate account based on his careful investigation and on the reports of eyewitnesses.

19. Wenham, *Redating Matthew, Mark and Luke,* 87.

It is therefore likely that Wenham is correct that many of the parables and stories that have a loose parallel between Matthew and Luke represent alternate versions of those stories from slightly different sources. But this would hardly apply to all the parables and teachings common to Matthew and Luke. For instance, Wenham suggests that Luke's Sermon on the Plain represents a separate tradition from Matthew's Sermon on the Mount, but, in view of the similar wording, order, and sense of the material, this seems highly unlikely. It also seems unlikely that there is a separate origin for the majority of stories in Luke's Journey to Jerusalem that have a sense similar to parallels in Matthew, even though they occur in a different order. As Wenham himself stated in the passage quoted above, Luke frequently alters Mark's wording, so there is every reason to believe that he would have altered Matthew's as well. So we are still faced with a large amount of material common to Matthew and Luke that needs to be accounted for.

Francis Watson has suggested that Luke would have used a wax tablet notebook, a common piece of equipment available to first-century authors, on which temporary notes could be made and then the wax could be smoothed over for later reuse.[20] Especially in his rearrangement of the Sermon on the Mount, Watson contends that Luke could have copied those portions he wanted to use later in his Journey to Jerusalem onto wax tablets, then consulted these tablets later in his work rather than having to scroll backward in Matthew. This is a plausible proposal, and one that is applicable to *any* Synoptic theory. As noted before, *someone* must have reordered the material of one or more other authors in order to produce all three Synoptic Gospels, and the use of wax tablets would have provided a mechanism that would have mitigated some of the difficulties involved.

Yet there is one simple solution for how Luke could have used Matthew as a source for material found in different orders in the two Gospels: Luke had simply memorized Matthew! He could then have drawn on any pericope from anywhere in Matthew at any time without having to have the text physically in front of him. Memorization of entire documents was a common practice in the cultures of Luke's day, both Jewish and Greek. Steve Mason, in his commentary on the *Life of Josephus*, discusses the use of memorization in the first century:

> Memory-work was a fundamental component of Greek, Roman, and rabbinic education—in preparation for public life in an oral culture. A num-

---

20. Watson, "Q as Hypothesis," 406. See also Richards, *Paul and First-Century Letter Writing*, 47–49.

ber of authors from Plato onward refer to the memorization of large sections of poetry. To become an effective orator, which was a primary goal of Roman education, one needed to rely upon one's memorization of a speech; hence, by the first century BCE memory had become one of the five parts of rhetoric. . . . On the later rabbinic side, the very name *tanna* ("repeater, reciter") draws attention to the skill of this teacher—a figure from the mid-second century CE—in memorizing vast stretches of *halakhah*.[21]

This practice of memorization is well documented. Indeed, just in the short passage quoted above, ten different references have been removed that Mason had included to support his statements. In a culture where books were scarce, it should not be surprising that vast amounts of writing were commonly committed completely to memory. Memorization of the entire Torah was a standard element of Jewish education in the first century. As the quotation above indicates, it was not merely the Scriptures that were often memorized but any useful text.

In this vein, the author of 2 Maccabees says in the introduction to his work, "We have aimed to please those who wish to read, to make it easy for those who are inclined to memorize, and to profit all readers" (2 Macc 2:25 NRSV). The implication here is that, regardless of whether this book should be considered sacred or inspired, there would be those in the culture of that day who would choose to memorize an entire book. Second Maccabees is about two-thirds the length of Matthew, so Matthew would not have been considered a daunting text to memorize completely. Based on Luke's skill as an author, we would expect that he was sufficiently intelligent to have accomplished the task of memorizing Matthew.

It is not at all unreasonable, therefore, to suppose that Luke might have had the entire Gospel of Matthew committed to memory, a book that, if not yet considered sacred, *did* record the life of Luke's Messiah. Luke would certainly have had a clear motivation for memorizing it, especially if he was a traveling Christian missionary who would have had reason to recall portions of it frequently in his preaching and teaching. According to tradition, as recorded by Eusebius, Luke was a native of Antioch, which is where most scholars believe the Gospel of Matthew was written. Either having lived in the precise location of its origin, or at least having traveled widely among early Christian

21. Steve Mason, *Life of Josephus: Translation and Commentary* (Leiden: Brill, 2003), 13.

communities, Luke could easily have come across a copy of Matthew's Gospel (even if it had only recently been published) and would thus have been afforded the opportunity to memorize it. Under such circumstances, then, it is highly likely that Luke had memorized Matthew's entire Gospel.

We usually assume that the Gospel authors, if working from other texts, would have had those texts in front of them as they wrote. While this may be true to some extent, the practice of ancient authors seems to have been to have no more than one particular source text in front of them at any one time. They would have drawn on other texts from memory (even if they would have needed to read some unfamiliar texts immediately prior to writing).[22] If Luke *had* memorized Matthew, even if he had the physical text of Mark in front of him as he wrote some of his narratives, he could easily have drawn on his memory of Matthew at any time to enhance his own version, thus incorporating the Minor Agreements in such passages (assuming that it was his procedure to follow Mark for the most part).

But Luke's procedure may have also been entirely different in the middle portion of his Gospel, his Development section, which is structured quite differently from his narrative sections. His careful interweaving of themes here suggests that, rather than working from written sources at all at this point, Luke may have been drawing on his apparently considerable acquaintance with oral tradition, and in the same way likewise drawing on his memorized knowledge of Matthew's Gospel, perhaps supplemented by his use of wax tablets. Hence, just as all the New Testament authors had also memorized much of the Old Testament and did not need to have such texts in front of them as they wrote, Luke would not have needed to have Matthew's Gospel physically in front of him when he was writing. No one supposes that the Gospel writers would have needed constantly to scroll through all the Old Testament texts in order to find the quotations they were looking for, so there is nothing to prevent Luke from following the same method with Matthew if he was already intimately familiar with its text. This would thus make perfect sense of how Luke pulled parables and teachings from disparate parts of Matthew's Gospel in an order that has no correspondence to their order in Matthew. No physical scanning back and forth would have been necessary at all.

Indeed, Luke probably knew these pericopes far better than we do

22. R. A. Derrenbacker, Jr., *Ancient Compositional Practices and the Synoptic Problem*, Bibliotheca Ephemeridum theologicarum Lovaniensium 186 (Leuven: Peeters, 2005), 37–39, 46–47.

today, and yet any of us who are relatively familiar with Matthew's Gospel would be able to quote (with greater or lesser faithfulness) many of these same pericopes, even if we were hard-pressed to say exactly where in the Gospel each of them is located, or be able to list them in their correct order. Therefore, Luke's use of Matthew in his Development section is completely plausible and consistent with first-century writing procedures. Therefore, the second objection listed above to Luke having used Matthew as a source is sufficiently answered. Luke would have had no difficulty whatsoever in rearranging Matthew's pericopes as he desired in order to produce the type of work he intended.[23]

This also suggests an answer to the third objection above, that if Luke had had both earlier Gospels available to him, why would he have used Matthew and Mark in different and seemingly inconsistent ways? Goodacre believes that Luke would have done so because he was already more familiar with Mark than with Matthew: "Before Matthew is even written, Luke is used to interacting with Mark, reading from Mark, preaching on Mark, steadily getting Mark by heart. When a copy of Matthew comes into his possession, Luke begins to interact with the new Gospel too."[24] Goodacre is making this logical deduction based on the assumption that Mark was the first of the Synoptics to have been written, and so would have been better known by Luke. However, the quote from Clement of Alexandria discussed above suggests that, even if Mark had been *written* earlier, it was not *circulated* publicly until much later.

Hence, perhaps precisely the opposite of what Goodacre has suggested was actually the case. Regardless of when Mark's Gospel was written, it was Matthew's Gospel that was first circulated publicly. In this scenario, Luke was already familiar with *Matthew* to the point of having it completely memorized when (according to the hypothesis put forward above) he was personally given a copy of Mark's Gospel. Not being as familiar with it, Luke would have needed to have Mark's

---

23. It may be validly asked at this point, if it is possible for Luke to have completely memorized Matthew, then surely it is also the case for other theories that authors could have memorized some of their sources. In particular, proponents of the Q theory might well suggest that Matthew could have had Q memorized (a much shorter document than Matthew to begin with), which would have mitigated somewhat the extremely complex process required by him to both rearrange its material and at the same time conflate it with (also) rearranged material from Mark. Indeed, for every Synoptic theory, memorization seems to provide the only realistic mechanism for explaining how the Double Tradition material could be in such different orders in both Matthew and Luke, since someone at some point had to rearrange this material, and the physical procedures required to do so in the first century *without* memorization seem virtually impossible.
24. Goodacre, *Case against Q*, 89.

text in front of him as he wrote and would have had to follow it much more closely, whereas he could be much freer with Matthew's material, drawing from it at will whenever it was appropriate.

This, however, raises a further question. If Luke was so familiar with Matthew, why would he have used Mark at all, since virtually everything Luke would have taken from Mark would have been in Matthew already? This is, after all, one of the arguments for the Griesbach theory. Luke could have written his own Gospel based entirely on Matthew's; Mark could then have produced his condensed version from the other two. For now, one simple answer may be offered. Since Mark concentrates more on the stories *about* Jesus, whereas Matthew includes far more of the teachings *of* Jesus, Luke may have found that it was much easier to use Mark's more "uncluttered" narratives whenever he himself wanted to produce a straightforward narrative section. He perhaps would have saved his real effort for the far more complex job of combing through his knowledge of Matthew and oral tradition in order to present Jesus's teachings in the dynamic and dramatic way in which he had intended.

We have adequately answered the first two objections to Luke having used Matthew as a source: Luke's rearrangement of Matthew's material makes perfect sense, given Luke's intentions; and Luke would have had no difficulty implementing this rearrangement if he had already memorized Matthew's Gospel. We have also begun tentatively to address some of the remaining issues, but a full answer must await an analysis of how Luke used his sources, once we have provisionally determined what all those sources were.

## John?

We have now identified two potential written sources for Luke—Mark and Matthew—both of which qualify as being among the "many" narrative accounts Luke mentions in his Prologue. We do know of one other such account, of course: the Gospel according to John. Is it possible that this, too, was one of Luke's sources?

A growing number of scholars believe that this is a real possibility. John A. T. Robinson in his books *Redating the New Testament* and *The Priority of John*[25] has questioned the long-held belief that John's was the last Gospel to be written; he suggests that John may have begun writ-

25. John A. T. Robinson, *Redating the New Testament* (London: SCM, 1976), *The Priority of John* (Oak Park: Meyer-Stone Books, 1987).

ing his Gospel in the early years of the church, perhaps even before Matthew and Mark were written. According to Robinson, an early version of John, which we may refer to as "Proto-John," may well have existed at the time Luke wrote his Gospel, even if the final version of John was written at a later date.

Among those who support Robinson's hypothesis is Barbara Shellard, who suggests that similarities between Luke and John (particularly similarities in their passion narratives) are best explained if Luke was familiar with John's Gospel.[26] Joseph Fitzmyer lists a number of features common to Luke and John that are missing from Matthew and Mark, including "the anointing of Jesus' feet by a woman; the single account of the multiplication of the loaves and fish; the mention of Lazarus, Martha, and Mary; one of the twelve named Judas; no night interrogation of Jesus by the high priest; three nonguilty statements of Pilate during Jesus' trial; and postresurrection appearances of the risen Christ in the Jerusalem area."[27]

It is an attractive proposal for a number of reasons. It brings John into the "family" of the Synoptics instead of treating it as an entity separate from and foreign to their world. It increases the count of Luke's prior narratives to three, a better number for a believable "many" than just two. And it adds weight to the idea that the early Christian church was not divided into isolated individual communities where different traditions developed apart from one another but was instead a vibrant network of interrelated communities sharing ideas.

The analysis of Luke's Development section also suggests that there might be more connections between Luke and John than have been supposed in the past. Luke's style in this section bears more than a passing resemblance to the "spiraling" technique that John often employs in his Gospel (where the same themes recur but in slightly different lights as new elements are added). In addition, the central theme of Luke's Development section, the faithful versus the unfaithful, is strikingly similar to the theme in John's Gospel (and his first letter) of a somewhat dualistic contrast between the children of light and the children of darkness. There are other minor thematic connections between Luke and John as well.

If John's Gospel *was* a source for Luke, however, it would have had a

---

26. Barbara Shellard, *New Light on Luke: Its Purpose, Sources, and Literary Context,* Journal for the Study of the New Testament: Supplement Series 215 (London: Sheffield Academic Press, 2004).

27. Joseph A. Fitzmyer, "Luke, The Gospel According to," in *The Oxford Companion to the Bible,* ed. Bruce M. Metzger and Michael D. Coogan (Oxford: Oxford University Press, 1993), 471.

much more subtle influence than either Matthew or Mark, and would have left only a few scattered clues here and there. It was certainly not a major source for Luke, and, for this reason, the impact of this possibility on the issues dealt with here would not be significant.

Even if John was not a *written* source for Luke, it is certainly not out of the question that Luke was familiar with some of the same specific traditions that influenced John. Nor can we rule out the possibility that John (if his *was* the last of the canonical Gospels to be written) was familiar with Luke's Gospel. The most that can be said at this point, to account for some of their similarities, is that there does seem to be some point of contact between Luke and John (or between their sources). As Fitzmyer also concludes, "Although there is no real evidence that the Johannine evangelist knew the Lucan gospel, some contact in the oral traditions behind both the Johannine and the Lucan gospels is not impossible."[28]

## Other Gospels?

Beyond Matthew, Mark, and John, there is also the possibility that Luke may have used other written sources that were not later included in the New Testament canon. Unlike the hypothetical Q or other proposed hypothetical source documents for which there is no evidence, there did exist in the early centuries of Christianity a number of "gospels" that were rejected by the church as spurious or heretical (and usually both) but that were accepted by breakaway groups. Many of these are often referred to collectively as the "Gnostic Gospels." Is it possible that any of these could have been among Luke's "many" accounts? For this to be the case we would need to establish that two conditions existed: We would need to show, first, that such potential sources had been written prior to Luke's Gospel, and, second, that they contained material that may have influenced Luke. But neither of these conditions appears to be the case.

A growing number of Q (and associated) scholars have suggested that some of these gospels may reflect very early traditions, representing an alternative but valid Christian approach that differs from the version of Christianity portrayed in the canonical books of the New Testament. In particular, the so-called Gospel of Thomas (usually classed separately from the Gnostic Gospels proper) is believed by some to contain early traditions that are perhaps more faithful to Jesus

28. Ibid., 471–72.

himself than are the canonical Gospels. If this were true, the ramifications for the church and for all of Western culture would be significant. But is there evidence that might support this idea?

Regarding dates, there is no evidence that any of these documents existed before the second half of the second century, with the earliest evidence for the Gospel of Thomas being the early third century. Indeed, Bart Ehrman, who claims that "there were other books written as well, with equally impressive pedigrees—other Gospels, Acts, Epistles, and Apocalypses claiming to be written by the earthly apostles of Jesus,"[29] dates all four canonical Gospels to the first century, yet his own list of rejected texts places none of these "alternate" gospels or other writings in the first century.[30]

It was Irenaeus, who became bishop of Lyons in about 180 CE and then published his most famous work, *Against Heresies*, who gives the first account of the Gnostics' spurious gospels (which he numbered at around fifty). Before Irenaeus, there is no mention by any author, Christian or non-Christian, of any of these documents. This implies strongly that these were recent writings and that "Christian" Gnosticism was a new development in Irenaeus's day.

Of particular note in this regard are two specific early heretics, Marcion and Valentinus, who had each broken away from the Roman church around the year 150 CE (only a few short decades before Irenaeus's work), neither of whom makes any mention of any of these alternate "gospels" but both of whom did rely on canonical texts. This is especially significant, since Valentinus was considered to be one of the earliest Gnostics, and Marcion's own beliefs were also not unlike the Gnosticism Irenaeus would later describe. If Gnosticism actually represented a truer, earlier version of Christianity, which had by this time produced written gospels, we would certainly expect some mention of such texts. But instead, Valentinus is said to have later written his own gospel (the Gospel of Truth). Particularly relevant in the current discussion, Marcion accepted one and only one gospel as authoritative—the Gospel according to Luke—but only after he had purged from it any passages with which he disagreed. Thus, in Marcion's day the Gospel of Luke was clearly in circulation, whereas at this same time there is no sign of any of the Gnostic Gospels.

Internal evidence regarding the Gnostic Gospels also strongly sug-

29. Bart D. Ehrman, *Lost Christianities: The Battles for Scripture and the Faiths We Never Knew* (Oxford: Oxford University Press, 2003), 3.
30. See ibid., xi–xv.

gests a date for their writing well after the writing of the Synoptics, since they frequently seem to take for granted background information (such as the calling and roles of the various disciples) that does appear in the Synoptics but not in any of the Gnostic Gospels themselves. Hence, the Gnostic Gospels may be safely discounted as sources for Luke. If there is any dependence, it is the late Gnostic Gospels that are dependent on the early Synoptics, not the other way round.

But what about that one unique document, the Gospel of Thomas? The earliest reference to Thomas was by Hippolytus of Rome in the early third century, and we have no indication that the Gospel was known before this date. It is not mentioned, for instance, by Irenaeus, who wrote just prior to this time specifically about spurious Gospels. Three small extant fragments of Greek versions of the Gospel of Thomas date from the early to middle years of the third century. But even the texts of these fragments vary somewhat from the complete fourth-century Coptic text found at Nag Hammadi in 1945. Yet, in spite of the late date of all this evidence, some scholars have speculated that the Gospel of Thomas actually originated in the very early years of Christianity and represents a version of Christianity consistent with that of Q.

Indeed, some modern Q scholars have actually linked Q and Thomas directly, suggesting that an early version of Q may have been a source document for the Gospel of Thomas itself. This possibility is reflected in the way the editors of *The Sayings Gospel Q in Greek and English* have included not only parallels between Q and the Synoptic Gospels, but with the Gospel of Thomas as well.[31] Speculations about a community of "Q Christians" and "Thomas Christians" who existed at least as early as or earlier than "Markan" or "Lukan" Christians dominate much of the current Q scholarship.

Is there any evidence, however, that the Gospel of Thomas was an early Christian work, or even that it relied on early traditions? There are only two arguments for an early date, neither of which is based on any evidence. The first is that Thomas is similar to Q, which, if it existed, had to be an early document. But if there is no evidence that Q existed, there is no reason to use this argument in favor of Thomas. Hence, if we concluded, based on our investigation, that Luke used Matthew directly as a source, there would be no reason to postulate

---

31. James M. Robinson, Paul Hoffmann, and John S. Kloppenborg, *The Sayings Gospel Q in Greek and English: With Parallels from the Gospels of Mark and Thomas* (Minneapolis: Fortress Press, 2002). See especially Robinson's discussion of the work of Helmut Koester in his Introduction, 56–57.

the existence of Q, and therefore no reason on this basis to think that Thomas was an early document.

The second argument is based on the fact that Thomas does not seem on the surface to be derived from the other Gospels. It does contain numerous sayings that are similar to those in the Synoptics; other sayings are somewhat similar but twist the sense of the saying to reflect a different (and often contradictory) meaning from what we read in the Synoptics. Still other sayings have no parallels in the canonical Gospels. To some Q and Thomas scholars, this suggests that the Gospel of Thomas reflects a different, independent tradition (probably initially oral) from what lies behind the Synoptics, and hence could potentially indicate an early date.

This second argument shows that, for our present purpose (determining possible sources for Luke), Thomas must be ruled out. Regardless of its date, if it represents an independent tradition from the Synoptics, then it did not influence Luke. Scholars who maintain that Thomas was based on an early version of Q have not typically suggested that it then became a direct source for any of the other Gospels, since it is so different in its outlook. In addition, Thomas, even more than Q, is not an "account" of any sort; its content is limited to sayings. We may safely conclude, therefore, that, regardless of anything else that may be said of Thomas, it was not one of Luke's sources.

If the Synoptics were not influenced by Thomas, then, can we say for certain that Thomas was not influenced by the Synoptics? As with Luke's relationship to Matthew, one of the arguments often given for Thomas's independence from the Synoptics is the complete lack of a common order of any of its sayings when compared to the Synoptics. But is this a valid argument? We can only speculate about the circumstances under which the Gospel of Thomas may have been written, but if it was perhaps a "stream of consciousness" document, would we expect to find any specific order to its sayings? The author may have been moved to write by the Spirit (like the prophetesses of the Montanists) or even by his own internal wisdom (and perhaps even composed over a period of time, not unlike Muhammad writing the Qur'an). If parts of Thomas were intended to "correct" the Synoptics (and again a parallel with the Qur'an in this regard would not be out of the question), the differences between its versions of sayings and those in the canonical Gospels would be completely understandable, as would its lack of a discernible order.

The author of Thomas may therefore have been familiar with the

Synoptic Gospels and their content and so drew on his memory of certain sayings from them, using the sayings as freely or as faithfully as he wished depending on their suitability for his own beliefs and purpose and mixing them with his own ideas. Indeed, such a free rearrangement and reworking of Synoptic passages is just as likely a sign of the author's imagination as of any historically independent *tradition* that might supposedly lie behind Thomas. Further, it would be consistent with a Gnostic-friendly, individualistic, and ahistorical concept of religion, which many might consider to be the legitimate expression of the internal faith of the author of Thomas. Such characteristics would be appropriate to his worldview, whereas they would not have been appropriate for the Synoptics, which reflect a more historically grounded and community-centered Hebrew worldview. (We do not, for example, find any claim in Thomas that it reflects careful research or that it is a historically accurate account, in contrast to the claims made by Luke in his Prologue.) Hence, although the character of Luke and the other Synoptics argues forcefully against their being influenced by Thomas, the reverse seems possible. Under such circumstances, then, both a late-second-century date for the Gospel of Thomas and its author's familiarity with the Synoptic tradition would make perfect sense but would have no bearing on the Synoptic Problem itself or on the writing of Luke.

## Oral Sources

We are left, then, with two major potential written sources for Luke (these being Matthew and Mark), and one possible minor one (a Proto-John). There is also reason to believe, however, that Luke relied heavily on oral sources as well. Oral tradition does after all stand behind all the Gospels, especially if some of them drew directly on the testimony of actual eyewitnesses, since those witnesses had heard what Jesus had said orally and would (at least initially) have given their own testimony orally. Acknowledging the primacy of this oral tradition, Luke mentions in his Prologue traditions that had been passed on, both to himself and to those who had written down the other "many" accounts, by eyewitnesses. As discussed earlier, Luke's usage of the word παραδίδωμι ("to entrust or deliver") throughout his writings does not necessitate a lengthy process of transmission. Instead his wording suggests that he had personally received these traditions directly from disciples who *were* eyewitnesses. His Prologue also implies that he had done considerable "investigative reporting" in order to be assured of the accuracy of his information.

Oral tradition (possibly directly from some of the original apostles), therefore, accounts adequately for the material in Luke's Gospel that has no parallel or has only a loose parallel with pericopes in Mark or Matthew. Even if Luke did find some of this material in a written form that has no longer survived, there is clearly an oral tradition behind any such written sources, so we may safely refer to all of it as originating from an oral source.[32] And Luke (again in his Prologue) has staked his whole argument on the reliability of this tradition.

It is often assumed that oral tradition is less reliable than written sources and is more subject to change and development, but this is largely due to the philosophical framework within which biblical scholarship has operated during the past century and a half. This framework was dominated by Enlightenment religious philosophy and culminated in the view of scholars such as Rudolf Bultmann, who asserted that Christian communities frequently invented sayings of Jesus: "Thus tradition shaped and handed down, in the form of words of Jesus, conceptions actually arising from the faith of the community."[33] This view, however, is particularly out of touch with the realities of the culture of first-century Judaism, which relied heavily on the continued faithful transmission of oral tradition. It also assumes that such traditions were handed down over the course of several generations. Yet, as Richard Bauckham observes:

> The Gospels were written within living memory of the events they recount. . . . This is a highly significant fact, entailed not by unusually early datings of the Gospels but by the generally accepted ones. One lasting effect of form criticism, with its model of anonymous community transmission, has been to give most Gospels scholars an unexamined impression of the period between the events of the Gospel story and the writing of the Gospels as much longer than it realistically was. We have been accustomed to working with models of oral tradition as it is passed down through the generations in traditional communities. We imagine the traditions passing through many minds and mouths before they reached the writers of the Gospels. But the period in question is actually that of a relatively (for that period) long lifetime.[34]

---

32. The appendix at the end of this work lists this unique Lukan material.
33. Rudolf Bultmann, *Jesus and the Word* (New York: Scribner, 1926), 340.
34. Richard J. Bauckham, *Jesus and the Eyewitnesses: The Gospels as Eyewitness Testimony* (Grand Rapids: Eerdmans, 2006), 7–8.

Likewise it is often assumed that parables and other teachings of Jesus that have somewhat different forms or senses of meaning in the different Gospels reflect either the authors' own altering of the traditions or different and contradictory strands of tradition from different "communities." Much discussion has been devoted to the attempt to determine which version must be the original (or at least *more primitive*) and which is derivative. But this, too, seems to be based on an invalid assumption. As we have seen, Luke seems especially passionate about transmitting the traditions as faithfully as possible, and there is no reason to suspect that the other Gospel writers were any less concerned with being faithful to their sources and traditions.

The invalid assumption here is that any given saying would have been said once and only once by Jesus, and so there is only one valid "original" form. But there is no reason to suppose that Jesus would have told any given parable only once, or that if he repeated it in a different context that he would not have ever altered it in order to make a slightly different point. N. T. Wright writes:

> Another mould to be broken here is the idea that Jesus only ever said the same thing once, so that similar stories or parables must be parallel developments from a single original. . . . The point here is that good, pithy parables and allegories are much harder to construct than you might think—even the rabbinic parallels are flat and mundane by comparison, and it would be surprising if Matthew or Luke possessed a talent for composition comparable to that of Jesus rather than to that of their Jewish contemporaries—and partly of course that Jesus, as a wandering teacher in the days before mass media, naturally said similar things over and over again, no doubt developing them this way and that as he went along.[35]

It is at least as likely (if not more likely) that the handful of variations in parables and teachings in the Gospels (of which there are only about half a dozen significant examples) reflect instances of Jesus saying similar things at different times rather than the imagination of the Gospel writers or changing traditions in different Christian communities. In this regard, if the traditionally ascribed authors did write the Gospels called by their names, then Matthew, Mark (having written based on Peter's recollections), and John would each have based his Gospel on the witness of one particular person, and only Luke would have researched and drawn together the remembrances of multiple witnesses. It is precisely this variation of witnesses that the church val-

---

35. N. T. Wright, *The Scriptures, the Cross, and the Power of God* (London: SPCK, 2005), 13–14.

ued so highly, especially in light of the command in the Torah that truth was not to be established on the basis of one person's testimony, but that "only on the evidence of two witnesses or of three witnesses shall a charge be established" (Deut 19:15 ESV). This applied not only to establishing legal matters but to establishing any truth within the community.

Different witnesses to the same events will frequently produce slightly different accounts of those events, but this does not necessarily indicate that one or another witness has altered the "true" account. Rather, the witnesses have remembered the event differently. Hence, minor contradictions in different Gospel accounts should be expected. There will, however, also be cases where authors have chosen to edit their narratives in different ways in order to emphasize different aspects of events.

For example, the Synoptic Gospels all place Jesus's cleansing of the temple immediately after the triumphal entry into Jerusalem, whereas John places this event at the very beginning of Jesus's ministry, probably about three years earlier. Attempts have been made to try to reconcile these accounts, such as by suggesting that Jesus performed this cleansing twice, once at the beginning of his ministry, then again at its end. But such attempts at reconciliation are unnecessary. The Gospels are recounting the same event but are emphasizing different aspects of it.

In John's Gospel, Jesus makes frequent trips to Jerusalem for the various Jewish feasts. In the Synoptics, Jesus is only specifically said to have been in Jerusalem as an adult the one time at the very end of his life. Hence, any event that occurred in Jerusalem needed to be told in the context of Jesus's final days. This allowed the Synoptic authors to concentrate all their material relating to Jerusalem together in one place and to connect it all theologically to Jesus's conflict with the Jewish leaders and with his warnings of coming judgment on Jerusalem. Yet, in all four Gospels, the cleansing of the temple is Jesus's first act upon entering Jerusalem for the first time as an adult, so in that sense the accounts *are* all consistent.

Thus, some variations among the Gospels may be the result of Jesus saying the same thing in different contexts; some may be due to the authors wishing to emphasize different aspects of the same event; and some may reflect conflicting reports by different eyewitnesses, such as the contradictions in some of the birth and resurrection narratives. We do not have to choose one version as the "original" or the "true" one, nor do we need to absolutely reconcile the accounts for them to be historically accurate witnesses of events, any more than we would expect two modern individuals to give identical accounts or interpretations of the same historical event.

What all of this suggests, then, is that Luke may well have collected a considerable amount of information about the life and teachings of Jesus beyond what he found in the Gospels of Matthew and Mark, most of it oral but perhaps some of it having been written down (although we have no evidence for this). According to Luke, most of this information was apparently passed on to him directly by eyewitnesses to the events. From this vast pool of resources, then (some of which may have contradicted the memories of other eyewitnesses), Luke would have set about his task of choosing which material to trust and to use for his purpose of convincing Theophilus of the truth of Christianity.

Having thus provisionally established Luke's sources, we may depict them as follows:

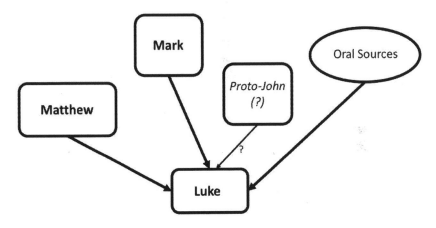

Fig. 3.1. The Proposed Hypothesis of Luke's Sources

This is consistent with Luke's Prologue, in which he claims that he has "carefully investigated [or followed] everything from the beginning [or for a long time]" (1:3). This could mean that he has investigated the entire matter from start to finish, or it could mean that he has spent a long time himself following and investigating the matter. Long before he had ever written his own Gospel, he could indeed have obtained an in-depth knowledge of all the traditions, having memorized Matthew's Gospel and having sought out eyewitness testimony concerning Jesus's life. Again, if the author of Luke was an itinerant preacher, he would have had many opportunities in his travels to encounter eyewitnesses (even if his Gospel was not finally written down until the later decades of the first century). Thus, when the opportunity presented itself, he had already "done his homework" and was ready immediately to begin his task of presenting an orderly account of the Gospel to Theophilus.

# 4

---

# The Writing of Luke

Given our list of the most likely sources Luke would have used, we may now address the particulars of *how* he would have actually gone about writing his Gospel, keeping in mind the procedures an author in the first century would have needed to follow.

## Luke's Material

It is usually assumed that Luke used Mark as the framework or "skeleton" for his Gospel, adding in other material around it. According to the Q theory, this other material would have come from Q (and other sources including possibly *L*), which Luke would have had to interweave with Mark. But even those who believe that Luke also had Matthew available to him still usually assume that, for the most part, he followed Mark, only supplementing it with material from Matthew when Mark was lacking. Perhaps even this assumption is worth reconsidering, however. If Luke had both Mark and Matthew to work from, would he necessarily have used Mark as his primary source, only occasionally referring to Matthew?

In this regard, the way in which the Synoptic Problem is typically defined tends to lead us in one particular direction. Resources that attempt to show the relationships between the Synoptics generally divide the material into Triple Tradition, Double Tradition, and unique material to each Gospel, with the implied assumption that these are realistic categories from which obvious conclusions may be drawn.

For example, Allan Barr's classic *Diagram of Synoptic Relationships* charts the various pericopes in the three Gospels in colors corresponding to the categories of Double or Triple Tradition or unique material. In this (and other representations), Mark's whole Gospel comes to represent the Triple Tradition, and, apart from the few pericopes that are unique to Mark, his entire Gospel is represented by one color. When we look at Luke on such a chart, the colors lead us to suppose that Luke took all his Triple Tradition material from Mark. Indeed, although Barr draws connecting lines from Mark to both Matthew and Luke to compare their orders of Triple Tradition material, in his comparison of Matthew and Luke he connects *only* the Double Tradition material between them, *not* the Triple. The possibility that there might be some connection between Matthew and Luke regarding the Triple Tradition is not even remotely contemplated. In his introduction, Barr says, "The Diagram therefore does not profess to delimit sources, either by way of inclusion or exclusion, but to present the facts on which such delimitation may proceed."[1] Yet the diagram already precludes the possibility that Luke drew any of the Triple Tradition material from Matthew, since it fails to show any such potential connections. In fact, the very concept of Minor Agreements between Matthew and Luke assumes this to be the basic situation, since these agreements are considered to be exceptions to the "rule" of Luke taking his Triple Tradition material from Mark.

Hence the way in which Barr has chosen to "present the facts" already has one and only one solution in mind (the Q theory). Yet even the definition of the Triple Tradition material is deceptive as it is normally conceived. We would expect that Triple Tradition material really is only material that is included in *all three* Synoptic Gospels. Yet a fair amount of the so-called Triple Tradition is present in only *two* of the three Gospels. There is a small amount that is shared only by Mark and Luke but is not present in Matthew, and a much larger amount that is common only to Mark and Matthew but is not present in Luke. Whereas about 630 of Mark's 662 verses are usually categorized as Triple Tradition, the number of verses that are clearly parallel in all three Gospels is closer to 340,[2] only a little more than *half* of

---

1. Barr, *Diagram of Synoptic Relationships*, 1–2.
2. All statistics are from Barr, *Diagram of Synoptic Relationships*, 4.

Mark. Thus, because of the connections usually drawn between Mark and Luke, as well as the definition of virtually all of Mark as Triple Tradition, the actual correspondence between Mark and Luke is overexaggerated as a "fact" even before any evaluation is done.

As part of the analysis for this book, I have created simplified charts of the Synoptics, similar to Barr's, using the pericopes of Aland's *Synopsis Quattuor Evangeliorum* as a guide. A few pericopes have been subdivided when one portion of the pericope is common between certain Gospels while another is not. Because pericopes may vary in length from a single verse to more than twenty, the actual length of documents may not always be faithfully represented in these charts.

Figure 4.1, "Luke's Hypothetical Use of Sources" (online at http://fortresspress.com/lukethecomposer) is similar to Barr's but includes also Q, M, and L (green, blue, and yellow respectively) to show the "Four-Source Hypothesis" and how these correspond to the four traditions of material present in the Synoptics. Connecting lines between pericopes have been eliminated, however.

The Triple Tradition as it is commonly understood is shown in indigo in the chart, and hence virtually all of Mark (at the bottom of the central column) is shown as indigo. Grey areas on the left and right sides of Mark show Triple Tradition material that has been "omitted" from Matthew and Luke respectively and, hence, technically is not Triple Tradition at all. The few pericopes unique to Mark (with no parallels in either Matthew or Luke) are shown as red. The contents of Q (at the top of the central column) conforms to *The Critical Edition of Q*[3] and include several "Mark/Q overlaps," also shown in indigo.

When we look at this chart, it is tempting to believe that it gives us an indication of Luke's procedures. His introductory material is all his own (yellow). Then the Exposition (approximately the top third of Luke in the chart, after the Introduction) consists predominantly of Triple Tradition pericopes, where Luke presumably followed Mark, often in lengthy blocks but with a few scattered additions of Luke's own and a few isolated pericopes from the Double Tradition (drawn from Q according to this theory), the largest of which is the Sermon on the Plain. The middle part of Luke, the Journey to Jerusalem, is quite different, now with only a few scattered Triple Tradition pericopes but many more Double Tradition and unique passages all mixed together. It is only at the very end of this section that we once again see large

---

3. Robinson et al., *Critical Edition of Q*.

blocks of Triple Tradition material, which continues to the end of the passion narrative (the bottom portion of Luke in the chart), with virtually no Double Tradition material in evidence at all, which suggests that Luke followed Mark almost exclusively for this entire section, ending with unique Lukan pericopes for the resurrection appearances.

But what if this was not Luke's procedure? If he *did* have both Mark and Matthew to work from, would he necessarily have taken all the so-called Triple Tradition material from Mark, turning to Matthew only when Mark failed him? Perhaps he may have taken some of it from Matthew instead of from Mark. Indeed, perhaps the entire concept of the Triple Tradition is simply a red herring that would certainly not have been an idea shared by Luke himself (since this "tradition" did not exist until after his Gospel was completed and he had made his own choices about what material to include and what to omit). Perhaps he did not rely on Mark as his skeleton after all, especially considering that (even according to Barr) he actually used only about half of Mark's material (and this would have been the case even if all the Triple Tradition *did* come from Mark).

Therefore, if Luke did have both Mark and Matthew in front of him (and, as I suggested above, even had Matthew memorized), there is no reason to suppose that he would have sorted through all the pericopes in both Gospels and then decided that, for anything that was common between the two of them he would use Mark's version, turning to Matthew only as a last resort. He could just as easily have used Matthew's version for much of what we now call the Triple Tradition material, simply skipping over any parallel pericopes when he did turn to Mark. Perhaps, given this possibility, it would be better to look at the evidence itself, rather than making an assumption beforehand about Luke's procedures.

To test this idea, I have conducted an analysis, pericope by pericope, comparing Luke's version against both Matthew and Mark to see which of the other two is closer to Luke in each individual case. This would seem to indicate which of the two would have been Luke's source for that particular pericope. In cases where no discernible preference between the two could be found, I have assumed that the source is the same as for the previous pericope, with the rationale (especially when such pericopes were consecutive in the Gospels) that Luke would have continued to use the same source until there was a clue that he had switched.

THE WRITING OF LUKE

## Exposition

The following tables give details of the comparisons made for Triple Tradition pericopes, highlighting those that seem to deviate from the "norm" of Luke following Mark. The first table involves pericopes in Luke's Exposition section (3:1–9:50).

**Table 4.1. Luke's Exposition Section (3:1–9:50)**

| Verses | Pericope | Commentary |
|---|---|---|
| Matt 3:1–6<br>Mark 1:1–6<br>Luke 3:1–6 | John the Baptist | Luke agrees with Mark in including the specific phrase "preaching a baptism of repentance for the forgiveness of sins" (κηρύσσων βάπτισμα μετανοίας εἰς ἄφεσιν). Luke agrees with Matthew, however, in placing the quotation from Isaiah after John's preaching instead of before it, as Mark does. Likewise, Luke agrees with Matthew in beginning this quotation with "The voice of one crying . . ." against Mark, who begins with a verse from Malachi preceding the verse from Isaiah. Thus, Luke has similarities to and differences from both, but in general is slightly more in agreement with Matthew. |
| Matt 3:11–12<br>Mark 1:7–8<br>Luke 3:15–18<br>[Acts 13:24–25] | John's Messianic Preaching | Although Luke agrees with Mark in saying "to loose the thong of his sandal" (λῦσαι τὸν ἱμάντα τῶν ὑποδημάτων αὐτοῦ), he agrees with Matthew in placing the phrase "I baptize you with water" earlier in the pericope than does Mark. The wording of this phrase is also closer between Matthew and Luke (ἐγὼ μὲν ὑμᾶς βαπτίζω ἐν ὕδατι in Matthew, ἐγὼ μὲν ὕδατι βαπτίζω ὑμᾶς in Luke, and ἐγὼ ἐβάπτισα ὑμᾶς ὕδατι in Mark). Mark ends with John saying, "He will baptize you with the Holy Spirit," but both Matthew and Luke add "and with fire" (καὶ πυρί) and then go on to describe the winnowing fork. Luke is clearly closer to Matthew here than to Mark. (Interestingly, however, the parallel passage in Acts 13 is closer to Mark than to Matthew.) |

| | | |
|---|---|---|
| Matt 14:3–4<br>Mark 6:17–18<br>Luke 3:19–20 | The Imprisonment of John | Luke's wording is not similar to either Matthew or Mark here and is not discernibly closer to either one. Either this should be considered a unique Lukan addition or a loose, displaced parallel drawn from Luke's memory of Matthew's description of John and Herod. |
| Matt 3:13–17<br>Mark 1:9–11<br>Luke 3:21–22 | The Baptism of Jesus | Here again, Luke's wording is not similar to either Matthew or Mark except in a few short phrases. Luke agrees with Matthew that the Spirit descended "upon him" (ἐπ' αὐτόν) rather than Mark's "into him" (εἰς αὐτόν), but Luke agrees with Mark that the voice said "You are my son . . ." (σὺ εἶ ὁ υἱός μου) rather than Matthew's "This is my son . . ." (οὗτός ἐστιν ὁ υἱός μου), with the corresponding necessary grammatical changes required for the difference in person. This may represent a unique Lukan version of Jesus's baptism more than either a Matthean or Markan one. |
| Matt 4:1–2<br>Mark 1:12–13<br>Luke 4:1–2 | In the Wilderness | The wording here is not similar in any of the three Gospels, but the *elements* present are similar between Matthew and Luke, but not Mark. Both Matthew and Luke agree against Mark that Jesus fasted during the forty days, whereas only Mark says that he was with wild beasts. So Luke is clearly closer to Matthew here than to Mark. |
| Matt 4:12<br>Mark 1:14–15<br>Luke 4:14 | The Journey to Galilee | Once again, there is little common wording here. All three Gospels include the phrase "into Galilee" (εἰς τὴν Γαλιλαίον), but only Mark and Luke include the name Jesus, instead of simply saying "he." Given the many dissimilarities, the inclusion of Jesus's name is hardly significant, and this is basically a Lukan verse. |

| Matt 13:54–58<br>Mark 6:1–6<br>Luke 4:16–22 | Jesus' Preaching at<br>Nazareth | Although the main portion of this pericope loosely parallels the passage from Matthew 13, the unusual form Ναζαρά for Nazareth appears in the New Testament only here in Luke and in Matt 4:13 (the verse after the previous pericope), so this must be considered an important parallel. Otherwise there is little in common between Luke and either Matthew or Mark here, apart from the main thrust of the story, although Luke agrees with Mark that this was on the Sabbath, which Matthew does not specifically say (but which could be taken for granted). Hence, this is once more a Lukan pericope with only loose parallels to the other Synoptics, except for the significant form of Nazareth, which indicates a clear dependence on Matthew. (Indeed, even the editors of the *Critical Edition of Q* recognize the significance of this connection and assign this one word to Q.[4]) |
| Matt 26:6–13<br>Mark 14:3–9<br>Luke 7:36–39 | The Woman with the Ointment | This isolated pericope is only loosely parallel to the account in either Matthew or Mark, and it has no specific points of similarity with one against the other. It is clearly a Lukan pericope, but since the many pericopes prior to this one had all been drawn from Matthew, it is more likely that Luke would have had Matthew's version in mind here rather than Mark's. |

The first six pericopes here are all part of the section relating to Jesus's baptism and temptation. Except for the third of these (the Imprisonment of John, which comes at a later point in both Matthew and Mark), this is one continuous narrative in Mark (as the verses indicate), whereas in both Matthew and Luke there is additional common material added between some of the elements. The much more detailed agreement between Matthew and Luke overall therefore outweighs the few places where Luke does seem to agree more with Mark than with Matthew (which includes only "preaching a baptism of repentance for the forgiveness of sins" in the first pericope, the loosing of the thongs of the sandal in the second, the phrase "You are my son . . ." in the fourth, and the one inclusion of the name Jesus in the sixth).

---

4. Robinson et al., *Critical Edition of Q,* 80.

Although it seems clear that Luke was influenced by Mark in some of these cases, these must count as only Minor Agreements between Mark and Luke here in an extended passage where Luke agrees with Matthew against Mark in a total of twenty verses out of thirty-one, but with Mark against Matthew in only three or four. Luke may have read through the Markan version (the first few verses of Mark's entire Gospel), or even had it in front of him, and so incorporated these few details from it, but he definitely relied far more on Matthew throughout this entire passage, and even within the specific pericopes mentioned.

The final two pericopes listed above are only loosely parallel to anything in Matthew or Mark but have a slightly greater affinity with Matthew than with Mark.

## Development

The few pericopes in Luke's Journey to Jerusalem (9:51–19:27) that have parallels with both Matthew and Mark are isolated individual stories. Most of them appear to be from a different tradition than either Matthew or Mark, but, where there are parallels, they are always stronger parallels to Matthew than to Mark, except in the case of one unusual pericope.

Table 4.2. Development in the Journey Narrative

| Verses | Pericope | Commentary |
|---|---|---|
| Matt 22:34–40<br>Mark 12:28–34<br>Luke 10:25–28 | The Lawyer's Question | Luke agrees with Matthew that it was a "lawyer" (νομικός) who asked the question, instead of Mark's "scribe" (γραμματέων), and in both Luke and Matthew he called Jesus "teacher" (διδάσκαλε), instead of no form of address in Mark. Luke also agrees with Matthew in omitting the Shema ("Hear O Israel ...") in Jesus's answer, which Mark includes. The rest of the quotation from Deuteronomy is slightly different in all three Gospels, with Luke sometimes closer in his version to Matthew, sometimes to Mark (which may be because they are each translating it themselves rather than relying on each other's translations). Jesus's final answer |

is different in all three Gospels. Luke's version of this pericope is therefore definitely more similar to Matthew's than to Mark's.

| | | |
|---|---|---|
| Matt 12:22–30<br>Mark 3:22–27<br>Luke 11:14–23 | The Beelzebub Controversy | There are numerous points in this passage where Luke agrees with Matthew against Mark, including the occasion of the conflict, Jesus knowing his opponents' thoughts, the question of how his opponents cast out demons, and the conclusion that whoever is not with Jesus is against him. There are no agreements of Luke with Mark against Matthew. |
| Matt 16:5–12<br>Mark 8:14–21<br>Luke 12:1 | The Leaven of the Pharisees | Luke agrees with Matthew in using the verb προσέχετε rather than Mark's βλέπετε, both meaning "to beware." Apart from this, there is no indication that Luke is following either one or the other, so, once again, if Luke is closer to either it is to Matthew. |
| Matt 12:31–32<br>Mark 3:28–30<br>Luke 12:10 | The Sin against the Holy Spirit | Luke agrees with Matthew in including the saying that whoever speaks against the Son of Man will be forgiven, which Mark omits. There are no agreements with Mark against Matthew. |
| Matt 13:31–32<br>Mark 4:30–32<br>Luke 13:18–19 | The Parable of the Mustard Seed | Luke agrees with Mark in using the term "kingdom of God" rather than Matthew's "kingdom of heaven," but this is a difference that is consistent throughout all three Gospels and, hence, cannot indicate that Luke is here specifically dependent on Mark. Luke then agrees with Matthew against Mark in using the phrases "which a man took" (ὃν λαβὼν ἄνθρωπος) and "in its branches" (ἐν τοῖς κλάδοις αὐτοῦ), neither of which is used by Mark, indicating that Luke is again far closer to Matthew here than to Mark. |
| Matt 5:32; 19:9<br>Mark 10:11–12<br>Luke 16:18 | On Divorce | The sense of the verse in Luke is closer to Matthew 5:32 than to either of the other parallels, since it refers both to divorcing one's wife and to marrying a divorced woman (and there is no mention of marrying a divorced woman in either Matt 19 or Mark 10). The precise wording |

of the Lukan verse, however, is closer to Matt 19:9 and Mark 10:11 (both of which are nearly identical to each other, except that Matthew adds the extra stipulation about unchastity). In addition, Mark is the only Gospel that goes on to mention a woman divorcing her husband. All in all, then, Luke is definitely closer to Matthew than to Mark here.

| | | |
|---|---|---|
| Matt 18:6–9 | Warning against | Luke agrees with Mark that the millstone is "hung around" (περίκειται) the neck, rather than using Matthew's word "suspended" (κρεμασθῇ). Likewise he agrees with Mark that the offender should be thrown "into the sea" (εἰς τὴν θάλασσαν) instead of being drowned "in the depths of the sea" (ἐν τῷ πελάγει τῆς θαλάσσης), as Matthew says. |
| Mark 9:42–50 | Offenses | |
| Luke 17:1–2 | | |

This is therefore the only "unusual" pericope in the entire journey, prior to the very last sequence, that seems to have been taken from Mark rather than from Matthew (unless it too represents an independent tradition).

| | | |
|---|---|---|
| Matt 17:20; 21:21 | On Faith | This is a loose parallel between Luke and different sayings from both Matthew and Mark, but there are no specific common phrases either between Luke and Matthew or between Luke and Mark, so this is almost certainly a saying from a different source than either Matthew *or* Mark. |
| Mark 11:23 | | |
| Luke 17:5–6 | | |

| | | |
|---|---|---|
| Matt 24:15–28 | The Day of the Son of | In this passage, Luke has six verses that parallel various scattered verses in Matthew but have no parallel in Mark, plus two verses that parallel verses in both Matthew and Mark. Luke agrees with Matthew once against Mark in using the phrase "look here" (ἰδοὺ ὧδε) but agrees with Mark once in using the phrase εἰς τὰ ὀπίσω instead of Matthew's single word ὀπίσω to mean "back," but this could be a stylistic choice and so is not significant. There is therefore far more agreement between Luke and Matthew here, but half of the verses in this passage have no parallel at all, indicating that Luke is probably drawing on an independent oral source, perhaps merging it with his memory of verses from Matthew. |
| Mark 13:14–23 | Man | |
| Luke 17:22–37 | | |

132

In addition to these pericopes, there is also one isolated verse in the Journey to Jerusalem where there is a loose parallel between Luke and Mark for which there is no parallel in Matthew. This is a reference to Jesus being "baptized with a baptism" in Mark 10:38 and in Luke 12:50. But the contexts, and even the wordings, are completely different, so it is obvious that Luke's saying is from a completely different source.

## Recapitulation

An evaluation of Luke's Recapitulation (19:28–23:56) is not as clear-cut as was his Exposition. There is far more material unique to Luke throughout this narrative, which seems to be merged with material from Matthew and Mark. It is difficult to tell whether certain pericopes are based on the other Synoptics or on separate oral sources. Assuming, however, that Luke has used Matthew and Mark as his *primary* sources here, it seems that Luke tends to favor Mark over Matthew up to the Last Supper. After the so-called Words of Institution, the situation changes. From this point until Jesus is condemned by the Sanhedrin, there are definitely more similarities between Luke and Matthew than between Luke and Mark, and they are more substantial similarities, definitely pointing to Luke's use of Matthew rather than Mark for this passage.

**Table 4.3. Luke's Recapitulation (19:28–23:56)**

| Verses | Pericope | Commentary |
|---|---|---|
| Matt 26:21–25<br>Mark 14:18–21<br>Luke 22:21–23 | Jesus Foretells His Betrayal | Luke agrees with Matthew against Mark in mentioning the "hand" (χείρ) of the betrayer. There are no agreements with Mark against Matthew; hence, this saying appears to have come from Matthew rather than from Mark. |
| Matt 20:24–28<br>Mark 10:41–45<br>Luke 22:24–27 | Precedence among the Disciples | No exact parallels, either in wording or in sense, exist between Luke and one of the other Synoptics against the other. The similarities with Matthew in the pericopes before and after this one, however, indicate that Luke continued to use Matthew as his source here. |

| Matt 19:27–30<br>Mark 10:28–31<br>Luke 22:28–30 | The Rewards of<br>Discipleship | Only Luke and Matthew include statements by Jesus that the disciples will sit on thrones, judging the twelve tribes of Israel. There are no agreements with Mark against Matthew in this entire pericope, and hence it is clearly from Matthew and not from Mark. |
| --- | --- | --- |
| Matt 26:31–35<br>Mark 14:26–31<br>Luke 22:31–34 | Peter's Denial<br>Predicted | There are no agreements with Mark against Matthew here, but Luke does agree with Matthew in limiting the cock crow to one time rather than Mark's two times, a significant detail, indicating that Luke is following Matthew here. |
| Matt 26:36–46<br>Mark 14:32–42<br>Luke 22:39–46 | Gethsemane | Jesus's first prayer in Luke agrees with Mark in using the verb "remove" (παρένεγκε) against Matthew's "pass" (παρελθάτω) in reference to the "cup," but Luke agrees with Matthew in using "nevertheless" (πλήν) against Mark's "but" (ἀλλ'). Luke then agrees with Matthew against Mark that Jesus came to the "disciples" (μαθητάς) but agrees with Mark that he asked if they were "sleeping" (καθεύδετε). Luke then agrees with Matthew's "enter" (εἰσέλθητε) against Mark's "come" (ἔλθητε). Hence, Luke appears to be slightly closer to Matthew overall than to Mark. |
| Matt 26:47–56<br>Mark 14:43–52<br>Luke 22:47–53 | Jesus Arrested | Luke agrees with Matthew against Mark that Jesus replied to Judas's kiss, but the responses are slightly different. Likewise, Luke agrees with Matthew against Mark that Jesus rebuked the one who cut off the slave's ear. He also agrees with Matthew against Mark in not reporting the young man who left his tunic and fled from the scene naked. Luke is therefore much closer to Matthew here than to Mark. |

| | | |
|---|---|---|
| Matt 26:69–75<br>Mark 14:66–72<br>Luke 22:54–62 | Peter's Denial | Luke agrees with Mark against Matthew in not naming Caiaphas as the high priest, then again in mentioning the fire in the courtyard. Luke agrees with Matthew against Mark that the second question to Peter was not asked by the same maid who asked the first, and again in recounting Peter's response. Luke agrees with Mark against Matthew that the third question identified him as a "Galilean" (καὶ γὰρ Γαλιλαῖος). Luke agrees with Matthew against Mark that the cock crowed only once and, then in the most exact parallel of all, agrees with Matthew against Mark that "he went out and wept bitterly" (καὶ ἐξελθὼν ἔξω ἔκλαυσεν πικρῶς). Luke's agreements with Matthew are therefore more numerous, more exact, and more significant. |
| Matt 26:57–68<br>Mark 14:53–65<br>Luke 22:63–71 | Jesus before the Sanhedrin | Luke agrees with Mark against Matthew that Jesus was "blindfolded" (περικαλύψαντες). Luke agrees with Matthew against Mark that the guards said, "who is it that struck you" (τίς ἐστιν ὁ παίσας σε)?, then again in mentioning the "elders of the people" (πρεσβυτέριον τοῦ λαοῦ). Luke agrees with Mark against Matthew in mentioning "scribes" (γραμματεῖς). As in the previous pericope, Luke's agreements with Matthew against Mark are far more detailed and exact, and hence much more significant than his agreements with Mark. |

Here, as with Jesus's baptism, we therefore have an extended passage where Luke exhibits similarities to *both* Mark and Matthew but overall is much closer to Matthew. In a sequence of fifty-one verses in Luke, Luke is closer to Mark in seven verses (limited only to "remove" this cup, Jesus asking the disciples if they are sleeping, *not* naming Caiaphas, the fire, Peter accused of being a Galilean, Jesus being blindfolded, and the scribes present at the Sanhedrin). None of these correspondences amounts to more than a word or two. But Luke is closer to Matthew in at least sixteen verses, including the lengthy exact letter-for-letter correspondences καὶ ἐξελθὼν ἔξω ἔκλαυσεν πικρῶς ("He went out and wept bitterly") and τίς ἐστιν ὁ παίσας σε ("Who is it that struck you?"), plus several common verses where there is no parallel (either loose or exact) in Mark.

135

For clarity, the following table lists the agreements between Luke and Matthew against Mark in this passage.

Table 4.4. Luke and Matthew Agreeing against Mark

| Matthew | Luke | Agreements against Mark |
|---|---|---|
| Matt 26:23 | Luke 22:21 | the "hand" (χείρ) of the betrayer |
| Matt 19:28 | Luke 22:28–30 | You will sit on thrones, judging the twelve tribes of Israel |
| Matt 26:34 | Luke 22:34 | one cock crow, not two |
| Matt 26:39 | Luke 22:42 | "nevertheless" (πλήν), not my will |
| Matt 26:40 | Luke 22:45 | Jesus came to the "disciples" (μαθητάς) |
| Matt 26:41 | Luke 22:46 | Pray that you may not "enter" (εἰσέλθητε) into temptation |
| Matt 26:50 | Luke 22:48 | Jesus questions Judas's kiss |
| Matt 26:52 | Luke 22:51 | Jesus rebukes the one who cut off the slave's ear |
| Matt 26:56 | Luke 22:53 | no young man who left his tunic and fled the scene naked (as in Mark 14:51) |
| Matt 26:71–72 | Luke 22:58 | The second question to Peter was not asked by the same maid who asked the first, plus Peter's response is quoted |
| Matt 26:74 | Luke 22:60 | The cock crowed only once |
| Matt 26:75 | Luke 22:62 | Peter "went out and wept bitterly" (καὶ ἐξελθὼν ἔξω ἔκλαυσεν πικρῶς ) |
| Matt 26:68 | Luke 22:64 | "Who is it that struck you" (τίς ἐστιν ὁ παίσας σε) |
| Matt 27:1 | Luke 22:66 | the "elders of the people" (πρεσβυτέριον τοῦ λαοῦ) |

The evidence therefore does not support the idea that Luke is following Mark here with only occasional references from Matthew; the situation is quite the opposite. If there are any Minor Agreements here, they are between Luke and *Mark*, but with Luke following Matthew in the main. Luke's version of the resurrection also exhibits similarities both with Matthew and with Mark, but there are enough differences from both that it seems that Luke's whole version appears to have come from a separate source (a separate eyewitness account). Indeed, in many details Luke's resurrection account is closer to John's than to either Matthew's or Mark's.

All other Triple Tradition pericopes throughout Luke seem to support the idea that Luke was dependent in these cases on Mark rather than Matthew. Since it is the common view that Luke did frequently rely on Mark, these pericopes need not be discussed individually.

Based on this analysis, then, if the assumption is *not* made that all the so-called Triple Tradition material in Luke came from Mark (with Luke only turning to Matthew when there was no parallel in Mark), it turns out that there is a great deal of material (including in the passion narrative) that Luke seems to have taken from Matthew rather than from Mark. The concepts of the Triple Tradition and of Minor Agreements therefore turn out to be misleading, and in the end completely unhelpful. Agreements between Luke and Matthew do not represent phrases or words Luke borrowed from Matthew in order to insert into Markan pericopes but instead are usually evidence that an entire pericope has come from Matthew rather than from Mark. Similarly, it seems highly unlikely that Luke was paying much attention to whether a particular story existed in both Matthew and Mark when choosing whether to include it. Rather, Luke was drawing what he wanted from one of his sources at one point, then doing the same with the other (but obviously tending to pass over material that was similar to what he had already used, or was planning to use, from the other).

There are a few cases, but only a very few (depending on how significant we count some of the similarities), where there are actually pericopes including both Matthean and Markan material merged together (probably three in the passages dealing with John the Baptist and another three in the passion narrative). These are definitely the exceptions, but in these instances there do seem to be certain details that Luke wanted to combine from both his sources in order to produce a fuller account.

## A New Luke

The results of this analysis are shown in Figure 4.2, "Luke's Hypothetical Use of Mark Q vs. Luke's Hypothetical Use of Mark Matthew" (online, at http://fortresspress.com/lukethecomposer). This second diagram of Luke's Gospel compares the "Q" Luke with this new "Matthew-Mark" Luke, and when the data are displayed graphically the results are quite startling! The first column is taken directly from the previous chart and uses the traditional method of showing Triple and Double Tradition material. Luke's unique material is shown in yellow. Triple Tradition pericopes are shown in indigo. The Double Tradition material is shown in green.

In the second column, material unique to Luke is again yellow. But now *no* material is displayed as Triple Tradition (indigo). Instead, those pericopes where Luke is closer to Mark than to Matthew are displayed as orange (corresponding to the intersection of yellow for Luke and red for Mark), while pericopes where Luke is closer to Matthew are displayed as green (Luke's yellow plus Matthew's blue). Thus, the green pericopes still include all the Double Tradition material (now also a less than useful term) but also include all the additional Triple Tradition pericopes Luke took from Matthew instead of from Mark. To help make better sense of this diagram, and the analysis carried out in this book, an outline of how the structure of Luke's Gospel corresponds to sonata form has also been included between the columns.

This chart now shows a rather different (and surprisingly "tidy") picture beginning to emerge of Luke's procedures for composing his Gospel. From this analysis, the evidence seems clear that Luke did employ a "block" pattern of using his sources for narrative passages in both his Exposition and his Recapitulation sections, alternating blocks between Matthew and Mark.[5] This is especially significant in the passion narrative, where the traditional view of biblical scholarship has been to see no evidence of Luke's possible use of Matthew at all except perhaps for a few of the supposed Minor Agreements inserted into an otherwise wholly Markan passage.

Also remarkable is the almost total lack of Markan influence in the entire Journey to Jerusalem, until we reach the Retransition point (starting at 18:9), where Luke begins to reuse Mark (with 18:15 picking up at Mark 10:13) as Jesus prepares to enter Jerusalem. As discussed above, in this entire one-third of Luke's Gospel there is only one "unusual" pericope that parallels Mark more closely than Matthew (the Warning against Offenses). This strongly indicates that, when Luke was writing the Journey to Jerusalem passage, he would have been able to draw at will from oral sources and from his knowledge of Matthew's

---

5. Indeed, this analysis is actually similar to that of B. H. Streeter in his *The Four Gospels*, chapter 8. Important disagreements with Streeter analysis include the passion narrative and the one "stray" pericope from Mark in the Journey to Jerusalem. Otherwise, the Markan blocks here do correspond fairly closely to Streeter's. My conclusions drawn from the current analysis, however, are rather different from Streeter's own.

Gospel without *any* written sources in front of him at all until he neared the end of the journey.[6]

It is also highly significant that, when we look now at all the passages throughout Luke's Gospel where he appears to be using Mark, there is now no displacement of Markan material, except for two slightly rearranged pericopes: The Call of the Disciples (Mark 1:16–20 and Luke 5:8–11) is shifted some twenty verses later, from before Jesus's teaching in Capernaum to just before the Cleansing of the Leper (at Mark 1:40–45); then in another section the saying about Jesus's True Kindred (Mark 3:31–35 and Luke 8:19–21) is shifted forty verses later, from before the parable of the Sower to just after the entire series of parables and before the Stilling of the Storm (at Mark 8:22–25).[7]

Additionally, if we now look carefully at the one "unusual" pericope in the Journey to Jerusalem, where Luke appears to be closer to Mark than to Matthew (the Warning against Offenses in Luke 17:1–2, derived from Mark 9:42), this turns out to be the very next pericope in Mark after the one where Luke had left off before beginning the Journey to Jerusalem (the Strange Exorcist, Luke 9:49–50, from Mark 9:38–41). This passage also comes just a few verses before the pericope where Jesus blesses the children (at Mark 10:13–16), the point at which Luke once again begins to follow Mark (Luke 18:15–17). Thus, even this one "exception" turns out to follow Luke's pattern exactly! So Luke could have been keeping his place in Mark's scroll all along, waiting for just this moment to utilize the next passage on his list.

Indeed, all of the passages in his Gospel where Luke significantly alters the order of pericopes (such as Jesus Rejected at Nazareth or the Woman with the Ointment) now turn out to be passages where Luke is drawing on Matthew, not Mark (and is usually adding his own significant details as well). This is particularly telling when we consider the passion narrative, since otherwise there would appear to be no good reason for Luke to have switched back and forth between using Mark and Matthew here. But the only place in the passion where Luke pulls material from elsewhere in his sources is in Jesus's discourse at the Last Supper. In particular, Jesus's saying that the disciples will "sit on thrones judging the twelve tribes of Israel" (Luke 22:30 NRSV) could

---

6. It should be noted, however, that since most of the supposed "Mark/Q overlaps" occur in the Journey to Jerusalem, and since the Q theory asserts that Luke would have taken these from Q rather than from Mark, most Q proponents would also agree that Luke made very little use of Mark throughout this entire portion of his Gospel.
7. A detailed table of pericopes upon which this chart is based is included in the appendix at the end of this work.

only have come from Matthew (19:28), not from Mark. Luke's desire to include such sayings at the Last Supper would have given him a good enough motive for switching to Matthew's account at this point, and the frequent agreements with Matthew in the subsequent passages (such as only one cock crow, Peter's weeping "bitterly," and the famous "Who is it that struck you?" [Luke 22:34, 61–64; Matt 26:34, 68, 75]) indicate that Luke continues to follow Matthew rather than Mark until Jesus is brought before Pilate. It is also significant that it is only in this portion of the passion, where Luke is drawing from Matthew instead of Mark, that he departs from Mark's order of events.

Although I stated earlier that we would not necessarily expect to find parallels between Luke's Exposition and the structure of the Exposition segment of sonata form, it turns out that there *is* a parallel after all. Just as in sonata form there are two theme groups in two different keys, which are then usually repeated, we see that Luke has alternated between Matthew (for his first "theme group") and Mark (for his second) and then has repeated this pattern exactly, even with a corresponding "Codetta" (the transfiguration), which brings his Exposition to a logical conclusion. No great significance should be drawn from this parallel, but it does provide further evidence that Luke's aesthetic sense of symmetry and contrast led him to create a structure for his Gospel similar to what the classical composers would later consider to be a "natural" (even "inevitable") musical form. Although Luke's Recapitulation also exhibits similar alternation between his sources, in this case these do not correspond quite so neatly to the pattern of sonata form. Instead, the two-part structure of Luke's Recapitulation focuses first on Jesus's confrontation with the Pharisees in Jerusalem (all taken from Mark) and then, second, on the passion (some from Matthew and some from Mark).

## Luke's Method

We are now able to address not only *what* material Luke took from which of his sources but *how* he went about doing so. Based on this analysis, a clear pattern emerges. Figure 4.3, "Luke's Method," (online at http://fortresspress.com/lukethecomposer), attempts to show more specifically the relationships between Luke and his sources. Matthew is shown to the left of Luke, with Mark on Luke's right. Pericopes in Mark and Matthew that have no parallel in Luke (which Luke therefore chose to omit) are shown as grey. Of the pericopes Luke did use, those that are parallel in both Mark and Matthew are purple or indigo in their columns. If a parallel pericope was taken by Luke from Mark, that pericope appears in Mark as purple, but in Matthew as indigo, with the reverse true if Luke used Matthew's version of the pericope. Hence, the first few pericopes in Mark's column, which recount Jesus's baptism, are indigo because Luke took this material from Matthew rather than from Mark. The corresponding pericopes in Matthew are therefore purple. Pericopes unique to Mark are red, and pericopes unique to Matthew are blue.

Luke's column, although based on the previous chart, now shows in more detail how he used material from his two written sources. Pericopes that he took from Mark but altered or expanded are shown in orange, whereas pericopes that remain faithful to Mark's version are shown in red. Similarly, pericopes that he took from Matthew but altered are shown in green, whereas pericopes that remain faithful to Matthew are blue.

The colored lines between the columns connect the corresponding pericopes from their location in the source documents to their location in Luke. The red and blue lines show pericopes from Mark and Matthew, respectively, that Luke has kept in their original order. Black lines indicate pericopes that have been displaced in Luke. However, because all the Matthean pericopes Luke used in his Journey to Jerusalem have been displaced, black bars beside the columns show which pericopes were used but do not show precisely which pericope in Matthew corresponds to which pericope in Luke. This allows us to see more clearly how Luke used Matthew in his Exposition and Recapitulation sections without the tangled confusion of his Development displacements.

This chart now allows us to make numerous interesting observations. We see that Mark, with which Luke was apparently not as familiar as he was with Matthew, was used almost exclusively for narrative passages and was always used exactly in order, except for the two slight rearrangements mentioned above (both of which we now see were the first pericopes respectively in the two blocks of Markan material Luke used in his Exposition). Even the few pericopes from Mark that Luke included in the last part of his Journey to Jerusalem came from Mark in exact sequential order. It is also evident now that Luke's use of Mark does not represent a skeleton or framework for his Gospel at all. Instead he used Mark in four specific continuous blocks of narrative material, except for the one "unusual" pericope in the Journey to

Jerusalem (and even that pericope appears near the end, after Luke has nearly exhausted the Matthean material he uses in the journey).

Luke was able to draw material from Matthew, however, with which he was almost certainly thoroughly familiar through memorization, and from any portion of Matthew at any time. In every case where Luke followed Matthew's narrative (both in the Exposition and Recapitulation), he included additional material from elsewhere in Matthew's Gospel (as the black lines indicate). In his Development section, Luke drew Matthean material at will from every portion of Matthew's Gospel and placed it in his own preferred storytelling order. Hence, Mark seems to have been the "easy" choice for certain narrative sequences where Luke wanted to keep the action going in his story. But any time Luke wanted to include more of Jesus's teachings or place a modified version of a pericope in a different location, he turned to Matthew. When we compare Luke's use of Mark and Matthew, therefore, it is apparent that, whenever Luke uses Mark, he follows him closely within a limited scale, whereas with Matthew he feels free to draw on material from anywhere at any time.

We may also look at this same information in another way using the following table. This table divides Luke's Gospel according to the structure of sonata form as described above. For each section, the passages Luke has taken from either Matthew or Mark are displayed, in the order in which they appear in Luke but with no indication about any of Luke's own unique material (and ignoring the many passages from Matthew in the Journey to Jerusalem). To make it clearer how Luke used this material, those passages that Luke has displaced, arranging them in a different order than they appear in Matthew or Mark, are highlighted in bold and italics. I have represented these relationships in the following table as well. We see that, throughout his Gospel, only two of Mark's pericopes appear displaced in Luke, whereas in every Matthean block, at least two pericopes have been displaced each time.

| Table 4.5. Luke's Displacements of Matthew and Mark | | |
|---|---|---|
| *Sections of Luke as per Sonata Form* | *from Matthew* | *from Mark* |
| **Introduction: Luke 1:1–2:52** | | |
| *Introduction:* Luke 1:1–2:52<br><br>The Nativity | loose parallels with parts of Matt 1–2 | |

| Exposition: Luke 3:1–9:50 | | |
|---|---|---|
| *1st Theme Group:* Luke 3:1–4:30<br><br>The Baptism and Temptation | Matt 3:1–12<br>*Matt 14:3–5*<br>Matt 3:13–4:17<br>*Matt 13:54–58* | |
| *2nd Theme Group:* Luke 4:31–6:16<br><br>Initial Ministry | | Mark 1:21–39<br>*Mark 1:16–20*<br>Mark 1:40–3:6<br>Mark 3:13–19 |
| *1st Group Repeated:* Luke 6:17–8:3<br><br>The Sermon on the Plain | Matt 4:24–5:12<br>Matt 5:38–48<br>Matt 7:1–5<br>Matt 7:15–20<br>*Matt 12:33–37*<br>Matt 7:21–27<br>Matt 8:5–13<br>Matt 11:2–19<br>*Matt 26:6–13* | |
| *2nd Group Repeated:* Luke 8:4–9:17<br><br>Parables of the Kingdom | | Mark 4:1–25<br>*Mark 3:31–35*<br>Mark 4:35–43<br>Mark 6:7–16<br>Mark 6:30–44 |
| *Codetta:* Luke 9:18–50<br><br>The Transfiguration | | Mark 8:27–9:10<br>Mark 9:14–41 |
| **Development: Luke 9:51–19:27** | | |
| *Development:* Luke 9:51–18:8<br><br>The Journey to Jerusalem | many parallels<br>with Matthew,<br>none in order | Mark 9:42–50 |
| *Retransition:* Luke 18:9–19:27<br><br>The Pharaisee and the Publican | Matt 25:14–30 | Mark 10:13–34<br>Mark 10:41–52 |
| **Recapitulation: Luke 19:28–23:56** | | |
| *1st Section:* Luke 19:28–21:38<br><br>In Jerusalem | | Mark 11:1–10<br>Mark 11:15–19<br>Mark 11:27–12:27<br>Mark 12:35–13:20 |
| *2nd Section, part 1:* Luke 22:1–20<br><br>The Passion – The Last Supper | | Mark 13:24–32<br>Mark 14:1–2<br>Mark 14:10–17<br>Mark 14:22–25 |

| *2nd Section, part 2:* Luke 22:21–71<br><br>The Passion – The Arrest | Matt 26:21–25<br>*Matt 20:24–28*<br>*Matt 19:27–30*<br>Matt 26:31–56<br>Matt 26:69–75<br>*Matt 26:57–68* | |
| --- | --- | --- |
| *2nd Section, part 3:* Luke 23:1–56<br><br>The Passion – The Trial and Crucifixion | | Mark 15:1–15<br>Mark 15:21–47 |
| **Coda: Luke 24:1–53** | | |
| *Coda:* Luke 24:1–53<br><br>The Resurrection | loose parallels with<br>parts of Matt 28 | |

In addition, it is also the case that, when Luke used Mark, he seldom made significant alterations to Mark's versions of stories (except that he frequently abbreviated them), *until* he reached the passion narrative. Up to that point, there are very few orange pericopes in the chart, but once the passion begins there are very few red ones. In contrast, there are more green pericopes than blue ones throughout his entire Gospel, indicating again that Luke felt much freer with material he took from Matthew, either altering it himself or perhaps often drawing on an alternate version from an oral source. We can also see that there are very few passages unique to Luke (yellow) placed within red Markan blocks, but such yellow pericopes are frequently interspersed among Matthean green or blue passages. Far from this being evidence that Luke only used Matthew tentatively, this suggests strongly that Luke was very familiar with Matthew's Gospel (again pointing to complete memorization) but was relatively unfamiliar with Mark's Gospel, which in all likelihood he had only recently come to know and, hence, needed to have physically in front of him whenever he was using it.

Additionally, the lack of lengthy blocks of unique Lukan material apart from the birth and resurrection accounts also makes it seem unlikely that Luke employed other *written* sources apart from Matthew and Mark (unless he also had these memorized). Instead, he seems to have been able to draw on his own apparently vast knowledge of oral tradition in order to add his own unique touches wherever necessary throughout the entire Gospel, usually (as already noted) interspersed among pericopes taken from Matthew. Rather than using Mark as his skeleton, then (adding material to it and occasionally omitting material from it), it now appears that Luke's method was more one of constructing his Gospel from large "building blocks" taken from his two major sources (Matthew and Mark) and occasionally supplementing these with material from his third major source (oral tradition). Luke therefore had no single "primary" source at all but drew on all his sources at different times, and in varying but appropriate ways, for specific purposes.

Figure 4.4, "Luke's Use of Matthew and Mark," (online at http://fortresspress.com/lukethecomposer) now reveals the rest of the picture, showing just how freely Luke used Matthew in his Development section, and showing the sharp contrast in how he utilized Matthew and Mark, for which we are now able to understand his reasons.

## Omissions

Scholars in the past have often assumed that Luke would have used as much material from each of his sources as possible, and hence any omissions from those sources were considered problematic. Given this new way of looking at how Luke produced his Gospel, however, it is far more appropriate to examine what Luke chose to *include* in his work, rather than what he chose to *omit*, since he was building a specific document for a specific purpose, not merely throwing together whatever stories or sayings he could find. Again, this is a significant departure from the conventional view that he used nearly all of Mark, all of Q and all of L.

Nevertheless, it may still be worthwhile at this point to look at what he did *not* choose to include from his sources and to speculate on why he may have passed over specific material (but noting the important distinction here between passively *not* choosing to include rather than actively choosing to omit). Luke ended up using about two-thirds of Mark and two-thirds of Matthew (counting all of the Triple Tradition material in both cases, since he would not be expected to have used a parallel pericope from one source if he had already used the same pericope from the other).[8] So why did he leave out the portions he did? It is impossible, of course, to know how much of the additional oral tradition at his disposal he rejected, so this must remain a complete unknown.

Luke's intentions for writing his Gospel are critical. Luke was not

---

8. The material Luke did omit from Matthew and Mark is listed in the appendix at the end of this work.

simply attempting to write a comprehensive compendium of all possible information relating to Jesus, his life, and his teachings. He was writing to convince the gentile Theophilus of the truth of Christianity, probably to convert him, and possibly to defend Christianity as a valid (indeed, *the* valid) sect within Judaism. This means that the material he chose to include or omit may have depended very much on its "Luke-pleasingness," as this term applies to his purposes in writing. In this light, then, at least some of the material he omitted should be expected to display some features of "Luke-*dis*pleasingness."

But there is also one additional and important factor to be considered. The length of Luke's Gospel is virtually identical to the longest practical scroll that could be produced in the first century. Luke was therefore not only limited by his own taste and purpose; he was seriously limited as to how much material he *could* include, even if he had wanted to include more. It is possible that Luke's original plan of what to include had to be scaled back, since he has pushed so close to his limit that he probably could not have included a single verse more. It may therefore be the case that among the material he rejected we will also find numerous passages that are indeed "Luke-pleasing" but which he reluctantly had to let go in order to keep his document to the requisite length.

How he may have chosen between two potential (and well-loved) pericopes might be subjective, and it may turn out to be unwise for modern scholars to attempt to second-guess Luke's decision-making process in this regard. For instance, faced with a choice of whether to include a parable such as the Laborers in the Vineyard (from Matthew 20), Luke may originally have intended to include it but ultimately decided that, in order to save space, he would have to let it go. Even though it was sufficiently "Luke-pleasing" and would have illustrated God's call to repentance, even at a late hour, along with God's promise to reward all those who do turn to him in faith (two of Luke's favorite themes), considerations of space prevailed. Luke may have decided that the parable of the Good Samaritan, for instance, was a far better use of his limited, and therefore precious, space.

Yet even this is making an assumption that may not be correct. Luke may not have gone through all the pericopes available to him and assessed whether they were worth including. He did have to work out carefully how he wanted his story to develop, especially in his Journey to Jerusalem, and how each pericope would relate to the ones before and after it. A parable such as the Laborers in the Vineyard, despite its "Luke-pleasingness," may simply never have entered his mind at any particular moment along the journey as making the specific point he wanted to make at that precise time. It therefore remained unused once the Journey to Jerusalem was completed.

For most "omitted" material, then, there is probably no significance at all to be attached to the fact that Luke "chose" to omit it. There are five categories of material, however, that perhaps do hold some significance and are worth examining: Matthew's birth narratives, material from the Sermon on the Mount, some of the parables of the kingdom (from Matthew 13 and Mark 4), Luke's "Great Omission" from Mark, and Matthew's unique material from the passion.

One of the most important objections that has been raised by scholars against Luke having used Matthew as a source is the obvious differences between their birth narratives. If Luke was following Matthew, why is there no common material here? The first answer to this question is that there actually *is* common material, but there are important differences as well. As Goodacre indicates, Luke need not have included any birth narratives at all, so their very presence is a basic agreement with Matthew already. But the shape of the narratives is also similar. God promises that Mary as a virgin will give birth to a son who has been conceived by the Holy Spirit. A command is given in both Gospels to name the child "Jesus" because he will be the savior. Jesus is born in Bethlehem, and his birth is marked by supernatural events that lead certain individuals to come to worship him. The family relocates to Nazareth, where Jesus grows up. Additionally, both Gospels include a genealogy of Jesus. Such numerous agreements in the overall structure of the narratives is surely significant, as is the specific agreement that both Matthew and Luke attribute virginity to Jesus's mother.

The command to name the child "Jesus" is also remarkable, because (although addressed to Joseph in Matthew and to Mary in Luke) the command in both Gospels is identical, word for word and letter for letter, except for the form of the initial verb: τέξεται ("*She* will give birth") in Matthew as opposed to τέξῃ ("*You* will give birth") in Luke. The rest of the verse is identical: υἱὸν καὶ καλέσεις τὸ ὄνομα αὐτοῦ Ἰησοῦν ("[give birth] to a son, and you shall call his name Jesus") (Matt 1:21, Luke 1:31). Regarding this exact correspondence, Goodacre writes:

> In Matthew καλέσεις ("you shall call," singular) is addressed appropriately to Joseph who, as Matthew will make clear later in the passage, will name the child. . . . In Luke, by contrast, καλέσεις ("you shall call," singular) is

addressed less appropriately to Mary who will not be solely responsible for the naming of the child. As Luke elsewhere makes clear, the naming of the child is either the sole responsibility of the father (1:13) or, at best, of both parents (1:59-66; cf. 2:21). In other words, this close parallel between Matthew and Luke points in the direction of Luke's familiarity with Matthew, from whom Luke has taken over a clause that was more appropriate in its original context in Matthew.[9]

If Luke had not been aware of Matthew's Gospel (as Q scholars contend), the inclusion of all these details seems to be quite a coincidence. But what, then, of the many differences between Matthew's account and Luke's? How are we to account for these? There seem to be two answers to this question.

The first is to return once again to Luke's Prologue, where he tells Theophilus that he is producing an accurate account. There is every reason to believe that Luke trusted his own sources over Matthew's regarding the nativity of Jesus, and that he is therefore attempting to give a more accurate account than the one in Matthew's Gospel. Even if Luke respected Matthew's Gospel and had memorized it, there is no reason to think that he considered it to be so sacrosanct that it could not have contained errors. We have no idea what Luke's sources were for his birth stories (or Matthew's for that matter), and so we do not have available to us the information Luke had in order to make such a judgement. It may turn out in the end that Matthew's account is more accurate, but Luke himself thoroughly believed that his was the truer of the two.

Luke's desire for accuracy and his belief that the accounts he had gathered from oral sources were more accurate than Matthew's (regardless of whether they really were more accurate) give us a sufficient explanation for the differences between Matthew and Luke. But there is another factor involved that has already been mentioned in regard to Luke's own account: Luke was reluctant to portray early in his Gospel any of the political implications of Jesus being the Messiah because of his Roman (and possibly *legal* Roman) audience (even though admittedly, Gabriel *does* tell Mary that "the Lord God will give to him the throne of his ancestor David" [Luke 1:32 NRSV]). Hence, Matthew's genealogy, which presents the Davidic dynastic line, the Magi heralding Jesus as king, Herod's reaction to this treasonous idea, and the move to Nazareth in order to avoid political repercussions would all seem to be "Luke-displeasing" concepts this early in his narrative. Luke therefore would have had good reason to follow a different path than Matthew's in his birth narratives. Given these factors, then, it should not surprise us that Luke would have chosen to omit many of the elements present in Matthew's version.

The next category of omitted material in Luke is a number of sayings from the Sermon on the Mount that Luke did not include either in his Sermon on the Plain or in his Journey to Jerusalem. All of these sayings have to do either with the interpretation of the Torah or with Jewish religious practice. As such, they qualify as "Luke-displeasing." As discussed earlier, Luke uses the temple as his reference to show that Christianity is a valid sect within Judaism, but he carefully avoids the matter of following the Torah, particularly the question of whether gentile Christians need to follow the Torah. Again, this is a Roman-friendly position, and so Luke's omission of such potentially controversial topics is not surprising.

Next, although Luke includes the parable of the Sower and its explanation (plus the next parable from Mark, the Lamp on the Stand), he includes none of the additional parables of the kingdom from Matthew 13 or Mark 4, except for the Mustard Seed, which he does include later in the Journey to Jerusalem. Here it is the context that is important. Luke includes almost no teachings in his Exposition section except for the Sermon on the Plain and the parable of the Sower, and this seems intentional. The Exposition (as in the corresponding musical sonata form) is intended to present his main themes briefly, and with *little repetition*. Any development or repetition of themes is saved for the Development section, the Journey to Jerusalem. Hence, the Sermon on the Plain is short and succinct, and so is this one important parable of the kingdom. That Luke chose not to return to any of the other parables (except the one) later on is simply an indication that they did not meet his needs at any particular point in his journey.

Luke's so-called Great Omission from Mark probably represents a similar situation. In his two large blocks of Markan material in his Exposition, Luke follows Mark faithfully from chapter 1 to chapter 6, omitting only a few scattered pericopes or ones parallel to similar ones from Matthew. Then suddenly he jumps from Mark 6:44 to 8:27, omitting everything in between. In the traditional view of seeing Mark as Luke's skeleton, this gap is viewed as highly significant, since we would expect Luke to include nearly all of Mark. Thus, this Great Omission is often seen as indicating either that Luke's manuscript of Mark was defective or that our version of Mark has been augmented ( a "Deutero-Mark").

But this "omission" need not be an indication of any such thing. There are two straightforward and interrelated reasons why Luke may not have chosen to include these pericopes. First, Luke was *not* using Mark as his skeleton and was under no obligation to use all or even most of his Gospel. Luke took those portions that suited his purpose, and his purpose in his Exposition section was (as just stated) to set out his main themes with little repetition. This need not mean simply repetition of teachings, but repetition of events as well. It is obvious that Luke leaves out the odd healing miracle from Mark from time to time, all of which he may have felt were simply unnecessarily repetitious. So in the Great Omission we see as well that there is repetition of several stories similar to what Luke has included earlier, such as the miraculous feedings, nature miracles on the Sea of Galilee, and others. Luke may never have intended to include these stories, in order to keep his narrative brief, dynamic, and interesting.

On the other hand, he *may* have wanted to include some or all of these stories but decided the he simply did not have enough space. As has been stated a number of times, Luke's Gospel is *precisely* the length of the maximum scroll available to him. It would have been a tremendous coincidence if his original plan for his Gospel had proved to be a perfect match when he actually came to writing down his account. Hence, it seems far more likely that he overestimated what he could include and then had to trim back some material in order to keep the work to the proper length.

The story where Luke picks up the thread just after the Great Omission is Peter's Confession that Jesus is the Messiah, a very important pericope that marks the beginning of Luke's "Codetta" at the end of his Exposition, preparing for the transfiguration and the Journey to Jerusalem. It is not out of the question, therefore, that, having attempted his original version of his Gospel, and finding it a bit too long, he then worked from this point backwards, editing out whatever amount of material was needed to reduce the length of his Gospel in order to fit on his scroll. This would have been an especially appropriate place to make this edit because of its somewhat repetitious nature.

John Wenham comes to a similar conclusion:

> He had big stores of information and he knew that to keep his material within the limits of one scroll would require much self-denial. . . . It was

probably when he came to the final editing that he discovered that he had considerably exceeded the length of a scroll and decided that something must be dropped. It was natural to hold on to all the new material and drop something from the Galilean ministry, hence the Great Omission of Mark 6:45–8:26, which apart from the healing of a blind man at the end is fully covered by both Matthew and Mark. This is a sensible omission since there are obvious similarities between Mark 4:35–6:44 and 6:45–8:10. There are two feedings of a multitude, followed in each case by a voyage, a conflict with Pharisees and an act of power.[10]

Thus there is no reason to speculate about alternate versions of Mark in order to "explain" this "omission."

The final items Luke did not include in his Gospel are Matthew's unique material in the passion and resurrection accounts. Like the birth narratives, the perceived lack of such material in Luke's Gospel is often considered evidence that Luke could not have been familiar with Matthew's Gospel. But, as we have seen, this is simply not true, since Luke *does* follow Matthew from the Last Supper to the Sanhedrin. Nevertheless, there are specific elements unique to Matthew's version of the passion that Luke passes over. These include the death of Judas, Pilate's wife's dream, Pilate washing his hands, and the guards at the tomb. Again, all of these "omissions" are logical; moreover, they all occur in portions of the narrative where Luke is following Mark rather than Matthew.

Of course, Luke *does* give an account of the death of Judas, in Acts 1:18–19. Although this account is somewhat contradictory to Matthew's, both Luke and Matthew agree that Judas's death is associated with the "Field of Blood." As with the Birth narratives, then, Luke appears here to have been familiar with Matthew's version but chose to draw on a different tradition, perhaps intentionally in order to "correct" Matthew.

The details about Pilate and his wife appear on the surface to be "Luke-pleasing," as they would seem to exonerate Pilate and would thus be Roman-friendly. These details, however, could also have been interpreted by a Roman audience as portraying Pilate as weak and ineffectual, seeking to extricate himself from a difficult situation. Instead, Luke portrays Pilate as more prudent and juridical, eventually "granting their request" rather than giving in and "handing him over" to the Jewish leaders. Thus, in its careful neutrality, Luke's portrayal of Pilate is more Roman-friendly than Matthew's and, in particular, is more

10. Wenham, *Redating Matthew, Mark and Luke,* 209–10, 294.

friendly toward the Roman system of governance and justice (again important if Luke is concerned with legal matters in his Gospel). Similarly, the account of the guards at the tomb would not have served Luke's purpose, being related to the quashing of rumors spread among the Jewish people and requiring the bribery and collusion of Roman soldiers, thus putting the Romans in a bad light.

Luke's resurrection account, like his birth narrative, also has elements in common with Matthew's: the women coming to the tomb at dawn and a figure or figures appearing in radiant clothing to tell the women that Jesus is not there but has risen and to give them a command to report to the disciples (which includes a reference to Galilee). Other details in the two accounts, however, are not only different but contradictory. This again seems to be a case where Luke is familiar with Matthew's account but gives a different account from one of his oral sources (most likely an actual eyewitness of the events). Again, Luke's own concerns are evident. Instead of going to Galilee, the disciples remain in the temple praising God, emphasizing Luke's interest in continued worship in the temple by Jesus's followers. The differences are therefore not surprising.

Luke *did* omit material from his sources, but these omissions probably tended to be passive rather than active. Rather than choosing *not* to include certain material, far more often Luke simply chose what he *would* include, the omissions simply being the material left over after he had made these choices. Even "Luke-displeasing" material was more likely simply passed over than actively rejected. The only material he may have actively chosen to leave out would have been the Great Omission from Mark, and this would probably have been done mainly to save space.

## Inclusions

More significant than Luke's supposed "omissions" are his inclusions, the material he chose to use when composing his Gospel and the procedures he would have followed when putting it together.

As discussed above, Luke's birth narratives (which form his Introduction) appear to have been informed by Matthew's but on the whole seem to have come from other (oral) sources. On the basis of his Prologue, it seems likely that most of Luke's unique material in these narratives came directly from eyewitnesses, rather than from traditions gradually developing in isolated Christian communities. But what about the canticles included in these narratives? Did Mary and Zechariah spontaneously burst into song on the spot, as suggested in the text? This seems highly unlikely, but it is certainly not out of the question that Mary herself could have composed the Magnificat based on the song of Hannah from 1 Samuel 2 and on her own experience, and that she and others could have sung it in the early church in Jerusalem, since Luke himself tells us in Acts that she was a central figure in the infant church (Acts 1:14). Likewise, the other canticles could well represent authentic early hymns associated with the people involved (perhaps also remembered and sung by Mary), and that Luke is here transmitting a genuine primitive tradition.

Following his Introduction, Luke initially turned to Matthew's Gospel as he began his Exposition, since his account of John the Baptist and Jesus's baptism and temptation clearly follow Matthew's. But the few details Luke incorporated from Mark's version may indicate that he had already opened Mark's scroll, since he would not have needed Matthew's scroll physically in front of him if he had memorized it. Alternately, he may have simply read through Mark's version just before writing this segment of his Gospel, making mental notes of the elements he wanted to incorporate. Then, because he was working from his memorization of Matthew, he was able to pull from memory the extra information he wanted to include, such as a brief mention of the imprisonment of John from later in Matthew (since he himself would not be giving an account of John's death). He also included his own Roman-friendly (non-dynastic) genealogy of Jesus in the middle of this section.

Luke also wanted to begin his description of Jesus's actual ministry by describing his reception in his hometown of Nazareth, where he proclaimed that his coming was the fulfillment of prophecy, but where he was also rejected by those who had known him in his youth. Luke therefore pulled details from Matthew's version of this rejection, a story from much later in his Gospel, and merged them with Luke's own description. This did have the odd effect of having Jesus talk about his previous reception in Capernaum before Luke had ever given an account of Jesus having been in Capernaum. He "covered himself" by first giving a one-line description of Jesus's general ministry in Galilee before he had returned to Nazareth.

Having thus set the scene of Jesus's message and of opposition to that message, Luke was ready to give a more detailed description of some of the events in Jesus's early ministry in Galilee. If he had drawn on his knowledge of Matthew, this would have meant sifting through his memory of material from chapter 4 to chapter 12 in order to pull out the needed stories. Instead, by turning to Mark he was able to cover the same period by simply copying Mark from the middle of chapter 1 to the middle of chapter 3, leaving out one somewhat repetitious healing account in the process. He also made one other change. He wanted to include the miraculous draught of fish in his description of the calling of the first disciples, but he wanted to prepare for this "big" miracle with a few lesser ones. He therefore shifted the calling of the disciples a little further on in the narrative. Once again this had an odd effect, since Jesus was now made to visit Peter's home and heal his mother-in-law *before* he had actually called him. But this also turned out all right because it gave Peter a slightly longer relationship with Jesus before he chose to leave everything to follow him.

Jesus's ministry in Galilee thus begun, Luke now wanted to give a very brief exposition of Jesus's basic teachings, so he turned back to Matthew. Luke gives an abbreviated version of Matthew's Sermon on the Mount but locates it on a plain rather than on a mountain. As discussed earlier, this abbreviated sermon provides a succinct introduction to the major themes of Jesus's teachings that Luke would later develop during the Journey to Jerusalem, and so it is perfectly appropriate as it stands in its present context. As he often felt free to do with material from Matthew, Luke makes a few slight changes. He substitutes a slightly different version of the Beatitudes, which is more consistent with his own concern for the poor, and which also includes the extra "woes," setting out the first contrast between the faithful and the unfaithful. He also imports one brief saying from later in Matthew's Gospel that he wants to include here, which also makes this contrast. Otherwise he is faithful to Matthew's order, and also ends with the same parable as Matthew's Sermon on the Mount. He even includes (this one and only time) Matthew's stock ending phrase, "After he had finished all his sayings. . ." (Luke 7:1).

Since he was now still drawing from Matthew, he included a few stories from the remainder of Matthew's "early ministry" section, up to chapter 12, stories that have no parallel in Mark but which are particularly "Luke-pleasing," especially the Roman-friendly Centurion of Capernaum. He also added a miracle story of his own (the Widow of Nain), ending this section with his own version of the Woman with the Ointment, which has a completely different emphasis here than in the other Gospels, although Luke is again able to draw on Matthew's version from much later in his account for certain details.

Luke could have stayed with Matthew at this point, but this would have required him to skip around a bit more from place to place and to leave out some intervening material, so again it was easier to go back to Mark, whose narrative is more straightforward. After the Sermon on the Plain, Luke wanted to recount the parable of the Sower as the other fundamental statement of Jesus's teachings. Mark's version of this and other related parables is briefer and more to the point than Matthew's, so Luke begins here. He wants to include the saying that comes just before this parable in Mark, a saying about Jesus's mother and brothers, but he saves this momentarily until he is finished with the parable. This allows the saying about "hearing God's word and putting it into practice" (Luke 8:21) to relate back to the parable rather than anticipating it (as it does in Mark 3:35). We have now seen the only two rearrangements of material from Mark that Luke would carry out.

It is noteworthy that Luke's treatment here of Mark's parable sequence is virtually identical to his treatment of Matthew's Sermon on the Mount. First, Luke changes the setting for the teaching, with no mention of the sea or of Jesus getting into a boat. Then he shortens the sequence considerably, from thirty-four verses (Mark 4:1–34) to fifteen (Luke 8:4–18). He saves some material from the passage for use later on (the parable of the Mustard Seed in Mark 4:30–32), but he eliminates other material altogether (Mark 4:26–29, 33–34), and he keeps what material he does include in its original order. The only technique he does not use here that he had used for his Sermon on the Plain is to insert any extra material (although this is consistent with his stricter use of Mark than of Matthew). Luke's treatment of this passage therefore demonstrates that his condensation of Matthew's Sermon on the Mount is completely consistent with his method throughout his Exposition section and, hence, gives a strong indication that Luke did base his Sermon on the Plain directly on Matthew's Gospel.

After the parable of the Sower, Luke continues with Mark's version of Jesus's extended ministry (Luke 8:22–9:50, based on Mark 4:35–9:41), skipping over material he does not want to incorporate (including his Great Omission), concluding with Peter's confession, the transfiguration, and the stories in the wake of the transfiguration. He then (at Luke 9:51) sets Mark aside for the time being but keeps his place in the scroll, as he will resume precisely where he left off once Jesus nears Jerusalem.

Luke is now ready for his well-planned journey to Jerusalem (9:51–19:27), in which he freely draws from oral sources and from Matthew's Gospel (possibly with no text physically in front of him but perhaps with the help of notes written on wax tablets) to weave his fascinating and effective Development section, in which he explores the theme of discipleship (as discussed in detail earlier). Under such circumstances, we would expect no discernible pattern in his use of Matthew, and this is just what we see. This "random" distribution is therefore not a sign that he was *not* using Matthew but is simply the result of the way in which he draws on this material in order to create his own desired effect. As he nears the end of this section, however, he includes the saying from Mark, the Warning against Offenses (Luke 17:1–2, which in Mark is in the very next verse after Luke had left him, Mark 9:42, so that Luke still continues to follow Mark in exact sequence). He could have used Matthew's version of this saying, but he apparently preferred Mark's (which was, after all, right there in front of him). This is followed by more unique Lukan material, plus a group of sayings about the Day of the Son of Man drawn from several places in Matthew and then more material unique to Luke.

Luke has now reached his "Retransition" point (at 18:9), the point at which he begins to prepare for his Recapitulation section, and here he once again opens up Mark's scroll (skipping just a few verses) to include especially the story of the Rich Young Man (from Mark 10:17–22 in Luke 18:18–23), which Luke then contrasts with his own story of Zacchaeus (19:1–10) to emphasize the two choices that might be made in response to Jesus. To end his Development section, Luke uses a variation on one more parable from Matthew (the Parable of the Pounds, Matt 25:14–30) to present the stark choice to Theophilus of either following or rejecting Jesus (Luke 19:11–27). We find, therefore, that there has been one Markan pericope in the middle of mostly Matthean passages, and now one Matthean pericope in the middle of mostly Markan passages, the only such alternations in all of Luke's Gospel, but these were dictated by the form and intention of his Development section, and especially by the way in which he wanted to make his transition back to his Recapitulation.

But in all of this, Luke has still been following Mark precisely in sequence, and he now returns solely to Mark's account again for the first part of his Recapitulation, beginning with the Triumphal Entry and continuing all the way to the Words of Institution at the Last Supper. Luke is a bit freer here than he had been before with Mark, not in rearranging material but in incorporating his own versions of events (perhaps influenced by John or perhaps from other eyewitness accounts), mixed in with Mark's version. Mark is again more conducive to Luke's purpose here than Matthew, since Luke would need to skip over more material (mostly parables and teachings that Luke had already used) in order to follow Matthew's narrative rather than Mark's. Luke skips over the Cursing of the Fig Tree, but little else in Mark's account (and after all, Luke *had* chosen earlier to include a *parable* of the Fig Tree).

After the Words of Institution, Luke wants to incorporate into Jesus's address at the Last Supper certain sayings from earlier in Matthew, particularly the saying that the disciples would sit on thrones judging Israel. This image is especially appropriate at the Last Supper, as the disciples are all gathered about Jesus with the imagery of the Passover and God's creation of the nation of Israel in their minds. Luke turns again to Matthew's Gospel for this and the next few pericopes, apparently preferring many of Matthew's details to Mark's, especially in his account of Peter's denial and weeping, and in his account of Jesus before the Sanhedrin where the guards mock him. But as had been the case with Jesus' baptism, there are a few Markan elements here as well, so Luke had probably at least read through Mark's version just before writing his own, thus incorporating some of Mark's details together with Matthew's.

Luke now returns one last time to Mark's narrative for the remainder of the passion. Mark is a bit more concise than Matthew here, and Luke is not interested in Matthew's unique material (as discussed above). He is very interested in his own material (from oral sources), however, and his text now bears even less resemblance to either Mark or Matthew and looks more like a separate oral tradition, even though there are still many points of contact with the other two Synoptics.

The same is true of Luke's resurrection narrative, but this departs even further from Matthew and Mark than had the passion, and once the initial encounter with the women has been described, there is little in common whatsoever with the other Synoptics. But again there are interesting similarities with John. (So Luke at least seems to be aware of some of the same events that would subsequently be written down by John, if John's Gospel did come later.) Finally, Luke takes us back to the temple at the very end of his Gospel, ready to pick up the story again in Acts.

One additional note about Luke's relationship to Mark may be mentioned at this point. Some scholars believe that the canonical version of Mark that we now possess may have lost its original ending. If so, it is probable that the copy Luke was working from would have included this now-lost ending, especially if Luke had received his copy directly from Mark himself. But would this have affected Luke's own ending? It seems doubtful, since what remains of Mark's ending is much closer to Matthew than it is to Luke, particularly since it includes the directive that Jesus would meet the disciples in Galilee, whereas in Luke's Gospel, the disciples remain in Jerusalem. It seems, then, that the original ending of Mark may have been similar to the ending of Matthew (except that it would not have included the guards at the tomb or the subsequent rumor that was spread by them) but that Luke chose to rely on different sources for his resurrection accounts.

Thus, based on this review of Luke's procedures, we can see that he was methodical, logical, and totally consistent in the way in which he went about putting his Gospel together (including using necessarily different methods required for his Development section as opposed to the rest of his Gospel, just as the classical composers would later do in sonata form).

Luke's procedures were also completely consistent with what is known of first-century writing techniques and practices. The physical process of actually writing a document would have been somewhat cumbersome. There is no evidence that writing desks were employed at this time, so a scribe would have been working on the ground, probably balancing his manuscript on his knees. Under such conditions it would have been extremely difficult for an author to have had more than one source document physically open in front of him at a time while also writing on his own. Authors tended to rely on their own memory of any secondary texts they might be using at any given time, unless they were able to employ an assistant to read such texts to them as they were writing.[11] In preparation for such work, ancient authors did often write draft notes of their intentions (typically on wax tablets, which could later be smoothed over to be used again) and would then consult with their associates regarding whether these were satisfactory before producing their final versions for publication.[12]

Luke's procedure of alternating between his two sources in large blocks (while hardly ever conflating them) means, therefore, that in this way he would have avoided the difficulty of needing to have two

11. Derrenbacker, *Ancient Compositional Practices*, 37–39, 46–47.
12. Ibid., 40–42, 75.

source scrolls open in front of him at the same time. His use of Mark almost entirely in exact order (with only two exceptions) would also have made sense if he was relatively unfamiliar with that specific text, which would have had no spaces between sentences or even words to help him find desired passages. His freer use of Matthew, still following it mostly in order for his narrative blocks (when he may have had the scroll open in front of him), but departing from its order wildly in his Development section, would have been made significantly easier if he had largely memorized Matthew's Gospel already, and (as Francis Watson has suggested) if he had already mapped out on wax tablets how he intended to organize this portion of his Gospel. Thus, Luke would have required no astonishing skills to produce his masterpiece apart from his own genius in organizing his material as the expert composer and storyteller he was.

# 5

---

# Evaluating Luke

Based on the above analysis, through which we have seen how Luke's Gospel would have been written with Mark and Matthew as his primary sources, we may now finally address all the various objections mentioned earlier to the possibility that Luke used Matthew directly as a source. These objections may be divided into three categories: arguments based on order, arguments based on content, and arguments based on invalid assumptions.

## Order

The objections relating to order have already been answered, but it will be worthwhile to review them briefly here.

### 1. Luke's "inferior" arrangement of the Double Tradition material

To emphasize this point one more time, the analysis of Luke's Journey to Jerusalem as analogous to the Development section of the classical sonata form provides us with a vehicle for understanding that the arrangement of material in Luke's Gospel is deliberate, logical, and effective as an aesthetic means of maintaining interest and building tension in Luke's story. Theologically the arrangement is also an effective means of giving a complete picture of what it means to be a true Christian disciple. Particularly with Luke's goal in mind of explaining Christianity to Theophilus (and thereby hopefully converting him), this arrangement is fit for Luke's purpose just as the arrangement of Matthew's Gospel is fit for his purpose of Christian instruction. Luke's arrangement therefore cannot be judged to be inferior to Matthew's, and so Luke would have been fully justified in rearranging material from Matthew in order to create this understandable sequence of pericopes. Hence, this objection can no longer stand as a legitimate argument that Luke could not have used Matthew directly as a source.

## 2. The physical difficulty of rearranging Matthew's material

The well-documented practice, widespread in both Greek and Jewish culture in the first century, of memorizing lengthy texts makes it highly likely that Luke could have fully memorized the Gospel of Matthew and so would not have needed to have it physically in front of him as he wrote his own Gospel. Just as all New Testament authors could quote passages from the Old Testament at will, so Luke was able to draw *any* material from *anywhere* in Matthew's Gospel at *any* time, thus removing any physical or procedural barrier to Luke's having used Matthew as a primary source. This is therefore also not a valid objection to Luke's direct use of Matthew.

## 3. The inconsistent use of sources

The use of Matthew, Mark, and oral sources by Luke as described in the above analysis is logical and consistent with his knowledge of those sources, and with his purpose. As with the first two objections above, we may briefly summarize what has already been demonstrated regarding this one. Perhaps because he had only recently received a copy of Mark's Gospel, Luke followed it closely whenever he used it, which was primarily for straightforward narrative passages. Except for the slight rearrangement of two pericopes, Luke used every pericope drawn from Mark *exactly* in order throughout his Gospel. His much greater familiarity with Matthew's Gospel and with his oral sources allowed Luke the freedom to draw material from them in whatever order he desired. Luke's use of Matthew's *narrative* material was often in the same order as it had been in Matthew, but Luke still occasionally rearranged such material when necessary to suit his intentions. Luke was then able to rearrange *teaching* material taken from Matthew at will in order to suit his apologetic and evangelistic goals rather than Matthew's instructional goal. Thus, this objection also cannot stand, since we can see clearly how and why Luke used his sources in the way he did.

## Content

The next several objections have to do with *how* Luke used the material he had taken from his sources, and they are the most serious objections remaining to the possibility that Luke could have used Matthew. We must therefore consider each of them carefully. The way that each of them is described, however, appears to be logically flawed regarding what is actually being suggested if we take them at face value. Before dealing with each in turn, then, let us see what these logical flaws are, since our perception of these flaws may affect how we evaluate the objections themselves.

The first of these objections is that there is a lack of Matthean content *outside* the Triple Tradition, which suggests that Luke was not familiar with Matthew's Gospel. But clearly Luke *did* use Matthean material outside the Triple Tradition, since the Double Tradition is by definition Matthean material that also appears in Luke but does not appear in Mark. Thus, all of the material ascribed to Q by the Q theory is material that Luke would have taken directly from Matthew if Matthew was one of his sources, and all of this is outside the Triple Tradition. The specific cases that this objection *does* address, then (in the birth and resurrection narratives), need to be approached not in isolation but in the context of all the material for which there are commonalities between Matthew and Luke.

The next objection concerns the lack of Matthean content *within* the Triple Tradition (since many Q scholars have argued that Luke relies entirely on Mark's version of the Triple Tradition rather than on Matthew's, except in those cases where there are "Mark/Q overlaps"). This, too, is a logically flawed argument because by definition the Triple Tradition is only material that appears in all three Synoptics, and hence it would be technically impossible for any unique Matthean material or Double Tradition material to be included as part of it, or for there to be Triple Tradition material that does not correspond to content present in Matthew. When examining this objection, then, we need to be careful not to define material too narrowly in terms of one preferred solution and then use such definitions as proof for that very same solution (such as by identifying Mark/Q overlaps).

The last of these three objections states that there is a lack of Markan content within the Double Tradition. But this argument as well appears to make no sense, since the Double Tradition is defined as material common to Matthew and Luke that does not appear in Mark, so once again it would be impossible by definition for Markan material to exist within Double Tradition material. In order to make any sense out of this objection, we must once again either be careful about how we define Double versus Triple Tradition, or perhaps abandon such designations altogether.

Each of these objections is actually more specific than is suggested by these brief descriptions, however, and has to do with specific instances where Luke appears to have used his sources in a particular way. We must be careful, then, to understand just how the Double and Triple Traditions are being defined by those who raise these objections, since they often already assume a particular way of looking at Luke's sources to be in operation (in other words, the Q theory).

## Outside the Triple Tradition

We will begin with the argument that certain narrative portions of Luke, specifically the birth and resurrection narratives, appear to be free of influence by Matthew.

### 4. Luke's lack of use of Matthean material *outside* of Triple Tradition contexts

This objection is not in regard to Luke's lack of use of Matthean material in general, but rather within the specific context of the birth and resurrection narratives, where Luke appears not to have followed Matthew's accounts. Yet, even in regard to these specific instances, this argument is seriously flawed and cannot be considered evidence against Luke's use of Matthew as one of his sources. This is because Luke's choice to use a *different* version of a story simply cannot prove that he was not also aware of Matthew's version but chose to ignore it.

When we consider Luke's birth narrative, for example, there are two initial possibilities: either he invented it entirely by himself, or he drew on an existing tradition (even if he then further shaped that tradition to suit his own purpose). If someone wanted to claim that Luke had invented the account himself, with no knowledge of Matthew's version, there would be an insurmountable obstacle in seeking to explain how he could have paralleled so many aspects of Matthew's version, especially the idea of the virginal conception accomplished by means of the Holy Spirit. Such a position would be untenable.

Luke therefore must have drawn on an existing tradition, either Matthew's account or an account from a different source that also existed within the early church. Michael Goulder has suggested that Luke could have written his account based entirely on Matthew's, but because of their differences this also seems highly unlikely. This leaves one remaining possibility: Luke's birth narrative is based primarily on an existing tradition within the early church that differed from Matthew's. (Its specific origin and what that origin's relationship may have been to Matthew's version need not concern us here, only that in the form in which Luke received it, it *was* different from Matthew's.) Both the Q theory and the present theory agree on this.

We may confidently affirm that there did exist within the early church at least two differing traditions regarding the birth of Jesus, one used by Matthew and one used by Luke. If we separated these two accounts from their respective Gospels it would not be difficult to determine which of the two was more compatible with the rest of Luke's Gospel. Clearly, the birth narrative that became part of Luke's Gospel is more compatible with his Gospel in general. It emphasizes the temple; it does not present Jesus's birth as a political threat to Rome; it exalts the poor and lowly (shepherds) above the rich and mighty (Magi); and it is, in general, more gentile friendly. Again, both the Q theory and the present theory would agree on this.

We are now faced with three choices: (1) Luke was aware of only one tradition (non-Matthean) and he chose to use that tradition in his Gospel; (2) he was aware of (at least) two traditions (one Matthean, one not), but he chose to use the one that was more compatible with his goals in his Gospel; or (3) he was aware of (at least) two traditions (one Matthean, one not) and he chose to conflate them. The Q theory would contend that there is not enough evidence to suggest that Luke conflated the two traditions, and for the moment we will provisionally accept this judgment (although we will question it later). This once again leaves us with two alternatives: (1) Luke had only one tradition at his disposal and utilized it; or (2) he had (at least) two traditions available and chose the one that was more compatible with his goal. Do we have any evidence that would tip the scales one way or the other? The answer is a very definite no!

There might be some *potential* evidence that could help us, but it turns out to be of no use whatsoever. For instance, if it had been Luke's normal procedure always to follow a written source unflinchingly, we would have to say that there was evidence that Luke could not have known of Matthew's account, since, based on this pattern, he would be expected to have chosen Matthew's written version over the other tradition. When we look at Luke's use of Mark, however, we see that there are definitely occasions when Luke departed significantly from Mark's version of a story, showing that he was willing to use a tradition different from his written source, Mark. One example is the story of the Woman with the Ointment, where not only the details but the entire sense of the story is completely different from the version in Mark. Luke's willingness to depart from Mark is seen even more clearly in his resurrection accounts, which are directly applicable to the matter at hand since one of the cases in question is Luke's resurrection account versus Matthew's. If Luke knew of Mark's resurrection account (and he must have known since Mark was one of his written sources) but chose instead to follow a tradition different from Mark's, we certainly cannot say that, if he had known of Matthew's version, he could not have chosen to follow a tradition different from Matthew's.

We might also *try* to suggest that, in every other known case, Luke was more likely to conflate two differing accounts rather than choose one over the other. If this were so, then this would then indicate that, if Luke had known both birth traditions, he would almost certainly have conflated them. But once again, the evidence points in the opposite direction. Luke rarely conflated his sources (the most obvious exception being Jesus's baptism and temptation). This again is recognized by both the Q theory and the present theory (and will be discussed in more detail below).[1] So again, Luke's decision not to conflate two differing birth narratives (if he *did* so choose) cannot help us to know whether he actually had *access* to both.

We might suggest that the nature of the early church would have made it impossible for Luke to have been aware of two differing versions of the same story about Jesus, but this would be an absurd claim. Nevertheless, it does appear that this might be the actual subconscious assumption underlying this entire objection, based on the philosoph-

---

1. See Streeter, *Four Gospels,* chapter 9.

ical idea of the Gospels having developed within their own isolated communities. Such a view, however, cannot possibly prove that Luke could not have had any exposure to traditions contrary to his own (and as we have seen he *did* have access to some traditions contrary to Mark).

We are therefore left with two possible scenarios: (1) Luke had only one tradition available to him regarding the birth of Jesus and chose to include that tradition in his Gospel, consistent with his other procedures and goals; or (2) he had (at least) two traditions available to him (one Matthean, one not) and chose to include in his Gospel the one tradition that was consistent with his other procedures and goals. His choice to use the non-Matthean version in his Gospel therefore cannot help us to know whether Luke had Matthew's Gospel available to him as a source but chose to reject it here. Based solely on this evidence, Luke's knowledge of Matthew must remain completely indeterminate.

Nevertheless, there do seem to be clues that Luke may have incorporated some Matthean elements into his accounts of Jesus' birth, genealogy, and resurrection, which suggests that Luke was familiar with Matthew's versions of all of these and that he did actually follow them in their basic outlines. In particular, the exact letter-for-letter wording of the command to name the boy "Jesus" is an indication that Luke may have borrowed this command directly from Matthew's account.

Yet Luke apparently chose to rely on a separate non-Matthean tradition for most of these stories for two reasons: First, he believed that this other tradition was more accurate; and, second, the other tradition was more in line with his own goals, and especially his desire to be "Roman-friendly." This is evident in the birth narrative, where Luke plays down the link between Jesus and David, avoiding at the outset a negative reaction from a Roman audience, which would naturally consider a Jewish "Messiah" to be a political threat. Luke would not have wanted to include the Magi worshiping Jesus as a king, Herod's reaction to the threat to his own kingship, the holy family escaping political persecution by fleeing to Egypt, or relocating in Nazareth for the same political reason. Therefore (as discussed earlier), Luke's alternate version of the birth narrative is consistent with a knowledge of Matthew's Gospel, since Luke provides alternate scenarios for each of these events: the shepherds *do* worship Jesus as the savior, there *are* movements by the holy family for political reasons (the census), and the family *does* ultimately relocate from Bethlehem to Nazareth.

Likewise, Luke's alternate genealogy makes perfect sense. Luke would not have wanted a genealogy of Jesus that highlighted the entire Davidic royal succession to the throne. Instead, Luke substituted a genealogy that traces Jesus's lineage not just to David and Abraham but back to Adam, the father of the gentiles as well as of the Jews. More importantly, although David *is* mentioned, Jesus's descent is recounted not through Solomon and the royal line but through an obscure son of David named Nathan. Thus, no other kings of Israel or Judah are included in this genealogy, although it does converge with Matthew's version on the name Zerubbabel, son of Shealtiel (Matt 1:12; Luke 3:27). This is significant because of messianic prophecies related to this "Prince" in Haggai and Zechariah (which would have been known to Luke's Jewish readers but probably not to his Roman audience). Luke's genealogy then departs from Matthew's again until we reach Joseph, the husband of Mary.

The theory has sometimes been put forward that Matthew (whose birth narrative focuses more on Joseph than on Mary) is presenting Joseph's lineage in his genealogy, whereas Luke (whose birth narrative focuses more on Mary) is presenting Mary's. There are three significant problems with this theory. The first is that Luke tells us that Mary is a relative of Elizabeth, whom Luke has told us was a descendant of Aaron, and hence from the tribe of Levi, not Judah. (This could be assumed to mean that Mary's mother was a Levite, but this is not supported based on Luke's account. Relationships in the Bible are almost always traced through the father.) The second problem is that Luke prefaces his genealogy by saying that Jesus was "the son (as was supposed) of Joseph . . ." (Luke 3:23 ESV). If he had been giving the actual lineage of *Mary*, this would be a true list, not what people "supposed." Luke is clearly attempting to give the true lineage of Joseph, the "supposed" father of Jesus. But the third problem is the most serious. It would be impossible, if the two genealogies did truly represent the lineages of Mary and Joseph, for them to depart after David, then *reconverge* at Shealtiel, then depart again, only to reconverge once more.

The most plausible explanation, then, and the one that fits both Luke's and Matthew's purposes, is that Luke was attempting to give the actual genetic lineage of Joseph, whereas Matthew was recounting the line of succession to the Davidic throne. Only in this way can the departures and convergences be explained. Matthew's goal in giving his genealogy was clearly to name Jesus as the heir to the Davidic dynasty. The first phrase in his Gospel claims to give "an account of the genealogy of Jesus the *Messiah*, the *son of David*, the son of Abraham" (Matt 1:1 NRSV). Luke, on the other hand, concentrates on Jesus as the savior of all humankind, as the "son of Adam, the son of God" (Luke 3:37). Regardless of how accurate either of these genealogies may be, they make perfect sense in their respective Gospels, and once again their differences point not in the direction of Luke's having no knowledge of Matthew, but in the direction of Luke's deliberately presenting a *different* tradition that supported his own purpose (but with full knowledge of what Matthew had already written).

When we turn to the resurrection narrative, there are again many similarities between Luke and Matthew, enough to suggest that Luke was at least familiar with Matthew's account but chose once again to tell the story in his own way, using alternate traditions about Jesus's appearances after the resurrection. Luke, as the expert storyteller, also goes about giving his account of the resurrection in a more audience-catching way than does Matthew. Jesus does not actually appear personally to the women at the tomb (24:1–11), nor does Peter see him when he runs to the tomb (24:12). It is not until we are on the road to Emmaus that Jesus actually appears (24:13–35). Thus, Luke is able to keep our interest and keep us wondering for a while what has really happened. Then, as has been mentioned, Luke is also intent on keeping the disciples in Jerusalem, close to the temple. Again, we must remember that Luke certainly was familiar with Mark's version of the resurrection but still chose to depart from it.

There is one additional parallel between Matthew and Luke in a context outside the Triple Tradition: the Death of Judas (Matt 27:3–10 and Acts 1:15–20). As in other cases, Luke's version is quite different from Matthew's, but there is also the significant feature that both link Judas's death with the "Field of Blood." Matthew, in typical style, links Judas's death with a passage from the Prophets but also indicates that Judas had repented of his betrayal and then hanged himself. Luke, on the other hand, gives no indication that Judas was the slightest bit repentant but instead suffered the fate of one struck down by God, giving us yet another one of Luke's examples of God's punishment of the unfaithful.

But would we still not expect that if Luke *were* familiar with all of these stories that he would have followed them more closely, even if he altered some of the details? Again we may point to Luke's treatment of Jesus's Preaching at Nazareth and of the Woman with the Ointment, which have very few points of contact with the parallel accounts in either Matthew or Mark, yet no Q scholar would suggest that Luke was unfamiliar with Mark's version of these stories, or with Mark's account of the resurrection.

There is clear evidence, then, that Luke was familiar not only with Mark but with alternate traditions (sometimes contradictory traditions) as well. Since he did not consider Mark's version of the Anointing at Bethany or of the resurrection to be sacrosanct but instead chose to include a version that conflicted with Mark, there is every reason to suspect that the same might be true in other situations. If Luke had had available to him both Matthew's version of the birth narrative and an alternate, somewhat contradictory version, it is logical and consistent for him to have chosen to use the version that complied more with his own goals than to simply follow Matthew's. At the same time, however, just as in the case of the Woman with the Ointment, there are enough points of contact to suggest that Luke was aware of Matthew's version, even if he chose to depart from it to a great extent.

When we look at all of these contexts "outside the Triple Tradition," we do not see a pattern of Luke being completely unaware of what Matthew has done, but quite the opposite. Luke seems very familiar with Matthew's versions of these stories but chooses to include his own material for his own completely understandable reasons. In the end, then, this objection to Luke's knowledge and use of Matthew fails the test miserably. It is more likely, based on this evidence, that Luke *did* know Matthew's Gospel than that he did not. But even if this evidence is ignored, there is still no basis for suggesting that, because Luke followed a tradition different from Matthew's in these cases, he did not *also* have Matthew's versions available to him directly but chose to reject them in favor of the alternate versions.

## Within the Triple Tradition

The next objection has to do with the fact that Markan and Matthean material present in Luke seldom appears to be mixed but instead is typically found in distinctly separate contexts.

### 5. Luke's lack of use of Matthean material *within* Triple Tradition contexts

The use of the term "Triple Tradition" has been demonstrated to be largely a misnomer, especially for Luke, who took some material from

Matthew and some material from Mark. But the question arises: If Luke did have both Matthew and Mark available to him, why did he consistently choose to use Mark's version of pericopes with no elements from Matthew inserted into them?

As the above analysis has shown, Luke clearly did use Matthew's version of so-called Triple Tradition material when it suited his purpose and method. Clear examples include John the Baptist and Jesus's baptism, the temptation, Jesus's Preaching at Nazareth, the Lawyer's Question, the Beelzebub Controversy, the Leaven of the Pharisees, the Sin against the Holy Spirit, the Parable of the Mustard Seed, the Day of the Son of Man, Jesus Foretelling His Betrayal, the Rewards of Discipleship, Peter's Denial Predicted, Gethsemane, Jesus Arrested, Peter's Denial, and Jesus before the Sanhedrin. This in itself is hardly an insignificant list.

Additionally, because Mark contains far less teaching material than Matthew or Luke—and hence proportionally more narrative material—the Triple Tradition is primarily heavily weighted with narrative material, since it cannot be "triple" unless it appears in Mark as well as in the other two Gospels. Because Luke did rely more frequently on Mark for narrative passages and more frequently on Matthew for teaching pericopes (which is rational and consistent and has been demonstrated in the above analysis), there is necessarily less Matthean material in Triple Tradition contexts than in other contexts. But such material is not lacking, merely less frequent.

Specific texts have been proposed by some Q scholars to illustrate passages where Luke would be expected to have included Matthew's enhancements of Markan pericopes if Luke had been familiar with Matthew. In his article "On Dispensing with Q?: Goodacre on the Relation of Luke to Matthew," John Kloppenborg lists the following passages where Luke has followed Mark's Gospel but has failed to include Matthew's enhancements to the Markan versions:[2]

---

2. Kloppenborg, "On Dispensing with Q?," 219.

Table 5.1. List of Luke's Failures to Include Matthew's Enhancements of Mark
(after John Kloppenborg)

| Verses | Pericope |
|---|---|
| Matt 3:15 [Luke 3:21–22] | The Baptism of Jesus |
| Matt 12:5–7 [Luke 6:1–5] | Plucking Grain on the Sabbath |
| Matt 13:14–17 [Luke 8:9–10] | The Reason for Parables |
| Matt 16:16–19 [Luke 9:18–21] | Peter's Confession |
| Matt 19:19b [Luke 18:18–23] | The Rich Young Man |
| Matt 27:19 [Luke 23:17–23] | Jesus or Barabbas |
| Matt 27:24 [Luke 23:24–25] | Pilate Delivers Jesus |

Except for the first, all of these examples occur in passages where Luke is using Mark in a narrative "block," and at such times Luke does not normally draw on Matthew but saves any of Matthew's additions that he does choose to use for his Journey to Jerusalem. This in itself seems to be the basic argument here against Luke's use of Matthew: Why would Luke not have included some of these additions of Matthew's right where they would occur in Mark's version of the story (especially if, as suggested in this book, Luke had memorized Matthew and was therefore free to insert anything anywhere he wanted)?

This argument is articulated by E. L. Bradby in his article "In Defence of Q":

> If St. Luke had Matthew as well as Mark before him when he wrote, we can picture him following Mark verbatim whenever he had him, and Matthew verbatim when he had not Mark. But what, then, would happen when he had rival versions of an incident from Mark and from Matthew? What we should *normally expect any conscientious historian to do* is to take the later and fuller version, in this case Matthew. . . . But if we find, as we have found . . . that there is not one clear instance in these sections of any non-Markan passage which Luke has derived from Matthew, we can hardly be blamed if we fall back, with relief, on the alternative hypothesis, that in many passages Luke has used Mark and in many others Luke and Matthew have each used a common source other than Mark, that is, Q.[3]

The answer to this argument is very simple. As our analysis has

3. E. L. Bradby, "In Defence of Q," *Expository Times* 68 (1957): 315–18, here 318 (emphasis added).

172

shown, whenever Luke uses Mark for his narratives, he uses him for quick, concise accounts, unburdened by any extra teaching material (which he has deliberately placed instead in his Development section). There was therefore no reason for Luke to have cluttered Mark's accounts at these points with Matthew's additions. Indeed, Luke even unclutters Mark's own accounts at some points, particularly in the section following the parable of the Sower, where Luke wants a brief, non-repetitious introduction to some of Jesus's basic teachings. In addition, in the final sequence of his Exposition, Luke likewise unclutters Mark's version of Peter's confession and the transfiguration. Luke's procedure, even if it does not comply with what we might "normally expect any conscientious historian to do," is logical, understandable, and completely consistent. (But is it not also possible that a "conscientious" historian would take the earlier and less-embellished version, which would be closer to the actual event instead of the "later and fuller version"?)

Indeed, it is even a recognized trait of Luke's that he tends not to conflate his sources (a tendency that stands regardless of whether those sources include Q or Matthew). As Streeter points out:

> When an editor combines sources that cover the same ground along some part of their extent, he has a choice of two methods. He can either accept the version given by one source and ignore the other, or he can make a careful mosaic by "conflating" the two. We noticed in a previous chapter ... that, when the same saying occurs in both Mark and Q, Luke commonly accepts the Q version and ignores Mark's. Matthew, on the other hand, usually conflates Mark and Q, though with a tendency to abbreviate.[4]

According to the present theory, the passages Streeter assigns to Q would have been known to Luke from Matthew's Gospel (whereas Matthew's source that corresponds to Q is at this stage unknown), and so Streeter also testifies to the fact that there are plenty of examples where Luke chose Matthew's version of a pericope over Mark's. Hence, by simply reidentifying Luke's non-Markan source as Matthew instead of Q, we can alter the quote from Streeter above to demonstrate that "when the same saying occurs in both Mark and Matthew, Luke commonly accepts the Matthean version and ignores Mark's. Matthew, on the other hand, usually conflates Mark and his other source."

This difference in approach may be summarized by the following rule: "Matthew conflates, Luke alternates." If it is recognized by the Q

4. Streeter, *Four Gospels*, 246.

theory itself that it is Luke's tendency *not* to combine accounts from his sources into a single account but to follow one source as he finds it and then to alternate with another, it is extremely unreasonable to expect that if Matthew had been one of Luke's sources instead of Q, Luke should have been required to follow the opposite procedure! Hence, knowing what we do about Luke's procedures, we would not expect him to include unique Matthean elements when he is following Mark, nor specifically Markan elements when following Matthew.

Nevertheless, let us examine each of Kloppenborg's examples briefly. Kloppenborg suggests that Jesus's statement to John the Baptist that his baptism was "to fulfill all righteousness" (Matt 3:15 NIV) would have been important to Luke to demonstrate that Jesus was greater than John and did not need to repent. Based on Luke's birth narrative, however, John represents Samuel the anointer and so would never have been confused with a "superior" to Jesus (just as Samuel was not "superior" to King David), nor would his anointing of Jesus have anything to do with whether Jesus needed to repent. The baptism would have been for the purpose of appointing Jesus to the Davidic throne, so this exchange between Jesus and John would have been superfluous and perhaps even confusing. (After all, does Matthew's answer, that it is "to fulfill all righteousness" really give an adequate explanation, especially for Luke's gentile audience?) Hence, it is not surprising that Luke would have eliminated it.

Additionally, given the vast number of elements Luke has taken from Matthew throughout the baptism and temptation narrative (one of the two places where Luke appears to have conflated Matthew and Mark to some extent), it is an absurd argument to suggest that Luke has failed to include Matthean elements here. If the argument were made that the other elements come from Q rather than from Matthew, this would not only be begging the question but would invalidate the entire procedure as well. If Q is defined as the intersection of Matthew and Luke minus Mark, then *by definition* Luke did include what was from Q but left out what was unique to Matthew. But if Luke used Matthew directly, then Q never existed and so all of the non-Markan elements throughout this passage that Luke has in common with Matthew would have come from Matthew and not from the non-existent Q! Hence, throughout this passage Luke *has* included most of Matthew's enhancements to the Markan version.

When we turn to Kloppenborg's next pericope—Matthew's extra statement in the story of the disciples plucking grain, stating that the priests legitimately break the Sabbath according to the commands of the Torah—this would also probably have been confusing to Luke's audience. Luke downplays much of Jesus's teachings concerning the Torah for his gentile audience, and eliminates many such statements from the Sermon on the Mount. So there is no reason here to suppose that Luke should have abandoned his normal procedure of alternating sources in order to include a "Luke-displeasing" element.

In the next instance, Luke omits Matthew's additional quotation from Isaiah after the parable of the Sower when explaining Jesus's use of parables, but Luke has also omitted much from this same passage, which does appear in Mark itself (again similar to his shortening of the Sermon on the Mount). Consistent with his desire to be brief and not repetitious in his Exposition section, Luke unburdens the narrative at this point but later picks up some of these themes during his Development. At that point (Luke 10:23–24), Luke *does* include some of the additions from the material in Matthew 13 listed above. This again works against Kloppenborg's argument, since it is definitely more in keeping with Luke's normal procedure of alternating sources to include Matthew's enhancements of Mark at a point when he is drawing on Matthew, rather than interrupting a "block" of Markan material to introduce elements from a different source (and this would likewise be true if Q had been his source instead of Matthew).

The passage from Matthew 16 appears to be the most "problematic" on the list, but only on the surface. Why does Luke omit Jesus's confirmation of Peter as "the rock," which is present in Matthew? Kloppenborg criticizes Goodacre for suggesting that Luke downplays the role of Peter, and rightly points out that "Luke in fact accentuates the role of Peter"[5] both in his Gospel and in Acts, so Jesus's statement that Peter is the rock would surely have been "Luke-pleasing." But this argument again assumes that Luke "ought" to have included whatever material he found. As has been noted earlier, however, Luke did not have unlimited space, nor was he bound to include whatever modern readers might suppose he should have done. Luke may simply not have felt a need to draw on Matthew at this point in his narrative (which again would have been contrary to his normal procedure), nor would it have been easy to bring up this statement in a different context later on, so Luke's desire to keep to a brief, concise narrative whenever he called on Mark meant that he simply let this saying go. He was under no oblig-

5. Kloppenborg, "On Dispensing with Q?," 221.

ation to include it, and it would not have fit the pattern of his method to have done so.

Perhaps even more significant, is that Luke not only omits Jesus's statement to Peter after his confession, but he also omits Peter's rebuke of Jesus's decision to go to Jerusalem and Jesus's counterrebuke of Peter, which *do* occur at this point in Mark's account **(Mark 8:32–33; cf. Luke 9:21–22)**. Any explanation for why Luke omits Jesus's statement to Peter in Matthew 16 therefore also needs to cover why Luke omitted the verses from Mark as well. So although both of these omissions do not mean that Luke is diminishing Peter's role, what they do indicate is that Luke is eager at this point to be brief and to keep his attention focused squarely on Jesus himself at this critical and climactic point of his Exposition section. This omission is therefore not problematic in the slightest.

Luke's omission of Matthew's addition of the saying to "love your neighbor as yourself" (Matt 19:19 NIV) in the list of commands quoted to the Rich Young Man should also not be a mystery. All of the commands that are included by Luke came directly from the Ten Commandments, whereas the command to love one's neighbor comes from elsewhere in the Torah. Luke's "omission" is therefore completely logical (and of course consistent).

The final two examples from the list, the dream of Pilate's wife and Pilate washing his hands, have already been discussed. Kloppenborg claimed that Luke

> . . . is keen to shift the blame from the Romans to the high priests. Pilate's wife's dream (Matt 27:19, inserting into Mark 15:10–11) and Matthew's hand-washing scene (27:24, added to Mark 15:15) would have served Luke's purposes admirably, especially since the dream declares Jesus to be δίκαος, which is precisely what Luke's centurion says of Jesus (23:47), and the handwashing scene has Pilate declare Jesus to be innocent."[6]

But what Kloppenborg has failed to grasp is that to include these passages would *not* have served Luke's purpose of being "Roman-friendly" because they would have shown Pilate to be a weak and ineffective governor, too afraid of the people. If Pilate had firmly believed Jesus to be innocent, then as a good governor he should have released him, not "washed his hands" of the matter in fear of a riot, as Matthew accused him of doing.

---

6. Ibid., 222.

None of these examples therefore offers a compelling reason to doubt that Luke could have read them and still have chosen not to include them in his Gospel, which is what this objection would require. Indeed, all of these so-called omissions are consistent and logical given the above analysis of Luke's intentions and methods. Further, the numerous examples listed at the beginning of this section of Luke using Matthew's version of specific pericopes instead of Mark's demonstrate that, if Matthew was one of Luke's sources, he most certainly did *not* fail to use Matthew within Triple Tradition contexts. So this objection, like those before it, cannot stand.

## Lack of Markan Content

The previous objections to Luke's use of Matthew all had to do with ways in which modern scholars expect that Luke *should* have used his sources, based on certain assumptions about his intentions and procedures. Since the proposed theory challenges some of these assumptions, these objections were not insurmountable. The next objection, however, presents a more significant obstacle.

## 6. Luke's lack of use of *Markan* material within *Double* Tradition contexts

It has been asserted by F. G. Downing, in his article "Towards the Rehabilitation of Q," that, when Luke includes pericopes where Matthew has expanded on Mark's version (note that admitting that such pericopes exist is a direct contradiction of the previous objection), Luke omits specifically material that is common to Matthew and Mark (in other words, material that Matthew has reproduced faithfully from Mark).[7] Downing's claim is that, if Luke is following Matthew in such passages, he must have deliberately "unpicked" the Markan material out of Matthew's version in order to omit it in these cases. Not only would such a procedure appear to be illogical, but it would also require a tedious word-for-word comparison by Luke of Matthew and Mark in order to isolate such common language in order to delete it, an absurd procedure.

Downing suggests that it is more reasonable to suppose that Luke

---

7. F. G. Downing, "Towards a Rehabilitation of Q," *New Testament Studies* 11 (1964): 169–81.

is not using Matthew in such cases but is using the same source that Matthew used to expand Mark in the first place. Downing concludes:

> We would suggest it is much more reasonable to suppose that Luke's apparent ignoring of every *clear* use by Matthew of Mark is due to Luke's ignorance of Matthew's use of Mark. Luke knew Matthew's source (or sources) "before" it had had its parallels with Mark conflated with the latter, and this source (or "these sources") is what has come to be known in part as *Q*.[8]

If Downing is correct about his analysis, this is a far more serious objection to Luke's use of Matthew than any of the previous objections, since it deals with how Luke actually *did* use his sources, not with how he *ought* to have used them.

To demonstrate his claim, Downing gives the four following examples of "Luke's supposed use of passages where Matthew has apparently conflated a Markan record of teaching with similar but distinct material of his own from some other source":[9]

Table 5.2. Luke's Use of Matthew's Conflation of Mark and a Source (after F. G. Downing)

| Matthew | Mark | Luke | Pericope |
|---|---|---|---|
| Matt 3:1–4:11 | Mark 1:1–13 | Luke 3:1–22; 4:1–13 | The Baptism and Temptation |
| Matt 9:35–10:16 | Mark 6:13–19; 6:6–11, 34 | Luke 9:1–5; 6:13–16; 10:1–12 | Commissioning the Twelve |
| Matt 12:22–45 | Mark 3:20–29 | Luke 11:14–26; 12:10; 6:43–45 | The Beelzebub Controversy |
| Matt 24:4–25:46 | Mark 13:5–37 | Luke 21:8–36; 17:22–37; 12:35–48; 19:11–27 | The Mini-Apocalypse |

In each case, Downing breaks down Matthew's material into three types: A, where Matthew follows Mark closely; B, where Matthew has altered Mark's version; and C, where Matthew has added entirely new material. He then looks at how Luke uses this material and finds that Luke omits nearly all of the A material, significantly alters the B material, but includes nearly all of the C material. Again, he concludes that this indicates that Luke is not using Matthew as his source but is using

8. Ibid., 285.
9. Ibid.

the same source Matthew used to expand Mark. But does Downing's analysis hold up?

The technique used in this book to determine which of Luke's pericopes came from Matthew and which came from Mark was based entirely on the similarity between Luke's version and the other two. Thus, by definition of this criterion, all of the pericopes where Luke used Matthew's version instead of Mark's will necessarily include C material or will at least be closer to Matthew's version of the B material than to Mark's. Downing's observation that Luke incorporates such material is therefore not merely *expected* by the theory proposed in this book but is *required* by it (or else the selected passages would not fall under the category to be analyzed in this way).

Likewise, the subtle distinction Downing makes between Luke's handling of B and C material is not entirely helpful. If it is true that Luke tends to rework B material but incorporates C material as is, this is far more easily explained by the theory that Luke is using Matthew directly than by the theory that he is using the same source as Matthew, because otherwise he could have had no knowledge that Matthew had made any alterations in the B material. If Luke were drawing on Matthew and Mark, we would presume that before writing he had read both accounts and was somewhat aware of extra material Matthew had included (the C material), and he may have noticed that there were variations in the material common to both (the B material). Having only one version of the C passages to work from, he may then have simply accepted such passages as they stood but felt freer to rework material where there were already two variant versions available, neither of which was "authoritative."

If Luke was *not* aware of how Matthew had expanded Mark, however, but instead was working from the same source Matthew used, then the B material would need to be explained in one of two ways. It might be material just from Mark that Matthew had reworked in his own way. In this case, it would be an incredible coincidence that both Matthew and Luke chose independently of each other to rework the exact same passages in Mark while at the same time choosing to leave intact the exact same other passages from Mark. This would be a far more absurd situation than the one suggested by Downing regarding Luke's treatment of the A material. The second possibility is that the B material represents material from Matthew's source (Q), which Matthew had intertwined with Markan material. In this case, it would again be quite a coincidence that both Luke and Matthew chose to mix together the exact same Q passages with Markan material (always doing so in variant ways, but never following Mark exactly), while at the same time choosing in the same other cases of "Mark/Q overlaps" to choose either the Q version or the Markan version *without* mixing them. Such coincidences of identical parallel behavior on the part of Matthew and Luke have always been a major difficulty for the theory that they wrote without knowledge of each other's work. Hence, if Luke does treat B material differently from C material, this is far more easily explained by the present theory than by the Q theory.

But it is not at all clear that Luke *does* treat B material and C material differently. In Downing's examples, there is B material included fairly faithfully by Luke and C material that has been reworked, and examples of both that Luke has omitted altogether. The distinction between B and C material thus begins to fade away. Under the theory that Luke used Matthew, it turns out to be material from Matthew that Luke has included or reworked, and under the theory that Luke used Q, it is probably material from Q that Luke has included or reworked. Therefore, the B and C material ceases to be problematic for either the Q theory or the present theory.

What is really in question, then, is Downing's assertion that Luke has omitted all of the A material. According to the present theory, Luke would not have been as familiar with Mark's versions of the pericopes in question, nor would he have consulted Mark's scroll when using Matthew's versions of stories (except in the cases of the baptism and passion passages, where he may well have read through Mark's version just before writing his own). Downing's assertion is, therefore, that, if Luke deliberately left out specifically that material which was common between Matthew and Mark, this would have been an absurd procedure and would strongly point away from Luke's direct use of Matthew as a source.

The A material that Downing has identified in each of his examples is as follows.

Table 5.3. Downing's "A Material"

| Verses | Pericope |
|---|---|
| Matt 3:3b, 4–5a, 6 | The Baptism and Temptation |
| Matt 9:36 | Commissioning the Twelve |
| Matt 12:29, 31a | On Collusion with Satan |
| Matt 24:4–9, 13, 15–25, 31–36 | The Mini-Apocalypse |

In the first three examples, Luke has (according to Downing) omitted all the A material except for Matthew 3:3b. Regarding the material from Matthew 12 (his third example), Downing writes that, if Luke were following Matthew, then "for some incomprehensible reason, he decides not to follow Matthew throughout, but to follow Matthew *only where the latter has added new material to Mark or has largely altered him*. He notes that one and a half sentences exactly quote Mark, and so omits them. It is not that he is going to use them somewhere else. He just arbitrarily excludes them".[10]

But Luke has not excluded Matthew 12:29; he has *reworked* it (in Luke 11:21–22). What Downing appears to be objecting to is that Luke has not reproduced the *exact wording* where Matthew and Mark agree exactly. For Luke to have done so, he would have had to compare Matthew to Mark word for word in order deliberately to include those phrases where they matched exactly. This is basically the same absurd procedure that Downing has suggested Luke would *not* have followed if he had used Matthew as a source. So if Luke was simply drawing on Matthew's Gospel at this point, he would not have known that Matthew 12:29 matched Mark 3:27 exactly, and so would have been just as free to modify it as he was to modify any other passage from Matthew. (Even if he had happened to notice that Matthew and Mark were the same at this point, this still would not have meant that he was not "allowed" to alter it.) Thus, in this passage, Downing is reduced to half a verse of A material that Luke has omitted.

Ken Olson, in his article "Unpicking on the Farrer Theory," also looks at Downing's examples and challenges his interpretation and conclusions. Olson considers the remaining half verse (Matt 12:31a):

It should be noted that Matthew 12:31 and Matthew 12:32 form a doublet, and it is a widely recognised characteristic of Luke to avoid repetition by

10. Ibid., 278.

eliminating one of the versions of doublets in his sources. . . . It seems unlikely that Luke would discard the version of the saying that speaks of Jesus and the Holy Spirit in favour of the one that does not.[11]

So there is a perfectly logical reason for Luke's omission of Matthew 12:31a that has nothing whatsoever to do with its parallel in Mark.

Also in connection with this pericope, Olson notes that the closest parallel between Luke 11:14-15 and Matthew is not in Matthew 12 but in the duplicate story in Matthew 9:32-34. Here Matthew 9:34 agrees word for word with Mark 3:22: ἐν τῷ ἄρχοντι τῶν δαιμονίων ἐκβάλλει τὰ δαιμόνια ("by the ruler of the demons he casts out demons"). Luke indeed reproduces this exact phrase in Luke 11:15.[12] Thus, in this pericope there are actually three verses of A material, two of which Luke *does* include (one exactly and one loosely), and one that he omits on grounds consistent with his procedures elsewhere. This pericope therefore does not support Downing's claims.

Regarding the first two examples (Matthew 3 and 9), Olson points out that the material excluded is all introductory, setting the scene, particularly Matthew 9:36:

> The omitted A material in Matthew 9:36 amounts to a single verse. Downing fails to note that Luke has no parallel to any of the material in Matthew's introduction, omitting the B and C material in verse 5 along with verse 36. This is not unusual for Luke, who shows great independence from his sources especially in his introductions to new sections.[13]

(Another clear example of this is Luke's failure to place Jesus in a boat when he tells the parable of the Sower in Luke 8, compared to Mark 4). What Olson does *not* note here, but which reinforces his case, is that Matthew's typical procedure regarding Mark's introductory material is just the opposite. Matthew often uses Mark's connecting material between pericopes even when he then alters the pericopes themselves. (Some other examples of this include Matthew 8:18; 15:21; and 16:1.)

It is therefore not surprising that in two of Downing's examples the only A material is introductory (since this is consistent with Matthew's procedures elsewhere). Nor is it surprising that Luke omits this introductory material (since this is also consistent with Luke's procedures

---

11. Ken Olson, "Unpicking on the Farrer Theory," in *Questioning Q: A Multidimensional Critiqut* (London: SPCK, 2004), 127–50, here 141.
12. Ibid., 140.
13. Ibid., 143.

elsewhere). Again, these cases offer nothing in support of Downing's claims. The omissions have nothing to do with whether Matthew agrees with Mark but are the obvious result of Matthew's and Luke's differing methods.

Indeed, we might expect to see precisely this situation recur, and it does in Matthew 16:1–4, which parallels Mark 8:11–13 and Luke 12:54–56. Here again, the only close parallel between Matthew and Mark is the introductory verse, setting the scene. This is precisely what Luke omits from his own account. We therefore have at least three clear examples of this phenomenon, all of which make perfect sense on the theory that Luke used both Mark and Matthew as sources and used and edited them in a consistent fashion, which has nothing to do with whether they agree at any particular point with each other.

This leaves only the Mini-Apocalypse (Matthew 24 and Mark 13). Here Luke has followed Mark's version fairly closely (although altering it at certain points for his own emphasis, including omitting the introductory setting, as is his pattern), and this necessarily includes considerable A material. He does, however, omit Mark 13:20–23 (which corresponds to Matt 24:22–25, all A material to which Luke alludes in chapter 17), and Mark's unique ending (Mark 13:33–37, to which Luke alludes in chapter 12, but which is not A, B, or C material since there is no parallel in Matthew). These omissions make sense under any theory, since Luke has used some of this material earlier.

But Matthew's additions to Mark's version appears at various points in Luke's Journey to Jerusalem (in chapters 12, 17, and 19). Downing's claim is that it is at these points that Luke has *not* included the A material that Matthew and Mark have in common, and so what he does include must have come from a separate non-Matthean source. But this is not an accurate assessment. The material in Luke 19 (the parable of the Talents) comes from Matthew 25, for which there is no Markan parallel. Hence, it cannot contain any A material and so has no bearing. In Luke 12, the A material (Matt 24:42) has been reworked (in Luke 12:35), not omitted, just as the following C verses have been reworked. In Luke 17, some of the A material has also been included (Matt 24:17–18 in Luke 17:31 and Matt 24:23 in Luke 17:23).

It is impossible based on these data to establish any pattern of inclusion or omission on Luke's part. His treatment of the Mini-Apocalypse is similar to his treatment of the parables in Mark 4 and Matthew 13. He used Mark's version but shortened it and included some of the leftover material elsewhere (in which case he has drawn more on Matthew's version than on Mark's, consistent with his practice elsewhere). We may safely conclude, then, that there is nothing in Downing's examples that points to Luke's *not* knowing Matthew or using it as a source. Yet to be complete we should also look briefly at those places not noted by Downing but which, according to the present theory, fit the requirements of his examples: in other words, other pericopes where Luke has apparently followed Matthew rather than Mark and where Matthew has expanded on Mark's version. The other passages that qualify are as follows:

Table 5.4. Other Places Where Luke Has Followed Matthew's Expansions of Mark

| Matthew | Mark | Luke | Pericope |
| --- | --- | --- | --- |
| Matt 16:1–12 | Mark 8:11–21 | Luke 12:54–56; 12:1 | The Pharisees Seek a Sign |
| Matt 22:34–40 | Mark 12:28–34 | Luke 10:25–28 | The Great Commandment |
| Matt 23:1–7 | Mark 12:38–40 | Luke 11:42–54 | Beware of the Scribes |
| Matt 26:21–25, 31–75; 20:24–28; 19:27–30 | Mark 14:18–21; 10:41–45; 10:28–31 | Luke 22:21–62 | The Passion (from after the Words of Institution through the trial before the Sanhedrin) |

The first portion of the first of these passages has been mentioned earlier and is consistent with Matthew's and Luke's patterns regarding Mark's introductory material. The remainder of the passage is part of Luke's Great Omission from Mark, and so it is not surprising that he has left this out. The saying "beware of the leaven of the Pharisees," however, which is A material, *is* included by Luke in 12:1. Thus, Luke has included some C material and some A material and has omitted the rest.

In the second case, Luke has reworked much of the pericope but has not omitted any of the material that would qualify as A material (which is in pieces scattered throughout the pericope). In the third passage, Matthew 23:6–7 would qualify as A material. Luke has included the end of verse 6 and the beginning of verse 7, half of the A material. In the final passage, the middle portion of the passion, there is a considerable amount of what would probably be categorized by Downing as A material: Matthew 26:22–24, 31–41, 45–49, 51b, 55–56, 58–62, 64b, 65b–67, 69–70, 74. This represents two-thirds of the whole passage, thirty-four of fifty verses. Of these thirty-four verses, Luke preserves about a dozen or so quite closely and another eight or so less faithfully (and so has included about two-thirds of the A verses in some form). The rest have been reworked considerably or have been omitted. Once again, no pattern based on Matthew's similarity with Mark is discernible regarding Luke's treatment of the material.

Having examined all of these pericopes, then, we see that Luke has included, altered, or omitted Downing's A, B, and C material throughout his Gospel in ways consistent with his overall practices but exhibiting no other discernible pattern. There is therefore no indication whatsoever that Luke has omitted material common to Matthew and Mark in a systematic way, or in a way that points away from his use of Matthew as a direct source for his Gospel. Once again, this objection does not stand.

## Expectations

Additionally, it is now possible to compare the various expectations of how Luke *ought* to have used Matthew as a source, according to the previous several objections. Downing suggests that Luke ought to have used what was common between Matthew and Mark as the strongest indication of a legitimate tradition. This appears to be precisely what Luke has done to a large extent in his passion narrative, eliminating most (but not all) of what is unique to either Mark or Matthew. But Luke is criticized by Kloppenborg for doing just this instead of including more of Matthew's unique material. Yet this criticism is based on the claim that Luke should have used specific unique material of Matthew's in the passion (Pilate's wife's dream and his handwashing), because, as it turns out, Luke actually did use some of Matthew's unique material (such as Peter's weeping bitterly and the question "Who is it that struck you?").

Therefore, not only have these criticisms from different scholars been shown to be unwarranted, but they are actually contradictory. It is hardly a valid objection to say that Luke *should* have acted in a certain way when that way is described in two contradictory fashions simultaneously: preferring to include specifically that material which is common between Mark and Matthew but at the same time preferring to include specifically that material which is unique to Matthew. Nor is it a valid objection to say that Luke should have included unique Matthean material in the passion and then attempt to explain away the evidence that shows that he did so. If we were to sum up all of the objections given so far, they would in effect be that, if Luke used Matthew as a source, he *ought* to have simply duplicated Matthew's Gospel as it stands rather than writing his own! This, then, appears to be the *real* objection to Luke's use of Matthew: His approach, his choice of material, his ordering of that material, and his theological emphasis are all different from Matthew's. Therefore, he could not have used Matthew as a source, because that would be simply copying Matthew as he found it (as it is claimed he simply copied Q).

Yet these objections also presuppose that Luke should not have simply copied Matthew as he found it, but that he should have conflated Matthew with his other sources (again a contradictory expectation given what was said in the previous paragraph). If Luke had been aware of Matthew's birth narrative, he ought to have conflated it with the alternate version that he in fact used instead. If he had been aware of Matthew's additions to Mark's pericopes, he ought to have conflated the two within his Markan blocks instead of using Matthew's additions separately in other contexts. As our analysis has shown, however, and as Streeter recognized in 1924, it was only rarely Luke's practice to conflate his sources, and so any expectation that he ought to have done so in any specific situation when he did not do so is completely unwarranted.

Lurking behind all these expectations are other assumptions that we may now likewise identify and call into question, since this entire line of thinking seems to be based once again on a specific philosophical position on how the Gospels came to be written. One of these assumptions is what James D. G. Dunn calls the "one document per community fallacy," that there was a specific "Matthew community," a "Luke community," and a "Q community," each of which is known to us by the specific document that developed in that community. Dunn writes:

> It simply will not do to identify the character of a community with the character of a document associated with it. Such a document will no doubt indicate concerns and emphases in the community's teaching. But only if we can be confident that the single document was the community's sole document (or traditional material) could we legitimately infer that the concerns and beliefs of the community did not extend beyond those of the document. And we cannot have such confidence.[14]

Dunn therefore challenges from a different angle the assumption that the Gospels could only have been written in different isolated communities. It is not only a fallacy but indeed an absurdity to suppose that the early church was made up exclusively of isolated communities, each with its own single, self-consistent set of traditions, and each with the inability to be aware of any alternate or contradictory traditions. Yet this is precisely the condition that seems to be presupposed by the Q theory (as we saw when examining objection 4 above), which does not appear able to accept the possibility that Luke could have been familiar with Matthew's Gospel and yet at the same time have chosen to depart from it on occasion. This is an absurd assumption, because it would require that Luke as an author could not have been aware of any conflicting traditions! Instead, he would have had to keep "safe" from coming into contact with any traditions from outside his own community about which he might have had to make a conscious choice whether to use or not.

There is no reason to suppose that Luke's "community" (if there was such a community) would have been isolated from other Christian communities and would have been aware only of its own specific traditions, which came to be encapsulated in Luke's Gospel. Hence, there is no reason to suppose that Luke (whether as a part of a specific geographically defined community or as an itinerant preacher traveling among communities—or perhaps we should say, *within* the single dispersed Christian community), would not have been exposed to many contradictory traditions regarding the life of Jesus and its interpretation. Certainly the early church as a whole did not have difficulty accepting the contradictory traditions regarding the birth and resurrection of Jesus present in Matthew's and Luke's Gospels as both valid (and eventually canonical).[15]

Yet, as we have seen, the tendency in biblical scholarship has been to avoid the (reasonable) possibility that the Gospel authors may have had contradictory versions of stories available to them from which to choose, and the possibility that such stories could have circulated freely throughout the widespread church. Instead, the tendency has

---

14. James D. G. Dunn, *Jesus Remembered*, Christianity in the Making 1 (Grand Rapids: Eerdmans, 2003), 150.
15. If it had been the common practice in the Christian community to depend only on one self-consistent Gospel account, then there would certainly have been vigorous disputes about which Gospel was more accurate than the others. It would then have been more likely that the canon would eventually have included a single harmonizing document such as Tatian's *Diatessaron* rather than the four different Gospels that were universally accepted from an extremely early date with apparently no objection from any quarter.

been to view every contradiction as an indication of a separate tradition, and hence a separate community, and hence (following Dunn's observation) a separate source document. But such a view would turn the early church into a bizarre patchwork of mutually exclusive communities, each inventing its own version of Jesus and each failing to share its ideas with the others, except in those rare cases when one document (such as Q) seems to have been "leaked" from one community to another. This is an entirely unrealistic scenario, especially given the level of communication and travel attested to in the New Testament itself.

Two other questionable assumptions related to all of this are the assumption that Luke used pretty much all of the material available to him and the assumption that there was very little overlap between the sources he used. These are carryovers both from the tendency to define the Synoptic Problem based on the concept of Double or Triple Tradition material (which is then perceived to provide a clear indication of the sources behind the Gospels) and from the idea that Luke was basically a "cut-and-paste" redactor, his Gospel being a compendium of all that made up his community's tradition (plus the "foreign" Q). Hence, Q is defined as the equivalent of the Double Tradition and is assumed to have been assimilated entirely into Luke (and Matthew) and therefore could have contained only that material which both Matthew and Luke have in common (with very little overlap with Mark). In the same vein, Luke's omissions from Mark are seen as problematic, in need of some "explanation" as to why they were left out of such a compendium. In this view, if Luke had used Matthew as a source, any omissions or alterations from that Gospel would be considered just as problematic.

Such a view fails to take into account the possibility that a significant number of variant versions of the same sayings or events in the life of Jesus may have circulated in the early church, whether in oral or written form. If a source such as Q had existed, there is no reason to suppose that it could not have included a birth narrative or a passion narrative or alternate versions of a number of stories also found in Mark but that these versions were not used by Matthew or Luke. Perhaps they were; perhaps Matthew followed Mark's passion narrative, but Luke followed Q's!

The same view also fails to consider the intelligence and judgment of the Gospel writers. Instead, it seems to see the whole process from the point of view not of the authors but of the documents themselves, which somehow "merged" with each other without much human intervention at all, another absurd way of approaching the writing of the Gospels. Yet numerous pieces of evidence demonstrate that the Gospel writers were very much in control of what they were doing and constructed their works in a very deliberate fashion.

Two aspects of Luke's Gospel in particular point away from the idea that Luke simply pasted together all the traditions he could find into one compendium. First, as has been mentioned before, the length of Luke's Gospel being the identical length of the maximum scroll available means that Luke could not have included any more material even if he had wanted to without expanding his Gospel onto a second scroll. This suggests that he carefully selected from the available material as much as he could fit, which implies that there was a fair amount of material left over when he finished. Second, Luke has told us in his Prologue that he has investigated everything carefully from top to bottom, again suggesting that he may have amassed a considerable amount of information from which he had to pick and choose very carefully what to include.

For all we know, therefore, he may have had available more than one version of the parable of the Good Samaritan, several conflicting resurrection accounts, and countless anecdotes that he abandoned altogether when writing. If such were the case, the amount that he did include from both Mark and Matthew may be an indication of how highly he esteemed these earlier documents over the numerous alternatives he may have had available to choose from; it is not an indication that he had no other choice. We do not know in how many cases Luke did choose to include Matthew's version of a particular pericope over against other available alternatives, because we no longer have such alternatives available to us for comparison. This is speculation, of course, but the point is that so is the assumption that Luke used virtually all of the material he had before him. We simply do not know, and there is no way of knowing for certain. The indications we have, however, seem to point away from Luke being just a redactor and toward him being a deliberate author making conscious choices when constructing his Gospel.

Hence, all of the arguments that Luke *ought* to have used Matthew in a certain way if it had been available to him break down. Furthermore, they break down without recourse to a nebulous concept of "Luke-pleasingness," which mysteriously defines some unknown plan that must have made sense to him even if it bewilders us. Instead, when we approach Luke on his own terms, then what would have been pleasing to him in a broad sense does seem quite evident, and from within that category the material he chose to include and the order in which he chose to place it also seem evident, logical, and artistic. We may therefore comfortably put all of the previous objections to rest, since it has been demonstrated that Luke had legitimate and understandable reasons for writing the Gospel he did and for using both Mark and Matthew as sources in the way that he did in order to do so.

## Invalid Assumptions

The remaining objections to Luke having used Matthew directly address different sorts of concerns, but all of them depend on certain specific assumptions being true, assumptions that are very much in question.

## Mutual Primitivity

The first of these objections has to do with the age of material found in Matthew and Luke.

## 7. Mutual primitivity

This argument is based on the idea that sometimes Matthew's version of a Double Tradition pericope seems to be earlier than Luke's version, but sometimes Luke's version seems to be the more primitive. If Matthew came first, and then Luke copied Matthew, we would expect that Matthew's version should always appear to be the more primitive. Instead, if Matthew and Luke had each used Q as their source independently of each other, then sometimes one author might alter a pericope (making it less primitive), and sometimes the other author might alter a different one. Thus, we would see a mixture of primitivity between the two, which is precisely what is claimed by many scholars to be the case. The two examples most frequently invoked of common pericopes where Luke's version is believed to be the more primitive are the Beatitudes and the Lord's Prayer.

But it turns out that this argument is based not merely on one invalid assumption but on a whole series of questionable assumptions. The first is that the versions of some pericopes in Luke are demonstrably more primitive than those in Matthew. In response to this, scholars from the Farrer school, such as Mark Goodacre, have shown convincingly that Luke's versions of these pericopes are not necessarily more primitive than Matthew's versions.[16] His arguments need not be repeated here, however, because this is only one minor aspect of the issue. To answer this objection it is not necessary to prove that all Double Tradition pericopes in Luke are less primitive than Matthew's, because the assumption that Luke's use of Matthew would require Matthew's versions to always be more primitive is invalid to begin with.

Even if Luke had either Matthew or Q available to him as a source for Double Tradition material, he also had other sources (whether L or oral sources, as suggested by various theories). There is no reason to assume that there were no overlaps between Luke's main Double Tradition source and his additional sources. Indeed, there is plenty of evidence that there were a number of such overlaps, since some of the parallels between Luke and Matthew are so loose that they can be accounted for only by having come from different sources. Cases where Luke's version of a pericope appears to be more primitive than Matthew's are frequently due to his version having come from a separate source other than Matthew (or Q). The differences between Luke's version of the Beatitudes (such as his inclusion of matching "woes") may be evidence not that Matthew has altered Q's version, which is faithfully reproduced in Luke, but that Luke is drawing on a different version from a source other than either Matthew or Q.

To go back to Luke's Prologue once again, he mentions not only other written narratives, but also the oral tradition handed on by eyewitnesses, and he has further told us that he has carefully investigated everything. We should not be surprised, then, that Luke should have heard different versions of certain sayings and parables from different eyewitnesses, especially if he was a traveler, not limited to one geographical location, and especially if he was seeking out such traditions, as he seems to be implying. As Goodacre also says:

> If we grant Luke's literary dependence on both Matthew and Mark, it is inherently plausible to imagine this literary dependence interacting with Luke's knowledge of oral traditions of some of the same material. . . . The difficulty is that scholars have routinely confused issues of literary priority with issues over the relative age of traditions. The theory of Luke's literary dependence on Mark and Matthew does not necessitate the assumption that his material is always and inevitably secondary to

---

16. Goodacre, *Case against Q*, 61–66, 133–51.

Matthew's and Mark's. Few scholars today would deny the likelihood that Luke creatively and critically interacted with the living stream of oral tradition when he was working with Mark, so too we should not think it odd that he might have interacted with Matthew in the light of his knowledge of similar material in oral tradition.[17]

Hence, if Luke did use Matthew as one of his sources we would also expect (based on Luke's own description of his method) that much of the material Luke drew from his own oral sources would be more "primitive" than similar material he found in Matthew.

Yet even the concept of primitivity itself in regard to such pericopes is also based on an invalid assumption—that Jesus only ever said a certain saying once, and so there must be one and only one "original" version of each saying, which is therefore the most primitive. As hinted before, the philosophical assumption of many scholars in regard to the way in which the Gospel traditions developed is itself invalid, but they also assume an extremely limited scope for Jesus's own ministry and teaching. If every possible parallel saying in the Gospels descended from only one original saying, and especially if many of them were later invented by the church and were not actual sayings of Jesus himself, we are left with only a tiny number of sayings that Jesus himself spoke. This does not seem to be a realistic picture of a traveling preacher whose followers referred to as their "rabbi."

A more realistic possibility is the one already described of Jesus frequently using the same parables and sayings over and over, often changing them to fit a particular context, and of teaching those parables to his disciples. Hence, the two versions of the Beatitudes are less likely to be versions altered by either Matthew or Luke (or by their communities) and more likely to be different versions spoken by Jesus himself at different times and then faithfully remembered by different witnesses (especially in a culture that valued the reliability of oral remembrance even more than written sources).

The analysis in this book of Luke's intentions and procedures has shown that frequently Luke does not seem to change the traditions he knows but instead records them faithfully. He may be selective about what he reports, but whatever he chooses to include seems to be faithful to his sources, whom he claims in his Prologue to have been eyewitnesses. We have no idea how many different versions of parables or other teachings Luke may have had at his disposal from investigating

17. Ibid., 64–65.

and interviewing witnesses; we only know those versions he decided to incorporate, presumably based on their suitability for his own intentions. When Luke disagrees with Matthew (such as in the form of the Beatitudes), it is therefore unlikely that Luke has taken Matthew's version and altered it; Luke is probably aware of a different version, which may appear more "primitive" to modern scholars, but which in reality simply represents the memory of a different witness, or the use of a similar technique by Jesus on more than one occasion.

This argument, however (that Luke does not tend to alter his sources), although based on the evidence that has been examined, cannot be conclusively proven and so does not carry the same weight as the other arguments. It does support the internal consistency of the present theory and so is valid as supporting the overall argument, but it cannot be invoked as proof of it.

What can be said confidently is that the assumptions underlying the objection from mutual primitivity are invalid because Luke's versions of parallel pericopes are more likely to represent separate oral sources rather than his own tampering with Matthew's (or Q's) versions. Likewise, Matthew's versions of parallel pericopes are more likely to represent different sources rather than his tampering with Q's versions. Therefore this objection to Luke having used Matthew fails because it cannot establish the very premise upon which its argument is based (the premise of "primitivity").

One of the responses to this line of reasoning by advocates of the Q theory is that in at least one case, the Lord's Prayer, Matthew's version is clearly superior to Luke's, and therefore if Luke had had access to Matthew's version, he would necessarily have used it instead of a more "primitive" version from a different source. Therefore, Luke could not have been familiar with Matthew's version at all. But here, yet again, we have the same aesthetic argument that has been made already in several different contexts: Luke could not have reordered Matthew's Gospel because Matthew's order is superior. Luke could not have chosen an alternate birth narrative because Matthew's version is superior. Luke could not have preferred a different version of the Lord's Prayer because Matthew's version is superior.

But did Luke think so? One suggestion made by some Farrer scholars is that he preferred a shorter, less-wordy version of the prayer, perhaps one he had learned before having read Matthew's Gospel. Or perhaps he felt that the shorter version made the point better of making simple prayers to God. There are any number of possible reasons why

Luke may have preferred his own version over Matthew's. Here is yet another case where the expectation is that Luke must necessarily have had the same aesthetic sense as Matthew. But this cannot be a valid argument since it denies Luke the ability to make his own choices about the contents of his own Gospel (and, of course, the analysis already carried out in this book has shown that Luke's aesthetic sense was quite different from Matthew's), nor can it prove that Luke could not have read Matthew's version of the Lord's Prayer and still have chosen to use a version from another source (as we have also seen in other cases). The assumption that Luke should have treated his material in the same way Matthew treated his simply cannot stand.

Another possibility, suggested by Ken Olson, is that the version of the Lord's Prayer in Luke 11 may actually be an intentional abridgment by Luke of Matthew's version. Luke often abbreviates speeches and parables of Jesus from his other sources and especially tends to eliminate repetitious material. As Olson argues, Luke may not here be attempting to preserve the liturgical practices of his or any other specific church[18] but may simply be offering a condensed version of the Lord's Prayer as an example of the simple, straightforward prayers Jesus recommends. Thus, Olson suggests, "Luke has identified the father as 'Lord of heaven and earth' in Lk 10.21. He did not need to repeat the identification 22 verses later in Lk 11.2. His audience would know from context which father is being addressed."[19] Similarly, Olson argues regarding Luke's omission of the third and seventh petitions of the prayer ("Your will be done, just as in heaven so also on earth" [Matt 6:10], and "deliver us from the evil" [Matt 6:13]) that these petitions "do not contain any new element of thought, but serve to restate the petitions that precede them. . . . They are repetitive, and Luke has a tendency to edit out repetition. He need not be concerned with retaining the parallel structures of the couplets any more than he was when he edited Mk 11.9-10."[20] Olson's argument therefore is that, if Luke has

18. Although Luke is very interested in liturgical practices in his Gospel (including the canticles in chapters 1 and 2, and the Passover ritual in chapter 21), these interests seem to be specifically tied to existing Jewish liturgical practices, showing the continuity between Judaism and Christianity. Hence, Luke's seeming disinterest here in preserving the liturgical form of the Lord's Prayer as recorded in Matthew is actually not inconsistent with this tendency, since this prayer has no significance for Luke in showing that Christianity is the true form of Judaism. It is possible, then, that Luke felt just as willing to abbreviate this prayer as he was to abbreviate some of the other teachings of Jesus that he found in Matthew and Mark.
19. Ken Olson, "The Lord's Prayer (Abridged Edition)," in *Marcan Priority without Q: Explorations in the Farrer Hypothesis*, ed. John C. Poirier and Jeffrey Peterson, Library of New Testament Studies 455 (London: Bloomsbury T&T Clark, 2015), 101-18, here 116.
20. Ibid., 113.

himself trimmed down Matthew's version of the Lord's Prayer, this is entirely consistent with procedures that we can identify Luke using elsewhere in his treatment of his written sources. Hence, it is impossible for us to make a determination that Luke's version of the prayer is more "primitive" than Matthew's, and indeed it may well be that its brevity is simply due to Luke's own well-established editing techniques. Again, the argument from mutual primitivity simply cannot prove that Luke could not have used Matthew as one of his sources.

## Resultant Characteristics

The last two objections to Luke's use of Matthew have to do with the results of the editing processes used by Matthew and Luke.

## 8. The occurrence of doublets in Matthew and Luke

The use of "doublets" (repeated verses or pericopes within a single Gospel) as an indication of sources in Synoptic studies is somewhat questionable and appears to be based on an assumption that authors tend to be careful and consistent whereas redactors tend to be sloppy and inattentive, which may not always be the case. It also fails to account for a tendency among Hebrew writers to revel in repetition and slight variation, a tendency that Matthew appears to display. Luke, however, tends to avoid unnecessary repetition (perhaps because of his desire to fit as much as possible onto his scroll), and so it may be relevant in Luke's case to examine doublets in his Gospel.

John C. Hawkins, in his book *Horae Synopticae*, identified eleven pairs of verses in Luke's Gospel that might be defined as doublets.[21] Barbara Shellard has added a twelfth to this list.[22] Harry T. Fleddermann identifies five more doublets in Luke, although he does not recognize all of the first twelve.[23] Putting all of these lists together gives us the following:

21. John C. Hawkins, *Horae Synopticae: Contributions to the Study of the Synoptic Problem*, 2nd rev. ed. (Oxford: Clarendon, 1909), 99–100.
22. Shellard, *New Light on Luke*, 74.
23. Harry T. Fleddermann, *Q: A Reconstruction and Commentary*, Biblical Tools and Studies 1 (Leuven: Peeters, 2005), 56–59.

| | |
|---|---|
| 1. Luke 8:16 = 11:33 | 10. Luke 21:14–15 = 12:11–12 |
| 2. Luke 8:17 = 12:2 | 11. Luke 18:14 = 14:11 |
| 3. Luke 8:18 = 19:26 | 12. Luke 18:18 = 10:25 |
| 4. Luke 9:3–5 = 10:4 | |
| 5. Luke 9:23 = 14:27 | 13. Luke 9:48 = 10:16 |
| 6. Luke 9:24 = 17:33 | 14. Luke 9:50 = 11:23 |
| 7. Luke 9:26 = 12:9 | 15. Luke 21:16 = 12:51–53 |
| 8. Luke 9:46 = 22:24 | 16. Luke 21:33 = 16:17 |
| 9. Luke 20:46 = 11:43 | 17. Luke 17:1–2 = 22:22 |

If the detailed table of all the pericopes in Luke in the appendix at the end of this work is examined carefully, it will be seen that in every case here, the first verse in each pair is in a pericope that has been identified as coming from Mark (the arrangement of the pairs in this way has been done deliberately, even though the second verse therefore sometimes comes earlier in Luke than the first). In cases 11 and 16, the second verse is in a unique Lukan pericope, but in all the other cases the second verse is in a pericope identified as having come from Matthew. Therefore, every doublet in Luke makes logical sense since they are seen to have originated in two different sources.

The argument, however, that the doublets disprove that Luke used Matthew and that Matthew and Luke each used Mark and another common source (Q) is put forward because several of these pairs (eight of them if we combine everyone's lists [3, 5–7, 13, and 15–17]) also have a corresponding pair in Matthew. The argument is that in each of these cases, one of the doublets comes from Mark (in both Matthew and Luke) and one comes from Q. Thus, each of the pairs here identified as coming from Matthew or from Luke's oral sources would, under the Q theory, have come from Q.

But this argument cannot be used to prove Q and disprove that Luke used Matthew because it is already based on the assumption that Luke did not know that Matthew existed. Indeed, if the evidence is examined carefully, it supports precisely the opposite conclusion. The theory that the common doublets between Matthew and Luke are due to their both having resulted from the independent conflating of Mark and Q by Matthew and Luke depends on two coincidences: First is the coincidence that both Matthew and Luke chose independently of each other to produce a Gospel by the process of conflating Mark and Q. The Q theory has never adequately explained why they each would have chosen to do such a thing, but this choice is required by the theory. The second coincidence is that, in the process of accomplishing this conflation, both Matthew and Luke ended up including most of the same doublets.

According to the present theory, however, no such coincidences are required. Matthew presumably was created by adding certain material to Mark, and in this process some doublets apparently resulted. Luke, on the other hand, had both Matthew and Mark available to him. He therefore had not only Mark's contribution to the doublets available, but both of Matthew's. In this situation he would be far more likely to duplicate some of the doublets from Matthew with which he was already familiar, than if, without knowledge of Matthew, Luke had coincidentally stumbled on the same repetitions Matthew had also made when expanding Mark. Luke would not, however, have been likely to create "triplets" by using Mark's verse plus both verses from Matthew. Matthew's doublets were already the result of using Mark as one of his sources, so one of each of Matthew's pairs had come from its similar context in Mark. Luke was careful not to include two versions of whole pericopes that were parallel between Matthew and Mark, and so would have eliminated one of each of these potential triplets in the process.

Hence, the claim that the doublets are best explained by the Q theory is not only invalid; it is blatantly false! The doublets are best explained by the theory that Luke used Matthew and Mark as his sources.

### 9. Q's distinct theology

The final objection to Luke's having used Matthew is based on the idea that Q evidences theological themes that appear to have different emphases than either Matthew or Luke. Q scholars therefore believe that Q was an independently existing document. This appears to be the only positive argument in favor of Q ever put forward. Instead of being the "only alternative" to Luke's having used Matthew (as all the other objections have been), this argument suggests that there is a discernible character present within Q itself that shows that it must have existed as a distinct document. This character is primarily that Q portrays Jesus not as a divine savior but as a wisdom teacher.

The invalid assumption here is that this is a positive argument

rather than a negative one. In reality, it turns out that the "distinct theology" of Q is not the result of its ever having existed but is the result
of the process of subtracting the theologies of Matthew and Luke that
do not appear in the specific pericopes assigned to Q.

To use an example of what this means, we could create a new document by collecting all the miracle stories from the Gospels and eliminating everything else. This document would then have its own "distinct theology." It would portray Jesus simply as a miracle-worker and
not as a teacher or a Messiah. We might then draw all sorts of conclusions about a community that held this view of Jesus, conclusions we
could back up by referring back to our new "Gospel," which differs so
dramatically in emphasis from the canonical ones.

This is exactly what has happened in the case of Q. Q is simply the
result of subtracting all the material from Matthew and from Luke that
is unique to their individual Gospels, along with all the material that
has parallels with Mark. The question is, Would such a process by its
very nature produce a document that *seemed* to exhibit its own dis-
tinctive character? The answer to this is a resounding yes, and it is
due not to the character of Q but to the character of the three Gospels
involved. Goodacre describes the result of this process in the formula:
"Q = (Matthew *minus* Mark) *divided by* 'Luke-pleasingness.'"[24] In other
words, if Luke used Matthew and Mark as his sources, Q is simply the
material Luke wanted to take from Matthew that had no parallel in
Mark and so displays the characteristics of Matthew (without Mark)
that Luke chose to include.

But there is a simpler way of describing much of the nature of this
material without recourse to either the Q or the Farrer theory, and
this is to consider the specific qualities of the Gospel of Mark. Mark
is unique among the four Gospels in that it contains very few teaching pericopes, and in particular few pericopes containing ethical teaching. (We may further note that even the few passages in Mark that
might be classified as ethical teaching are usually included not for the
sake of the teaching itself but in order to establish Jesus's authority
to give such teaching.) The larger Christian tradition from which all
four Gospels developed contained stories about Jesus, Jesus's teachings
about the kingdom of God, teachings about his own identity in relation
to that kingdom, and ethical teachings about how Christians are to live
in that kingdom. The other three Gospels contain a mixture of all four

24. Goodacre, *Case against Q*, 69.

of these (with John's ethical teaching being summed up primarily in the command to "love one another"), but Mark lacks material of this last category. Since John is more like Matthew and Luke in including such ethical teaching, even on a limited scale, it is obvious that Mark is the exception to this rather than the "rule."

Thus, because Mark concentrates so much on the events in Jesus's life, and because both Matthew and Luke used Mark as a source, there was little need for either Matthew or Luke to add much additional narrative material from other sources. They did, however, both want to include more teaching material, and specifically more ethical teaching material, which could not have come from Mark. Therefore, regardless of where such material came from, once we subtract the Markan material from both Matthew and Luke, it should not be surprising to find that there are few narrative stories about Jesus left over, but a significant amount of ethical teaching. This is exactly what we see in Q.

Because of the process involved in thus "extracting" Q from Matthew and Luke, and because of the unique nature of Mark, Q is dominated by Mark's missing category of material: ethical teachings. While this may appear on the surface to suggest that a document such as Q existed, with a distinct theology based on Jesus as an ethical teacher, it is simply a by-product of Mark's unique character. It is the criterion by which the Q material has been extracted from Matthew and Luke that has seemed to produce its characteristics, not something inherent in the supposed Q itself. There is therefore no distinct theology in Q any more than there is a distinct theology in our hypothetical collection of miracle stories, since both are merely extracts from larger works, based on arbitrary methods of extraction.

The argument that Q displays a distinct theology is therefore not a positive argument at all (if anything it is a negative argument against Mark!). It also has no bearing on how this ethical material came to be included in either Matthew's or Luke's Gospels (since it only addresses the content of a small subset of material, not the origin of that material) and so cannot be used as an argument against Luke's use of Matthew as a source.

## The Cumulative Argument

Each of the nine objections listed above has been addressed, and in each case it has been shown that there is no compelling reason to accept the objection as an indication that Luke did not or could not have used Matthew directly as a source. Indeed, the opposite is true, for in several cases the evidence that is supposed to point away from Luke's use of Matthew actually points instead in favor of Luke's direct use of Matthew.

One final aspect of these objections needs to be addressed, however, and that is their cumulative effect. Even if each one can be refuted individually, is it still not the case that, when they are considered in connection with each other, their combined weight is enough to tip the scales away from Luke's use of Matthew and toward his use of Q? Even if specific reasons can be given to refute each objection in turn, does not the very existence of so many objections indicate that there is something fundamentally suspect about the idea that Luke could have used Matthew? Some scholars would say that these objections are not offered as proof that Luke could not have used Matthew but only that the Q theory presents a better, more plausible explanation.

Such might be the case if the arguments against each objection were instances of "special pleading." If we had established a consistent pattern that Luke tended to follow, but then, in order to answer an objection, had said that in *this* case Luke *may* have followed a different pattern, we might have to conclude that the arguments against the objections turned out to be rather weak. But precisely the opposite has been the case. Time after time it has been the objections themselves that have insisted on inconsistent expectations of Luke's procedures. In order to answer them, it has been necessary only to show that in each suspected case Luke has consistently followed his own well-established patterns.

Nor have these patterns required an overly complex scheme on Luke's part. Instead, his procedures have been seen to flow naturally from just a few basic principles: Luke's primary goal was to present the truth of Christianity to his audience (the individual Theophilus, and perhaps others who might also read his work). This presentation had two purposes: to defend the early church against the charge of "atheism" (partly by showing through continued temple worship that Christianity was the "true" version of Judaism), and to convert Theophilus himself to become a Christian. Luke sought to achieve this goal by means of an artistic and dramatic story of the life of Jesus. To this end, he relentlessly illustrated the contrast between those who choose to be true disciples and those who do not do so, and the consequences resulting from such choices. He used three basic sources: Mark, Matthew, and oral (apparently eyewitness) testimony. He rarely conflated his

sources, but instead tended to alternate between them. He was relatively unfamiliar with Mark and so used it in limited narrative blocks,
nearly always in precise order, and seldom added additional material
into these blocks. He was far more familiar with Matthew, probably to
the point of having completely memorized it, and so was able to be
far freer with it, changing its order to suit his own goal and frequently
interspersing it with new or variant material from his oral sources.

By applying these few specific principles to the various objections,
they have each been refuted. It has been necessary to address each case
in detail simply because these objections and the assumptions underlying them have been so pervasive in the biblical scholarship of the
last century and a half, that each must be taken seriously and treated
accordingly. It has become evident, however, that each of these objections is due to one or another flaw in the basic way in which Luke, his
purpose, and his procedures have typically been approached. In each
case there has been a failure to treat Luke on his own terms but instead
a tendency to project certain foreign expectations onto him.

If the case for Luke's use of Matthew turns out to be so strong, and
the case against it so weak, why have scholars been reluctant for so
long to accept the possibility that Luke did use Matthew directly? Here
again, the answer to this seems to be because of the way in which the
Synoptic Problem has been defined, in terms of Double, Triple, and
unique Traditions. These have nearly universally been seen as realistic categories, each a pointer to a different source of materials, and
it is based on this assumption that the Q theory appears to be more
plausible than Luke's use of Matthew. From such a perspective, then, it
would be natural to suppose that Mark was the source for Luke of all
the Triple Tradition material and that Q was the source for the Double
Tradition. On these terms, Matthew is certainly problematic if viewed
simply as the source of the Double Tradition material. From this point
of view (but *only* from this point of view), the various objections all
seem reasonable, since they all point out that it would not have made
sense for Luke to have used Matthew simply as his Double Tradition
source. Even the way in which these objections have classically been
defined, such as by referring to the "lack of Matthean content within
Triple Tradition contexts" shows that this is the fundamental perspective from which the problem has come to be understood.

The analysis carried out in this book has shown that Mark was not
the sole source of Triple Tradition material for Luke, since Luke drew
much of it from Matthew instead of from Mark (and probably some

from his oral sources as well). Similarly, some of the Double Tradition material has come from Matthew and some from oral sources (hence, for example, Luke's alternate birth narrative and his Beatitudes are *not* problematic). This radically alters the way in which the Synoptic Problem needs to be addressed. Double Tradition, Triple Tradition, and unique material are no longer pointers to three different categories of sources but are merely the by-products of Luke's methods and choices, cutting across Luke's actual sources, as the following tables illustrate. (Note that the Q theory usually does not draw a distinction between the Triple Tradition and material common to Luke and Mark, even when such material does not appear in Matthew.)

| Table 5.5. Components of Luke according to the Q Theory | |
| --- | --- |
| From Mark | Common to Luke and Mark |
| | Triple Tradition |
| From Q | Double Tradition |
| From L | Unique to Luke |

| Table 5.6. Components of Luke according to the Present Theory | | |
| --- | --- | --- |
| From Mark | Common to Luke and Mark | Triple Tradition |
| From Matthew | Double Tradition | |
| From Oral Sources | | |
| | Unique to Luke | |

The standard categories are hindrances rather than helpers in reaching the correct solution to the problem. They are arbitrary and ultimately meaningless categories and need now to be recognized as such. They represent how we as later readers of the Gospels perceive different "traditions" flowing out of the Gospels to us (based on a simple count of how many Gospels contain a particular pericope), not streams of traditions present in the early church flowing into the Gospels (and so passing through the Gospels to us).

Hence, the cumulative effect of all the objections addressed above is simply to reinforce the assumed model of "Tradition equals Source," where the Triple Tradition is assumed to point to one distinct source, whereas the Double Tradition points to another. But does this model really make any sense? Is it reasonable to suppose that there were three different accounts of Jesus's life available to Luke (Mark, Q and L), plus a fourth one once we also introduce M (and regardless of the exact nature of L and M), all of which contained virtually no overlapping content? If we were to examine any other four documents, each written by an author who knew nothing about the others but all writing about the same historical figure, would we possibly find such a coincidence of mutual exclusivity? Yet this is what this model suggests (and ultimately requires, if we are to define Q's contents as virtually identical to the material common to Luke and Matthew that does not parallel Mark.

Once this model is abandoned, Luke's methods and intelligent choices begin to make more sense, the historical processes involved in the writing of the Gospels become more plausible, and the objections to Luke's use of Matthew as a source cease to carry any weight, individual or cumulative. The arguments from order bear no weight because Luke is now free to select alternate versions of stories from alternate sources and to rearrange those sources as he wishes to create his own order, rather than mechanically following his sources (and as we have seen, his own order is logical based on his self-published goals). The arguments from content bear no weight because all of the suggested "irregularities" make perfect sense based on Luke's acknowledged procedure of alternating his sources rather than conflating them, and especially once we understand that those sources do not correspond slavishly to the categories of the so-called Traditions. Likewise, the argument from "mutual primitivity" bears no weight once we accept that Luke's sources (especially his oral sources) may have overlapped and so may have contained alternate versions of pericopes also found in other sources.[25] The argument from doublets was never a valid argument against Luke's use of Matthew anyway, and the argument from Q's "theology" bears no weight once Luke's sources are liberated from

---

25. We may therefore also here briefly address one other minor Synoptic theory held by a small number of modern scholars, the so-called Jerusalem Hypothesis proposed by Robert L. Lindsey ("A Modified Two-Document Theory of the Synoptic Dependence and Independence," *Novum Testamentum* 6 [1963]: 239–63; *A Hebrew Translation of the Gospel of Mark: Greek-Hebrew Diglot with English Introduction* [Jerusalem: Dugith, 1973]). This theory holds that, because often Luke's versions of pericopes appear more primitive, and especially since Luke is often more easily translated into Hebrew from Greek than the other Synoptics, Luke's Gospel must have been the earliest of the Synoptics to have been written (followed by Mark, then by Matthew). But since Luke has, according to his own Prologue, interviewed eyewitnesses, it should not be surprising if his versions of stories and sayings often reflect a "primitive" version told to him directly in a Semitic language, which he then translated into Greek for his Gospel. All the other evidence (including his Prologue) points to Luke being the last of the Synoptics, so there is no compelling reason to consider the Jerusalem Hypothesis seriously.

being equated with the Traditions, since even if Q existed there is now no means of determining how extensive its contents (and hence its theology) might have been.

We may therefore conclude that there is no cumulative effect to these objections, because in the end they turn out not to be nine separate objections but simply nine different aspects of the single "Tradition equals Source" argument, an argument that is itself no more than a presupposition, and an exceedingly questionable one at that.

## Matthew or Q?

Having now examined all the objections to Luke having used Matthew directly, we find that none of them holds up against the analysis carried out in this book. Instead we can conclude that there is indeed every reason to suppose that Luke did use Matthew as a primary source, and that his use of Matthew in this light is both plausible and logical throughout his Gospel.

We may finally put to bed all the statements of ridicule heaped on Luke by his critics (and even the bewilderment of his advocate Farrer). Streeter had claimed that:

> If then Luke derived this material from Matthew, he must have gone through both Matthew and Mark so as to discriminate with meticulous precision between Marcan and non-Marcan material; he must then have proceeded with the utmost care to tear every little piece of non-Marcan material he desired to use from the context of Mark in which it appeared in Matthew—in spite of the fact that contexts in Matthew are always exceedingly appropriate—in order to re-insert it into a different context of Mark having no special appropriateness. A theory which would make an author capable of such a proceeding would only be tenable if, on other grounds, we had reason to believe he was a crank.[26]

As we have seen, Luke's method bears no resemblance whatsoever to Streeter's description. The material from Matthew was not limited to Double Tradition material, and it was never placed in a "context of Mark" at all by Luke. This whole idea is founded on the premise that Luke used Mark as his skeleton and added other material to fit around it. We have seen that this was not Luke's procedure (and, interestingly, Streeter himself recognizes this, and so should have known better than to have made the above statement in the first place).[27] Instead,

---

26. Streeter, *Four Gospels*, 183.

Luke turned to Matthew and to Mark in a consistent alternating pattern. Material from Matthew was never placed in the middle of material from Mark, or vice versa. Indeed, the contexts into which Luke did place material from Matthew were entirely of his own devising, based on his desire to tell his story and develop his themes effectively. Far from being a crank, Luke has proven himself to be a genius and a skillful composer.

Other accusations against Luke now look equally hollow. Martin Hengel suggested that, if Luke had used Matthew, he would have "in overweening vanity destroyed the grandiose architecture of the work along with its impressive theology."[28] Such an accusation might just as easily be leveled against the classical composers, such as Beethoven, who "destroyed the grandiose architecture" of their own Exposition sections when juxtaposing themes freely in their Development sections. Luke certainly did not "destroy" Matthew, since Matthew's Gospel as an independent literary and theological work still remains intact and in use by the church. Luke simply offers a different way of approaching some of this same material (and for a different purpose). There is, after all, no reason to suppose that Luke intended in any way for his own Gospel to replace Matthew (unless we were to revert to a theory that the Gospel writers had no intention except to collect every possible bit of "Jesus tradition" and to then present this material in a single anthology, but, as we have seen, this was not Luke's intention).

Similarly, Reginald Fuller said, "Matthew has tidily collected the Q material into great blocks. Luke, we must then suppose, has broken up this tidy arrangement and scattered the Q material without rhyme or reason all over his gospel—a case of unscrambling the egg with a vengeance!"[29] If we review the previous chart showing where Luke has taken material from Matthew and placed it in his own Gospel, we will see that it is actually Matthew, not Luke, who has this material (which appears blue in Matthew's column) "scattered all over his gospel,"

27. Ibid., chapter 8. It is indeed surprising that Streeter should have used this argument at all against Luke's direct use of Matthew since, according to Streeter's own hypothesis, all of the material in question was already in its present context in "Proto-Luke" before any material from Mark was even introduced. Hence, there was no such thing as a "context of Mark" into which Luke could have "re-inserted" it. Likewise, it is surprising that, after Streeter gives his second reason for rejecting Luke's direct use of Matthew (the argument of mutual primitivity), he proceeds to negate this reason as well (by arguing that pericopes where Matthew and Luke disagree, and hence exhibit varying degrees of primitivity, do not come from the same source at all). Streeter therefore subverts both of the main reasons he himself gives for rejecting Luke's direct use of Matthew as a source!
28. Hengel, *Four Gospels,* 177.
29. Fuller, *New Testament in Current Study,* 87.

whereas in Luke it is concentrated into two places: the Sermon on the Plain, and the much longer Journey to Jerusalem. Nor has this been done "without rhyme or reason," but in a purposeful, logical, methodical, and effective manner.

G. M. Styler likewise claimed, "If Matthew is Luke's source, there seems to be no commonsense explanation for his order and procedure."[30] As demonstrated above, both Luke's order and his procedure make perfect sense, and he has done a masterful job in achieving his goal. Indeed, it is the Q theory that offers no commonsense explanation for the order of material in Luke's Gospel. Even Farrer said:

> It may well be that we shall have to accuse St. Luke of pulling well-arranged Matthaean discourses to pieces and re-arranging them in an order less coherent or at least less perspicuous. St. Luke would not be either the first planner or the last to prefer a plan of his own to a plan of a predecessor's, and to make a less skilful thing of it.[31]

These disparaging comments seem especially harsh coming from a supporter of Luke's use of Matthew and have been shown by our analysis to be completely unfounded. Instead, by attempting to approach Luke on his own terms, paying attention to what Luke himself said about his own work rather than imposing our own expectations and assumptions on the evangelist, his genius and logic become apparent.

Given this analysis, then, we may now also ask how it would be possible under the Q theory for the many coincidences required by it to have happened historically. Why would both Matthew and Luke have chosen to produce new Gospels by combining the Matthew-and-Luke-friendly Gospel of Mark with the apparently Matthew-and-Luke-*unfriendly* sayings document Q? Why would they both choose to do so by appending birth narratives that stressed the virginity of Jesus's mother and Jesus's conception by the Holy Spirit, a divine command to name the baby "Jesus," divinely ordained visits by outsiders to worship the baby, a relocation from Bethlehem to Nazareth, and a genealogy? How is it that both Matthew and Luke, in combining Mark with Q, failed to notice the numerous doublets they commonly included completely independently of each other? How is it that in every case where Luke chose *not* to follow Mark's order of pericopes (except for two minor displace-

---

30. Styler, "Synoptic Problem," 726.
31. Farrer, "On Dispensing with Q," 65.

ments within a small block), Luke's version mysteriously resembles Matthew's (if he did not have it available to him) more than Mark's?

Even more remarkably, how is it that, in the portion of the passion story from after the Words of Institution to Jesus's condemnation by the Sanhedrin, Luke's version not only corresponds more closely to Matthew's than to Mark's overall but does so consistently throughout each individual portion of that passage, whereas in every other individual portion of the passion, Luke's account corresponds more closely to Mark's? And how is it that this very portion of the passion where Luke is closer to Matthew is also the only place throughout his passion narrative that Luke departs from Mark's order, and the only place where he introduces material not originally from a passion context? If Luke did not have Matthew's Gospel available to him (or if Q did not have a passion account that was virtually identical to Matthew's), the statistical probability of all these coincidences converging in order to create the illusion within Luke's passion narrative of a typically Luke-like block of Matthew-influenced material corresponding exactly in character to the similar blocks found in the early portion of Luke would be infinitesimally small!

Having thus "exonerated" Luke, we may now ask, What of Q? If it is possible and reasonable that Luke could have used Matthew as a direct source, is there still any reason to consider the Q theory at all? Or is it possible that it is still a better theory than the Farrer hypothesis? Even if Luke could have used Matthew as a source, does not the weight of a century and a half of scholarship show that the Q theory is actually more likely than Luke's use of Matthew, in spite of all its difficulties?

Here again we are in danger of making an invalid assumption, in this case the assumption that the Q theory has validity in and of itself. But it does not. Its only validity depends on the condition that Luke could not have used Matthew directly as a source. If Luke did know Matthew's Gospel, there is no reason to look for a different source for their common material (just as there is no reason to look for a common source behind Luke and Mark, since it is completely plausible that Luke used Mark directly).

As Farrer stated in his landmark article "On Dispensing with Q," "The hypothesis of St. Luke's using St. Matthew, and the hypothesis of their both drawing independently from a common source, do not compete on equal terms. The first hypothesis must be conclusively exploded before we obtain the right to consider the second at all."[32] This is strong language, but he is absolutely precise and correct. The burden of proof does not lie with the Farrer school to show that Luke *must* have used Matthew as a source. Rather the burden of proof lies with the Q school to prove that Luke *could not* have used Matthew as a source before we even have the right to consider the existence of Q.

Even Q scholar John Kloppenborg appears to acknowledge this. In his article, "On Dispensing with Q? Goodacre on the Relation of Luke to Matthew," he writes, "Q is a *corollary* of the hypotheses of Markan priority and the independence of Matthew and Luke, since it is then necessary to account for the material that Matthew and Luke have in common but which they did not take from Mark. The case for Q rests on the implausibility of Luke's direct use of Matthew or Matthew's direct use of Luke."[33] This is an admission that it is not a question of which theory is more plausible but rather that the theory of the independence of Matthew and Luke is itself dependent on the implausibility of Luke's use of Matthew (and the implausibility of Matthew's use of Luke), regardless of the plausibility of Q. Hence, if the plausibility of Luke's use of Matthew can be demonstrated, the hypothesis of the independence of Matthew and Luke is negated (regardless of how plausible it may be), and its corollary (Q) collapses altogether, with no argument either for or against Q itself needing to be considered. (In this light, the discussions above of a distinct Q theology and of Q's weaknesses are therefore also entirely irrelevant.)

Perhaps Kloppenborg has not been precise in his wording regarding his intended meaning, but he does appear here to be accepting Farrer's claim that the burden of proof lies squarely on proponents of Q to demonstrate that Luke's use of Matthew is implausible or even impossible. Or perhaps, given the history of biblical scholarship, Kloppenborg simply believes that the case has already been made for the impossibility of Luke's use of Matthew and hence the burden of proof ought to lie with those who suggest that it is plausible after all. Such could be a reasonable stance.

But surely the case has successfully been reopened by Farrer, Goulder, Goodacre, and others, with many demonstrations offered as to how Luke might plausibly have used Matthew as a source. As Farrer has pointed out, and as Kloppenborg seems to accept, that is all that is needed. It is not necessary to prove that any specific explanation of

32. Farrer, "On Dispensing with Q," 56.
33. Kloppenborg, "On Dispensing with Q?," 211–12. Interestingly, however, Kloppenborg's preferred name for the "Farrer" theory (213) is "Mark-without-Q," which implies that Q is the norm and that the Farrer theory is the deviation.

Luke's use of Matthew is more plausible than his use of Q, because Q in and of itself is already much less plausible than Matthew. The statistical probability for the existence of the Gospel of Matthew is 100 percent (in spite of Kloppenborg's claim that any specific "text" of an existing Gospel is itself a hypothetical reconstruction[34]). No matter how it may be calculated, the probability of the existence of Q is certainly less than 100 percent. Hence, the beginning probability of Luke's use of Matthew is statistically always higher than the beginning probability of his use of Q.

This further means that, once a plausible explanation for Luke's use of Matthew is offered, the burden of proof falls back on those who reject such use to demonstrate its impossibility, or at least its implausibility, not merely to offer reasons why the Q hypothesis offers "better" explanations for certain relationships between the Synoptics. Yet Kloppenborg in the same article states, "To conclude. Although Goodacre has presented an interesting case defending the possibility of Luke's direct dependence on Matthew, none of his arguments can be considered to be sufficiently weighty to displace the alternative scenario, which is at least as plausible, that Luke and Matthew independently drew on Q."[35] The key words here are "at least as plausible," because Kloppenborg now appears to be altering what he said earlier, namely, that "the case for Q rests on the *implausibility* of Luke's direct use of Matthew."[36]

By now contending that Q is "at least as plausible" as Luke's use of Matthew, Kloppenborg is (1) admitting that Luke's use of Matthew is plausible, and (2) putting the two theories on equal footing. Since the statistical probability of the existence of Matthew is 100 percent, however, and the probability of the existence of Q is less than 100 percent, if we multiply "at least as plausible" times the probabilities of their existence, the theory of Luke's use of Matthew automatically becomes "more plausible" than the theory of Luke's use of Q. Additionally, once the level of plausibility of Luke's use of Matthew crosses the threshold from "implausible" to "plausible," the statistical probability of the existence of Q drops to virtually 0 percent, since its existence (by Kloppenborg's own admission) is predicated on the implausibility of Luke's use of Matthew.[37] Hence, as long as Luke's use of Matthew remains even

---

34. Ibid., 215. The existence of the Gospel of Matthew is not dependent on the elimination of textual variants. Indeed, variant manuscripts themselves actually prove that the Gospel does (and did) exist.
35. Ibid., 236.
36. Ibid., 211–12 (emphasis added).

a hair above the threshold of "plausible," the probability of Luke's use of Q drops to virtually zero. Since even "highly plausible" times zero still equals zero, therefore "more plausible" times "virtually 0 percent" is significantly less than "less plausible" times 100 percent, and this is even assuming that there are arguments that Q is more plausible.

As we have seen, however, the historical conditions required by the Q theory are far less plausible than those required by the Farrer theory. Q requires that the early church would have been made up of numerous largely isolated communities, developing their own mutually contradictory theologies and encapsulating those theologies in mostly private documents that each purported to tell the story and teachings of Jesus but which reported virtually no overlapping incidents and hardly any overlapping teachings. It then requires Matthew and Luke, with no knowledge of each other, to combine the same two of these documents in nearly identical ways. Yet the evidence for the conditions in the early church suggest something very different: not a patchwork of largely isolated communities, but a network of interconnected communities sharing a common understanding and theology, linked by regular communication, particularly by means of itinerant missionaries traveling freely throughout the Roman Empire.

It is specifically such missionaries, frequently in touch with various communities and with each other, who were credited by the early church with the writing of some of the Gospels, including Luke. Within this milieu it would not be surprising to find authors drawing on the earlier works of others, expanding and modifying them in order to reach new audiences. This is precisely the setting suggested by the Farrer theory, according to which Luke would have drawn on oral (eyewitness) sources encountered during his travels, on the more basic Gospel of Mark, and on the very focused Gospel of Matthew (written largely for the instruction of Jewish Christians), in order to create his own work, written for his own distinct goal of converting gentile non-Christians. Thus, the Farrer theory is far more plausible historically and literarily than is Q. Hence, the comparison is now "less plausible" times virtually 0 percent for Q as opposed to "more plausible" times 100 percent for the Farrer theory, and so there is no contest. The analysis carried out in the present book therefore adds to the work of Goulder and Goodacre to refute further the claim that Luke could not have used

---

37. Q's existence cannot be ruled out altogether, however. There is still the tiniest of chances that scholars accidentally hit on the correct solution for all the wrong reasons, and in spite of its implausibility. Thus the probability of its existence can never drop all the way to zero.

Matthew. The analysis has shown instead that Luke's use of Matthew as a source is not only plausible but highly probable, and indeed almost certain.

## Luke's Achievement

Based on this examination of Luke's Gospel from the perspective that Matthew and Mark were most likely his major written sources, what conclusions may we draw about Luke, about the early church, and perhaps about Jesus himself?

## Luke and His Sources

One of the most obvious observations made in the exploration carried out here is that the pattern of correspondence between Luke's similarities to Matthew, then to Mark, then to Matthew again in large alternating blocks is a real, objective, and identifiable pattern, not an arbitrary structure superimposed on his Gospel from the outside (and which has nothing to do with whether any given pericope is "Triple Tradition" or "Double Tradition"). Further, this pattern is completely consistent throughout Luke's Gospel. The one case that seemed to be a possible exception to this pattern—the Warning against Offenses, a pericope where Luke corresponds more closely to Mark than to Matthew even though it occurs near the end of the largest Matthean block in Luke, the Journey to Jerusalem— has revealed itself to be completely logical and understandable, since in Mark it is the very next pericope after the end of the previous Markan block in Luke and comes just before the beginning of the next Markan block.

Furthermore, by examining this alternating pattern, it has been shown that the pericopes where Luke corresponds more closely to Mark than to Matthew—with the exception of only two pericopes, the first pericope in the first Markan block and the first pericope in the second Markan block—follow exactly in their Markan order throughout Luke's Gospel. This, again, is a real, objective, and identifiable pattern.

Equally, and in marked contrast to this, it has been shown by examining this pattern that in the blocks where Luke corresponds more closely to Matthew than to Mark, there are always displacements of Matthean material that Luke has transported from a different part of Matthew altogether. We have seen that there are frequently unique

Lukan pericopes (from his oral sources) included among the Matthean material, whereas it is only rarely that we find Lukan pericopes included among the Markan material.

The very real existence of these blocks and the observable characteristics that they display have given us a clear picture of how Luke went about composing his Gospel, alternating between his two written sources, Matthew and Mark. But what is especially surprising about this is that Luke's relationships to Mark and to Matthew seem to be just the opposite of what we might expect. Since, according to the evidence (and according to both the Farrer and the Q theories), Mark was probably written prior to Matthew, we would expect Luke to have been more familiar with Mark, and hence more free in his use of that Gospel, than he was with Matthew. Instead, however, Luke felt completely free to rearrange and rework the material he took from Matthew but followed Mark closely, indicating that he must have been far more familiar with Matthew's Gospel than with Mark's. This suggests that Luke almost certainly had Matthew memorized.

A valid historical explanation for Luke's greater familiarity with Matthew than with Mark was found in the testimony of Clement of Alexandria, which suggested that although Mark's Gospel may have been written prior to Matthew's, it may not have been accessible to Luke until much later, when Mark himself gave a private copy of his Gospel to Luke. Interestingly, this scenario also seems to fit the early church's traditions regarding the authors of the Gospels of Mark and Luke, that they were itinerant preachers, travelers among the various churches spread across the Roman Empire, rather than members of semi-isolated Christian communities that would have had little contact with other such communities.

Further, what Luke's use of Matthew and Mark has also revealed is that, although Luke obviously respected both of these previous Gospels greatly, since he drew on them to such a large extent, he nevertheless did not feel compelled to adhere to them slavishly. In a handful of cases, he did include versions of stories or parables from his oral sources that contradicted (or at least significantly altered) similar passages from his written sources. This should not surprise us, however, given what Luke tells us about himself and about his Gospel in his Prologue:

> Since many have undertaken to draw up a narrative of the things that have been accomplished among us, just as they were entrusted to us by

those who from the first became eyewitnesses and servants of the Word, therefore it seemed good also to me, since I myself have investigated everything from the beginning, to write an orderly account for you, Your Excellency Theophilus, so that you may know the certainty of the things about which you have been informed. (Luke 1:1–4)

Luke is telling us quite clearly here that his task was that of an "investigative reporter," combing through previous written accounts and interviewing eyewitnesses in order to produce the most accurate history possible of the life, death, and resurrection of Jesus. For the most part, he has corroborated those previous written accounts (Matthew and Mark), but he was not afraid on a few occasions to correct them when certain witnesses seemed to him to be more reliable than those written accounts (even though we cannot, from our vantage point two thousand years later, identify who those witnesses may have been).

Additionally, we have seen that the way in which Luke chose to present this material was indeed organized as a well-ordered account that presented to Theophilus not only the historical facts about Jesus but also the inevitable choice that Luke believed everyone who encounters this history must make: either to follow Jesus or to fail to follow him (and in so doing to oppose God). Luke was able to convey this message by skillfully presenting and then developing interrelated themes concerning Christian discipleship in the context of a well-woven and intriguing story. In other words, Luke was an expert artist and storyteller who knew exactly what he was doing and achieved precisely what he set out in his Prologue to accomplish.

This portrait of Luke the composer and investigative reporter is rather different from the picture the Q theory presents of Luke the compiler of traditions that had grown slowly over time within his own community (the "L" traditions). According to the Q theory, Luke then combined these traditions with those of two other similar communities (the "Markan community," developers of the Triple Tradition, and the "Q community," developers of the Double Tradition). But there are a number of reasons for preferring Luke the composer to Luke the compiler.

One reason is that, as we have already seen, the concept of these "traditions" is completely baseless. The three so-called traditions present in Luke do not correspond to different sources flowing into Luke's Gospel but are simply an artefact of Luke's own choices in editing the material he had available to him, regardless of whether the source of such material was Mark, Matthew, or eyewitnesses Luke had interviewed. Another reason is that the model of gradual development of "Jesus traditions" in semi-isolated Christian communities bears no resemblance to the evidence we have regarding the early years of the church. As Richard Bauckham has pointed out, there simply was not time for such "traditions" to have grown before the Gospels were written, which would have required several generations of processing the stories about Jesus in order for such development to have occurred.[38] Instead, the Gospels were written within the lifetime of those who would have been eyewitnesses of the events recounted, and (as Luke specifically tells us) it was those very eyewitnesses who were the sources for his and the other Gospels. Luke, as an itinerant missionary in the early church, would have had ample opportunities to meet such eyewitnesses and to record their memories.

It is also the case that the whole concept of the development of religious traditions as envisioned by the Q theory is dependent on a specific philosophy of religion that we inherited from the Enlightenment philosophers of the seventeenth and eighteenth centuries. This philosophy tends to divide human knowledge into two categories (based on the "Cartesian Compromise" of René Descartes). In the first category is scientific and historical truth, which is public, objective, and therefore verifiable. In the second category is spiritual and religious truth, which is personal, subjective, and therefore unverifiable. If we apply this model of human knowledge to the early church, it is easy for us to suppose that the New Testament authors were expressing subjective religious ideas that had developed over time in their own communities, which they themselves had individually internalized but which did not necessarily correspond to the historical facts about Jesus or his own (equally subjective) teachings.

It is evident that the early Christians, and especially the authors of the Gospels, did not accept such a dichotomy regarding human knowledge. In the Hebrew worldview (within which even the probably gentile author Luke operated), religious truth was considered to be no different from historical truth and was considered to be public, objective, and verifiable. Indeed, such truth was to be verified on the principle of multiple eyewitnesses. We see this expressed blatantly in Matthew 18:15–17 (quoting Deut 19:15), and we see this throughout the Gospel of John (including the important eyewitness statements in John 1:14; 19:35; and 21:24), and especially in chapters 5 and 8 of John's

---

38. Bauckham, *Jesus and the Eyewitnesses*, 7–8.

Gospel, where Jesus acknowledges that his own testimony about himself is invalid unless it is corroborated by other multiple witnesses. Of course, Luke's Prologue affirms the same by indicating that he is himself relaying the testimony of multiple eyewitnesses.

In this context, for a Christian author (or "community") to invent new sayings, and then to attribute those sayings to Jesus, would not have been an "innocent" undertaking, expressing new internal and subjective truths in the "spirit" of Jesus. Instead, such an endeavor would have been considered a false witness, claiming that Jesus had said or done something that he had not historically done. We must therefore take Luke's affidavit in his Prologue regarding the faithfulness of his report very seriously indeed, since he is giving us every indication that he is presenting his work as the reliable testimony of someone under oath in a legal context. In this vein, Bauckham writes:

> I suggest that we need to recover the sense in which the Gospels are testimony. This does not mean that they are testimony *rather than* history. It means that the kind of historiography they are is testimony. An irreducible feature of testimony as a form of human utterance is that it asks to be trusted. This need not mean that it asks to be trusted uncritically, but it does mean that testimony should not be treated as credible only to the extent that it can be independently verified. There can be good reasons for trusting or distrusting a witness, but these are precisely reasons for *trusting* or *distrusting*. Trusting testimony is not an irrational act of faith that leaves critical rationality aside; it is, on the contrary, the rationally appropriate way of responding to authentic testimony.[39]

Given Luke's meticulousness, therefore, his tendency simply to eliminate information that might be considered questionable by his audience (such as the charges against Jesus that he had claimed he would destroy the temple, or the beating of Jesus by the Roman soldiers) rather than altering it, and his solemn oath in his Prologue that he is presenting the true words of eyewitnesses, we do seem to have good reason to take Luke at his word and to trust that he has relayed this eyewitness testimony to the best of his ability. But how trustworthy were those eyewitnesses?

A detailed analysis of the historical accuracy of the events described in Luke's Gospel is beyond the scope of this book (although Luke himself may well have investigated whether the events reported to him had actually happened), but we may at least address briefly here the

39. Ibid., 5.

probable faithfulness of Luke in reporting the teachings of Jesus, which may have been relayed to Luke by eyewitnesses several decades after they had been spoken by Jesus. Do we have good reason to accept these as the true teachings of Jesus?

## Luke and Jesus

If there is one characteristic of Jesus about which all ancient writers agree (including the authors of the so-called Gnostic Gospels), it is that Jesus was a teacher. Yet the obvious implications of this simple fact seem to have escaped many modern perceptions about Jesus and about the Gospels. When we consider the impression given by films and other modern depictions of the life of Jesus, we may perhaps be forgiven for picturing Jesus as someone who roamed the countryside, occasionally blurting out words of wisdom, hoping that someone in the crowds might remember some of his words. But is such a picture reasonable? Would it not be more likely that Jesus would have employed the same teaching techniques as others in his culture? The Gospels indicate that Jesus frequently taught publicly in the synagogues on the Sabbath (indeed, the Gospels seem to indicate that most of his public healing ministry also probably took place on the Sabbath), but what about the other six days of the week? If Jesus was a teacher, with a group of formal students (his disciples), is it not likely that most of Jesus's time during the week was actually spent teaching those students? If so, the most common teaching technique used in the ancient world (and especially in Jewish circles) was memorization.

Along these lines, Birger Gerhardsson, in his book *Memory and Manuscript*, has conducted a study of the techniques used in rabbinic Judaism in the early centuries of the Christian era and has compared these techniques with what the Gospels tell us about Jesus. Gerhardsson affirms that, as was the case with nearly all forms of learning in the ancient world, memorization and repetition were the most common techniques employed by the rabbis:

> An ancient rule for the Rabbis' pupils was formulated in this way: "It is a man's duty to state (a tradition) in his teacher's words." . . . The pupil is thus in duty bound to maintain his teacher's exact words. But the teacher is also responsible for seeing that the exact wording is preserved. The oral material which the teacher really wishes to teach his pupils—whether his own doctrinal statements or passages of transmitted doctrine—is not merely to be read out quite generally in the course of preaching or teach-

ing. He must repeat it over and over again, until he has actually passed it on to his pupil or pupils; i.e. until they know the passage in question by heart.[40]

When a teacher's words are accorded considerable authority and when an attempt is made carefully to preserve them—and when instruction is concentrated generally on memorization—brevity and conciseness are important virtues. We see this very clearly in ancient Judaism, from the wise men . . . of the Old Testament and through the whole of Rabbinism. The tendency to concentrate teachings and texts, expressing them with the utmost brevity, is general. There was a very active consciousness of the importance of such concentration, of condensing material into concise, pregnant—and if possible also striking, pithy and succinct—sayings.[41]

It should not surprise us, then, that the vast majority of Jesus's teachings found in the Synoptic Gospels should consist of precisely this type of material: parables and short, pithy statements. Even the longer discourses of Jesus recorded in the Synoptics, such as the Sermons on the Mount and on the Plain and the three versions of the Mini-Apocalypse, would have been constructed by the Gospel writers from these shorter "building blocks" of Jesus's concise, memorable sayings. These statements do seem to present to a large degree Jesus's private teaching to his disciples, which would have been easily remembered and repeated. It seems almost certain that a large amount of the time Jesus spent with his students would have been in repeating and rehearsing his parables and sayings until they had been perfectly memorized.

The evidence strongly suggests that, during the time the disciples spent with Jesus, they would have learned and memorized Jesus's parables and important sayings. In the years and then decades after his resurrection, the disciples would have continued to tell those same parables and sayings in their teaching and preaching in the early church. According to the earliest sources, Mark's Gospel was based on the preaching of Peter, and it is possible that the few parables and other teachings found in that Gospel were indeed based on the actual preaching of the apostles. Similarly, the Gospel of Matthew, if not written by Matthew himself (who as a literate tax collector [Matt 9:9–13] could have served as a scribe among the apostles), was likely written deliberately so as to encapsulate the most important of Jesus's teachings

40. Birger Gerhardsson, *Memory and Manuscript: Oral Tradition and Written Transmission in Rabbinic Judaism and Early Christianity*, trans. Eric J. Sharpe, Acta Seminarii Neotestamentici Upsaliensis 22 (Copenhagen: Munksgaard, 1961), 130–31, 133.
41. Ibid., 136–37.

in a systematic way, based on the continued teaching of the apostles in the primitive church. Luke, who implies strongly in his Prologue that he had interviewed actual eyewitnesses, may well have filled in many of the remaining teachings of Jesus that had not been included in Matthew's Gospel. This scenario is highly plausible historically and is completely consistent with what we know of educational practices in Jewish circles in the first century.

Gerhardsson's analysis has been criticized by some scholars, however, on the basis that the concept of memorization of Jesus's exact words does not seem to account for the variations we find in some of Jesus's parables and sayings in Luke when compared with Matthew.[42] Surely this criticism imposes an unreasonable rigidity on Jesus's part regarding his own teachings, allowing him no room to vary his own parables to fit different situations (and to show his disciples that this is possible). There is certainly no reason why Jesus could not have asked his disciples to memorize more than one version of some of his parables. The number of examples of such variant teachings is actually very small. If we ignore the various versions of certain events in the Gospels (which can easily be accounted for based on the differing memories of eyewitnesses), we are left with only the following examples where Luke's version of a parable or teaching is significantly different from Matthew's:

**Table 5.7. Luke's Parables Different from Matthew's**

| Matthew | Luke | Pericope |
| --- | --- | --- |
| Matt 5:3–12 | Luke 6:20–26 | The Beatitudes |
| Matt 6:9–13 | Luke 11:2–4 | The Lord's Prayer |
| Matt 22:1–14 | Luke 14:15–24 | The Parable of the Great Supper |
| Matt 25:14–30 | Luke 19:11–27 | The Parable of the Talents or Pounds |

Other sayings, such as the various woes pronounced by Jesus against the scribes and Pharisees, would probably not have been part of Jesus's formal training of his disciples but may certainly have been repeated on different occasions with different details included each time, but similar enough to have left a permanent impression in the minds of

---

42. See Bauckham, *Jesus and the Eyewitnesses*, 251.

the disciples. As discussed earlier, Ken Olson has suggested that Luke's version of the Lord's Prayer may be one of several cases where Luke has abbreviated a saying of Jesus found in either Matthew or Mark by removing the second line of repetitive couplets. This leaves us with only two parables and the Beatitudes from the table above that represent variant versions of Jesus's teachings in Luke when compared to Matthew that cannot be accounted for either by the writing style of the different Gospel writers or by the memory of different witnesses. This is, indeed, a tiny number of such instances, and we may perhaps be amazed at how many different theories have been proposed by scholars to explain these few deviations. Here, as in many other cases, the simplest explanation is almost certainly the most likely. There is every reason to suppose that Jesus himself could have taught both versions of these three teachings to his disciples, asking them to memorize both versions.

We may then ask one further question, however, in regard to the teachings of Jesus as reported in Luke's Gospel compared to Matthew's: If Matthew's Gospel was intended as a systematic presentation of Jesus's teachings, and if the author of Matthew had fully memorized all of Jesus's formal teachings (whether that author was Matthew himself, who had been taught by Jesus directly, or whether that author was perhaps a student of Matthew or of one of the other original disciples), why were some of the teachings we find in Luke left out of Matthew? We may list here a number of such important teachings:

Table 5.8. Teachings of Jesus Included in Luke but Absent from Matthew

| Verses | Pericope |
| --- | --- |
| Luke 7:40–47 | Who Is Forgiven Little Loves Little |
| Luke 10:30–37 | The Parable of the Good Samaritan |
| Luke 11:5–8 | The Importunate Friend at Midnight |
| Luke 12:13–15 | Warning against Avarice |
| Luke 12:16–21 | The Parable of the Rich Fool |
| Luke 12:47–48 | Faithfulness |

| Luke 13:6–9 | The Parable of the Barren Fig Tree |
| Luke 14:7–15 | Teaching on Humility |
| Luke 14:28–33 | The Conditions of Discipleship |
| Luke 15:8–10 | The Parable of the Lost Coin |
| Luke 15:11–32 | The Parable of the Prodigal Son |
| Luke 16:1–9 | The Parable of the Unjust Steward |
| Luke 16:10–12 | On Faithfulness in What Is Least |
| Luke 16:19–31 | The Parable of the Rich Man and Lazarus |
| Luke 17:7–10 | We Are Unprofitable Servants |
| Luke 17:20–22 | On the Coming of the Kingdom of God |
| Luke 18:1–8 | The Parable of the Unjust Judge |
| Luke 18:9–14 | The Pharisee and the Publican |

Is it reasonable, if these were true teachings of Jesus, that Matthew would have omitted them from his Gospel? Two answers may be given to this question, and they are the same two that were given when we asked why Luke may have chosen to omit some of the teachings Matthew had presented in his Gospel. The first answer is that Matthew may not have made a conscious choice to omit any of these teachings; he may simply never have chosen to include any of them because they did not fit the theme he was trying to present at any particular point in his Gospel. We should not attempt, therefore, to attach any significance to the fact that he did not include them. The second answer is that there may be a quality common to these different teachings that made them less attractive to Matthew (they were less "Matthew-pleasing" than the teachings he did include). If we were to look for common qualities in these teachings, especially in the parables, we would find that many of them have a human-interest aspect, exuding a sense of pathos and emotion, and that many of them concentrate on the theme of God's mercy, especially his mercy toward those who are not yet a part of God's kingdom. These qualities do seem to be especially "Luke-pleasing" and seem especially appropriate to a Gospel intended to attract and convert non-Christians to Christianity. But these qualities may not have been as pleasing to Matthew, who (although he certainly also affirms God's mercy) seems to prefer more matter-of-fact parables and teachings over the more emotional ones we find only in Luke. We may note that the theme of God's mercy toward those outside God's kingdom would not have been quite as appropriate to Matthew's Gospel compared to Luke's, since Matthew seems to have been intended largely as a teaching tool for those already in the church, those who had already received mercy rather than those in need of mercy.

Thus, we find good reason to affirm that all three Synoptic Gospels seem to convey the true historical teachings of Jesus as memorized and proclaimed by his disciples. We may also affirm that the Gospels of Matthew and Luke complement each other admirably, one written primarily for the instruction of Jewish Christians, and one written primarily for the conversion of gentile non-Christians. Furthermore, the specific exploration of Luke's Gospel undertaken above has revealed it to be a masterful composition both as an engaging story and as a deep theological treatise, in which we, its readers, are challenged with the ultimate choice of either rejecting Jesus, the servant and Son of God, or becoming his faithful followers. Anyone who reads Luke's Gospel carefully cannot help being affected by its message.

# Epilogue

## *A Synoptic Theory*

We have now answered the two questions this book set out to answer:
(1) Why was Luke's Gospel written? The answer is that it was written
to convert Theophilus (and potentially any other gentile non-Christians) and to defend Christianity against a charge of "atheism" within
the Roman Empire. (2) How was Luke's Gospel written? The answer
is that it was written by using Matthew, Mark, and oral tradition as
direct sources. These answers will therefore have an impact on the
other questions raised in the prologue to this book: How and why were
Matthew and Mark written, and when and by whom were all the Synoptics written? Thus, we may now explore briefly what some of the
implications of the present analysis may be for the broader Synoptic
Problem.

This discussion has been relegated to a brief epilogue, rather than
to a full-fledged chapter, for two reasons. First, the suggestions made
in this epilogue will be tentative since, once made, they will require
a detailed inquiry of their own. The answers discovered in this book
may potentially point in certain directions, but it is only by subjecting
those implications to sharp scrutiny that it may be possible to confirm
or refute them. Since such scrutiny is well beyond the scope of a single
chapter, it will be impossible here to do justice to this task. It is not,
however, inappropriate to follow such implications briefly to see
where they may lead.

Second, the suggestions made here will expand the theory presented
in this book into new areas. It is important to understand, therefore,
that these suggestions are dependent on this book and not the other
way round. The arguments already made and the analysis already

given stand on their own. They do not depend on the truth or plausibility of what will now be suggested. If the tentative paths of exploration now to be proposed turn out to be dead ends, this will not invalidate what has already been established. It will simply mean that other possible paths need to be explored instead. It is therefore of great importance to understand that the suggestions made here are not necessarily the only possible implications resulting from this book but represent specific additional potential components of an overall Synoptic theory, of which the hypothesis presented in this book represents one standalone element. The additional components must stand or fall on their own merits as well; but if they do fall, this will not negate the hypothesis already proposed.

This epilogue therefore does not bear the same weight as the rest of the book. It is tentative and suggestive and, as such, provides a launching pad for further research, rather than representing the fruit of such research.

## Matthew and Mark

If we accept the conclusions reached earlier and acknowledge that Luke used both Matthew and Mark as sources, this opens up the question of what is the proper relationship between these two earlier Gospels? Why and how were *they* written?

The classic definition of the Synoptic Problem (as presented above in the prologue) divides the Gospel of Matthew (as it had Luke) into three types of material: Triple Tradition, Double Tradition, and unique. As we have seen, however, these classifications turn out to be largely meaningless. Once we have established that Luke did use Matthew directly as a source, there is no longer such a thing as "Double Tradition" material at all when we come to Matthew (since the Double Tradition would only come into existence at a later date based on Luke's choice of what non-Markan Matthean material to include). We are left, then, with only two types of material in Matthew: Markan and non-Markan.

The close similarities between Matthew and Mark (even closer than the similarities either of them has with Luke) indicate that there must be a direct literary relationship between the two. We are therefore faced with a seemingly simple choice. Either Mark came first and Matthew expanded it (as the Farrer theory suggests) by adding in the non-Markan material (from one or more other sources), or Matthew came first and Mark abbreviated it (as the Augustine theory suggests) by eliminating this material. When we look at these two Gospels side by side it makes much more sense to conclude that Matthew expanded Mark. The biggest problem with this, however, is the unanimous tradition of the early church that Matthew's Gospel was the first to be written. Those who advocate the Farrer theory tend to conclude that this tradition is simply not strong enough to outweigh the indications that Matthew expanded Mark, whereas proponents of the Augustine theory deem that it is.

When we look at the actual testimony of the early church fathers, from Papias and Irenaeus to Eusebius, the picture is not quite so simple. What these early fathers universally say is that (1) Matthew was the first to write a Gospel, but it was written in a Semitic language (Aramaic or Hebrew), not in Greek; and (2) Mark wrote his Gospel based on the preaching of Peter. (If we do not at this point want to pin down Mark's source to be specifically Peter himself, we could simply substitute "apostolic preaching" for "the preaching of Peter.") If we consider carefully what is being said here, it actually does not support the Augustine theory at all. If Mark based his Gospel on Peter's preaching, then he did not base it on the earlier Gospel of Matthew, which is what Augustine suggests (and, significantly, Augustine is the first of the church fathers not to mention Peter as the source of Mark's Gospel).

If we take the testimony of the earlier church fathers seriously, we actually have three mutually exclusive factors with which to contend here, and any two of them rule out the third. If there is a direct relationship between Matthew and Mark, and Matthew came first (the Augustine theory), then Mark cannot be based on Peter's preaching. Likewise, if there is a direct relationship between Matthew and Mark, and Mark is based on Peter's preaching (compatible with the Q and Farrer theories), then Matthew cannot have been written first (Matthew would then have to be a revision, and hence an expansion of Mark). Alternatively, if Matthew was written before Mark, and Mark was based on Peter's preaching, there cannot be a direct literary relationship between Matthew and Mark (an untenable position given their numerous close similarities).

The dilemma, then, is that, regardless of which of the tenable theories is adopted, it will inevitably contradict the external evidence of the church fathers in one way or another. Is there a resolution to this dilemma? The answer to this question may well be yes. There does indeed appear to be one simple resolution that makes sense if we once again look carefully at the actual testimony of the church fathers themselves. The universal testimony of the fathers is not that the Greek Gospel we now call Matthew was written first, but that the first Gospel was one written by Matthew in a *Semitic* language. If our extant Greek Gospel is not exactly the same as this original Semitic Matthew, then all of the conditions will be met. The first Gospel was written in a Semitic language by Matthew (and whether this was the "actual" disciple Matthew does not matter here). Mark's Gospel was then written independently of it, based on the preaching of Peter (or, if we prefer, based on "apostolic preaching"). The Greek Gospel we now know as Matthew was then produced by adding material to this Gospel of Mark. The Farrer theory appears to prevail.

There are two questions remaining, however: Is there any relationship between the Semitic Matthew and our Greek Matthew (or was the Greek Matthew simply mistaken by the early church for the by-then-lost Semitic Matthew)? And where did the material added to Mark to create the Greek Matthew come from? The simplest answer to both of these questions is that the non-Markan material present in our Greek Matthew did indeed come from Semitic Matthew, in which case it might be more accurate to say that Greek Matthew was produced by adding *Markan* material to Semitic Matthew and not the other way round!

This solution would satisfy all the conditions discussed above in order to make sense of both the internal evidence and the traditions of the early church. It would also explain why this new document (Greek Matthew) was still known by the same name as the original (Semitic Matthew). Additionally, there is a precedent in the history of Judeo-Christian sacred writing for such a phenomenon. Both the books of Esther and of Daniel, originally written in Semitic languages, were augmented with new material when translated into Greek. Yet they were still known as the same documents as the original Semitic versions. Esther is especially relevant, since the additions made to it are more integrated into its text than are the few additions tacked onto Daniel.

Esther does not exemplify precisely the same process suggested for Semitic Matthew, however, since the additions to Esther appear to be just that—additions. In the case of Matthew, we are suggesting instead that two separate documents were merged to form the new version. There is no specific precedent for such a process, but there is an antecedent: Tatian's *Diatessaron*, which was written at the end of the second century by conflating not only two texts but all four Gospels (which would certainly be much more difficult to accomplish than working with just two texts simultaneously).

If this is how Greek Matthew came to be written (and, since its non-Markan material had to have come from some source, Semitic Matthew is at least as plausible as any other potential source or sources), the analogy of Esther is even more applicable than is the *Diatessaron*, since the new document retained the title of the old. This suggests that the author of Greek Matthew was not attempting to create his own new document using Semitic Matthew and Mark as sources (comparable to what Luke would later do) but that he was attempting to *translate* Semitic Matthew (not just use it as a source), while at the same time augmenting it (with material from Mark), just as Esther had been augmented (with material from an unknown source).

This suggests that whatever we see in Greek Matthew that does not correspond to Mark is likely to have been present in Semitic Matthew already (rather than being invented by the translator or brought in from yet another source). Otherwise it would be more likely that the resulting document would have been known by the name of its redactor rather than by the author of the original document. If we remember Streeter's rule that "Matthew conflates, Luke alternates," it would seem reasonable that pericopes in Greek Matthew that appear to expand on the Markan version might actually represent stories that occurred both in Mark and in Semitic Matthew, but in somewhat different versions, which were then combined into one consistent version. We might also suppose that, since Mark was already in Greek, the translator often relied on Mark's wording when relaying a particular pericope rather than taking the effort to translate the Semitic version directly.

If this was the case, it should not be impossible to create a provisional reconstruction of the probable contents of Semitic Matthew, beginning by removing all the purely Markan pericopes from Matthew. We would then be left with a document about two-thirds the length of Greek Matthew (a little longer than Mark) with roughly one-quarter of its pericopes similar to ones in Mark, a text that is a complete Gospel, including the birth, passion and resurrection narratives. This would represent a document that could have been realistically produced completely independently of Mark, recounting a number of stories about Jesus that Mark also knew but concentrating much more on Jesus's teaching than Mark did.

These two original documents could also have been created realistically, given the historical setting of the time. Semitic Matthew would certainly have been written either in Judea or (perhaps) Galilee at a fairly early date when the composition of the church was still predominantly Jewish. The Gospel of Mark was written some time later, possibly in Rome (as tradition suggests), based on the preaching of the early church but with no knowledge of Semitic Matthew. At some still later date, as the church expanded more and more into the non-Jewish world, it would have been natural for someone to want to translate Semitic Matthew into Greek for a wider audience. If this unknown translator had also managed to get hold of a copy of Mark (which, as we have seen, was probably not in general circulation at the time), then he may have felt it advantageous not only to translate what Matthew had written but to combine it with the extra material he found in Mark, so as to create one consistent document. In order to keep this translation-and-augmentation to the size of a single scroll, he needed to abbreviate some of the material from Mark to some extent. He probably maintained all of the material that was present in Semitic Matthew (even if he may have made some minor adaptations to some of its material). Since his initial audience would have already been familiar with the Semitic version, they would have been able to confirm that this was simply an expanded version of the original. The new Greek version of Matthew, then, would have become very popular in the expanding church and so came to be a major source for Luke. As the makeup of the church became less Jewish, the original shorter Semitic Matthew would have been read less and less and was eventually lost.

This scenario is plausible historically and gives a reasonable explanation both for the writing of the Gospels as we know them and for the traditions about them that were transmitted by the early church fathers. Clearly, each of the steps outlined above needs to be examined carefully and in greater detail before we can be confident about such a theory. We do, however, have at least a potential single, self-consistent hypothesis regarding the relationships of the Synoptics, which may be illustrated as follows:

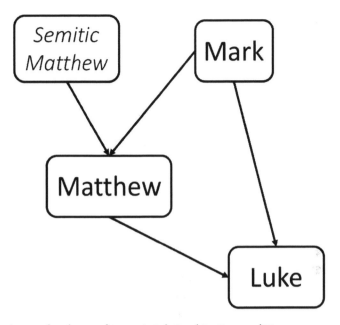

Fig. 6.1. The Theory of Synoptic Relationships Proposed Here

## Dating and Authorship

The theory suggested above outlines the relationships and relative order of the Synoptics, but it has not yet addressed the matter of when specifically any of the Gospels were written or by whom they were written. The historical context of first-century Christianity suggests two possible scenarios, each dependent on how we answer one critical question: Do the Gospel writers betray a knowledge of the destruction of the temple in 70 CE? This is not a simple question to answer, and it is as hotly debated as is the validity of the Q theory.

## Accepted Dates

The answer that most scholars would give is that at least Matthew and Luke do show signs of having been written after 70 CE, while Mark was probably written either just before or just after this event. If we accept this judgment, then the following scenario is suggested.

Semitic Matthew would probably have been written well before 70 (in Judea or Galilee), when the makeup of the church was still predominantly Jewish, perhaps as early as the 40s (the date many Q scholars assign to Q) or the 50s. Any clues in Matthew suggesting a later date of composition would have crept in during the translation process when Semitic Matthew was merged with Mark. Mark itself was composed (very possibly in Rome) either in the late 60s or the very early 70s. In spite of Semitic Matthew having been written some twenty years earlier, it would have enjoyed only a very limited circulation, confined to Semitic-speaking areas (perhaps only Judea, Galilee, and Syria). It is therefore possible that the Greek-speaking author of Mark, living in a more distant part of the Roman Empire, would not have had access to this document, and so could have remained unaffected by it.

In the following years of the 70s or 80s, however, some unknown individual with a Semitic background, who had perhaps recently obtained a copy of this Gospel of Mark, did make a comparison of these two Gospels and decided to merge them into a single Greek document. In doing so, he also made a few explanatory comments from time to time that reflected current conditions in the church. The location often suggested for the writing of Matthew is Syrian Antioch, poised as it was between predominantly Semitic- and Greek-speaking regions, and this seems to provide a plausible context for the creation of Greek Matthew. After this translation-and-augmentation was made, the new Gospel was immediately published for the church as a whole, and copies of it could even have spread throughout the empire in a matter of months rather than years.

One particular itinerant preacher could easily have come into contact with this new Gospel almost immediately and then have begun committing it to memory. Sometime in the ensuing years of the late 70s, 80s, or 90s, and after having also obtained a copy of the much rarer Gospel of Mark, this preacher had occasion to write his own version of the story of Jesus for the benefit of a specific gentile non-Christian, who may also have been an official who had heard rumors about this Christian sect with its questionable legal standing in the empire. So masterfully was this new Gospel of Luke written, that it was also then published widely in the church. Finally, the Gospel of Mark also came to be appreciated and eventually received its own wider circulation.

Such a scenario is historically plausible and does fit the time frame suggested by many scholars for the writing of the Synoptics. Given this picture, are we able to draw any conclusions regarding the actual authorship of the Synoptics? The disciple Matthew, as a literate tax collector, would be a plausible author for Semitic Matthew, and an early date of the 40s (or even the 50s) for its composition suggests that he could, indeed, have been the original author of such a document. Likewise, given the traditional date of 67 CE for the death of Peter in Rome, it would not be out of the question for the Gospel of Mark (if written just before or just after 70 CE) to have been influenced by Peter himself and written down not long after his death. Under such circumstances, the traditional author, John Mark, would also not be out of the question.

The anonymous translator of Matthew must remain forever a mystery, with no tradition or other clue to reveal his identity. Eusebius, the first to mention specifically the translation of Matthew into Greek, refers to the translator simply as "him who translated the scripture."[1] Eusebius, the collector of so many traditions of the early church, obviously had found no tradition regarding this individual, and so the translator must remain completely unknown to us.

And what of Luke? If he was indeed the sometime companion of Paul and had been a young preacher in his twenties when he first met Paul in the 50s, he would still only have been in his sixties during the decade of the 90s, the latest plausible date when the Gospel attributed to him might have been written. It certainly would not have been impossible for this Gospel to have been written by someone of that age (and ancient tradition holds that Luke lived to the age of eighty-four). Even if we accept the latest dates suggested by scholars for the writing of the Synoptics, and in the absence of any contrary evidence or traditions, there seems no compelling reason to doubt the traditional authorship of any of the Synoptics!

## Questioning the Dates

However, *should* we accept these late dates? As indicated above, these dates all depend on the judgment of some scholars that the Gospel authors do indeed betray a knowledge of the destruction of the temple in 70 CE. But is such a judgement warranted? There are dissenting opinions among certain scholars, such as John A. T. Robinson, who in his book *Redating the New Testament* suggests that not only the Synoptic Gospels but all the books in the canonical New Testament were written prior to this important event.

Robinson's argument calls into question the assessment that certain passages in the Gospels refer after the fact to the destruction of the

---

1. Eusebius, *On the Discrepancies of the Gospels*, Ad Marinum, Question 2, quoted in Wenham, *Redating Matthew, Mark and Luke*, 118.

temple, in particular the three versions of the Mini-Apocalypse found in Matthew 24, Mark 13, and Luke 21. He argues that the imagery employed in these passages does not reflect the conditions of 70 CE but instead calls to mind the proclamations of judgment pronounced by the prophets hundreds of years earlier around the time of the destruction of Jerusalem by the Babylonians, and again in writings from the time of the Maccabees relating to the threat of the Greek tyrant Antiochus IV Epiphanes. Robinson further argues that, since the "Coming of the Son of Man" predicted in the Mini-Apocalypse clearly *did not* come immediately after the destruction of the temple in 70 CE, as each of the Synoptics states quite emphatically would happen, this prediction could not have been written after that event.[2] So this one very simple fact provides extremely strong evidence that the Synoptics must have been written prior to the destruction of the temple.

Indeed, when we consider what purpose the Mini-Apocalypse serves in the Gospels, it seems unlikely that it was ever intended as a specific prediction of the destruction of the temple but was intended, rather, as a parable advising against depending on the physical temple as a guarantee of God's presence and favor. As Luke's Jesus said in an earlier passage, closely linked to the Mini-Apocalypse, "The kingdom of God is not coming with signs to be observed; nor will they say, 'Look, here it is!' or 'There it is!' For behold, the kingdom of God is in your midst" (Luke 17:20–21 NASB). As John the Baptist in both Matthew and Luke had said, "Do not suppose that you can say to yourselves, 'We have Abraham for our father'; for I say to you that from these stones God is able to raise up children to Abraham" (Matt 3:9 NASB). In precisely the same way, Jesus is now telling the disciples not to presume to say, "Look what wonderful stones and what wonderful buildings!" as if they were proof of God's continuing presence with his people, since "there will not be left here one stone upon another that will not be thrown down" (Mark 13:1–2).

Hence, instead of depending on such outward evidence, it is precisely when such evidence fails that the disciples should look for the kingdom of God in their midst. When the "abomination of desolation" appears (Matt 24:15; Mark 13:14), when the enemies of God's kingdom seem to have conquered, and when the physical signs of God's presence seem the weakest, it is at that very moment that we should turn to God and understand that in spite of the apparent outward signs, God's king-

---

2. Robinson, *Redating the New Testament*, 16.

dom is present in our midst. It is precisely at such a moment that the Son of Man does come.

All of this becomes even clearer when we compare the Mini-Apocalypse with chapter 7 of the book of the prophet Jeremiah. Indeed, such a comparison is already invited by each of the Synoptics, since the Mini-Apocalypse follows shortly after the Cleansing of the Temple in all three Gospels, and in each case Jesus alludes to Jeremiah 7:11 by saying that the temple has been made a "den of robbers" (Matt 21:13; Mark 11:17; Luke 19:4). Thus, when Jesus now tells the disciples not to presume to say, "Look what wonderful stones and what wonderful buildings!," he is closely echoing Jeremiah, who writes earlier in the same chapter: "Do not trust in these deceptive words: 'This is the temple of the Lord, the temple of the Lord, the temple of the Lord'" (Jer 7:4 ESV). The meanings of Jeremiah and of Jesus are precisely the same. The physical temple should not be taken for granted as a continuing sign of God's presence and favor. In Jeremiah's case, what is important is the care of the weak, the helpless, and the unfortunate by the nation of Israel. According to the Gospel writers, Jesus himself is now the embodiment of such care, and indeed the embodiment of God himself. It is Jesus's presence, therefore, not the presence of the temple that is the true indication of God's presence and care for his people (as he had also earlier claimed in Nazareth in Luke 4:16–21).

Thus, the Mini-Apocalypse is transformed from a prediction of specific historical events and of the "end of the world" into a simple parable. The key message of this parable is that "heaven and earth [including the temple] will pass away, but my words will never pass away" (Matt 24:35; Mark 13:31; Luke 21:33 NIV). When we see everything that seems most solid and secure to us crumbling before our eyes, even then (or, indeed, *especially* then) we can be assured of God's presence among us in Jesus himself. There is every reason, therefore, for us to conclude that Jesus could well have spoken these words and that the Gospel writers could have written them down long before the temple was actually destroyed.

In addition, there seem to be numerous instances in the Gospels that assume that the temple was still standing at the time of writing. For example, Luke appears to present the argument that, because Christians have continued to make sacrifices in the temple in Jerusalem, they cannot be accused of the crime of "atheism." Such an argument would make little sense if the temple were no longer standing, since

Christians could therefore not have still been making such sacrifices at that time.

If this is the case, then, and if Robinson is correct, 70 CE does not mark the date *after* which the Gospels must have been written but is instead the date before which they were probably written. Is it still possible under such circumstances to establish a realistic scenario for their writing? In this case we would not need to establish the date of the earliest and then work our way forward, but we would need to establish the date of the latest and work our way backward. Instead of beginning with Matthew or Mark, we must now begin with Luke. But Luke itself was not the last of the Synoptic-related texts to be written. That distinction belongs to the book of Acts, the sequel to Luke. Do we have any clues as to when this final document was written? If we put together a number of factors, we may have some very strong clues indeed.

Like Luke's Journey to Jerusalem, the ending of Acts has always been something of a puzzle. In his second book, Luke spends a good deal of time building up to Paul's anticipated trial before Nero, but he never gives any indication that such a trial actually occurred. Several solutions to this enigmatic ending of Acts have been suggested: (1) The work remained unfinished because of the author's untimely death (but the book does in fact come to a somewhat satisfactory conclusion, unlike the Gospel of Mark, which appears to end mid-sentence). (2) The true ending has been lost (but, like Matthew and Luke, Acts is very near the length of the longest practical scroll, and an account of Paul's trial could not possibly have fit at the end of the scroll needed for Acts). (3) Luke intended to write a third volume (but Paul's trial would not have warranted an entire third book). (4) There was no need to give an account of Paul's trial since everyone already knew the outcome, and what was important to Luke was not Paul's trial itself but the simple fact that Paul had brought the gospel to Rome.

This final solution appears to be the only logical possibility if Acts was written *after* 70 CE, but it simply makes no sense. Luke has emphasized both in his Gospel and in Acts that Christians would give their testimony before kings and rulers. Indeed, if we look carefully at Paul's first encounter with Jesus on the road to Damascus, we find that, just after that encounter, Jesus also appears to a certain Ananias (who heals Paul's blindness), and in a vision Jesus tells Ananias that Paul "is an instrument whom I have chosen to bring my name before Gentiles and kings and before the people of Israel" (Acts 9:15 NRSV). It is surely significant that three groups of people are named to whom Paul is specifically called to testify about Jesus: both Jews and gentiles, but also *kings*! It is for this very purpose, therefore, that all of the events in the last quarter of the book of Acts have been set in motion, in order to enable Paul's testimony to the Sanhedrin in Jerusalem, to the governors Felix and Festus and then King Agrippa in Caesarea, and ultimately to the highest king of all, the emperor Nero, in Rome. In the penultimate chapter of the book, an angel appears to Paul saying that he must stand trial and give his testimony before Nero, and so we would expect that Paul's testimony as a Christian before the emperor would be very important indeed. In addition, it is noteworthy that, when Paul reaches Rome, there are already Christians there, so he has not brought the gospel there. This solution seems inadequate. There is one and only one solution to the ending of Acts that therefore makes logical sense: Luke did not give an account of Paul's trial because Paul's trial had not yet taken place!

When we add this conclusion to one of the characteristics of Luke's Gospel that has been noted all along in this book, a *very* clear picture emerges. Language used in the Prologue to Luke's Gospel suggests that Theophilus, to whom the Gospel was addressed, was probably an important official involved with legal matters in the Roman Empire. Luke wrote his Gospel both to convert Theophilus himself to Christianity and to defend the church against a potential charge of "atheism" in the empire. If it turns out that this was one of the main charges to be directed against Paul in his imperial trial, Luke may not have been attempting to head off merely a potential charge, but a very real and dangerous situation not only for Paul himself but for the entire Christian community. If Nero were to find Paul guilty of atheism, this charge could then be leveled against every other Christian throughout the empire. It makes sense, then, that in order to prevent such a catastrophe, in order to defend Paul, and in order to persuade Theophilus himself to become a Christian, Luke wrote both his Gospel and Acts in preparation for Paul's trial, at which Theophilus was to be an important participant.

Such a scenario seems plausible, yet it limits the dates for the writing of the Synoptics. If this is the historical context in which Luke wrote, both his Gospel and Acts would have been written during Paul's house arrest in Rome during 60 to 62 CE. He would have needed to obtain a copy of Mark's Gospel by this time, but he would also have needed plenty of time to use and memorize the Greek translation of Matthew, itself therefore being dependent on an even earlier date for the writing of Mark.

Paul, in his letter to Philemon (and in the accompanying letter to the Colossians, if genuine), reported that both Luke and Mark were with him (Phlm 24; Col 4:10–14). These letters would have been written either very early during his house arrest in Rome or just before this time during his imprisonment in Caesarea in 57 to 59 CE. Thus, Paul himself confirms that there would have been an opportunity for Mark to have given a copy of his Gospel personally to Luke just before the time when Luke would have begun writing his own Gospel.

But what of Mark? Robinson draws on the work of George Edmundson's *The Church in Rome in the First Century*, which suggests that the apostle Peter had first gone to Rome and founded the church there in 42 CE, based on the enigmatic verse in Acts 12:17 where Peter is said to have gone to "another place" after his miraculous release from prison in Jerusalem.[3] This date corresponds to other early testimony and accounts for Peter's traditional twenty-five-year bishopric over Rome, if he was executed in 67 CE. If Acts was indeed written in preparation for Paul's trial, then Luke may not have wanted to implicate Peter directly as the founder of the Roman church and so was being deliberately vague at this point in Acts about Peter's destination in order to protect Peter. If this chronology is correct, then it is possible that the Gospel of Mark could have been written during Peter's *first* visit to Rome. Robinson himself concludes:

One must therefore, I believe, be prepared to take seriously the tradition that Mark . . . accompanied Peter to Rome in 42 as his interpreter and catechist, and that after Peter's departure from the capital he acceded to the reiterated request for a record of the apostle's teaching, perhaps about 45.[4]

We therefore have very specific dates, within a year or so, for the composition of both the Gospels of Mark and the Gospel of Luke, 45 CE and 61 CE, respectively. We may also be fairly confident in supposing that Semitic Matthew was written right around 40 CE, since tradition suggests it was written not long before the execution of James son of Zebedee in 42 CE, the precipitating event that led Peter and the rest

3. George Edmundson, *The Church in Rome in the First Century: An Examination of Various Controverted Questions Relating to Its History, Chronology, Literature, and Traditions; Eight Lectures,* Bampton Lectures for 1913 (London: Longmans, Green, 1913).
4. Robinson, *Redating the New Testament,* 114.

of the original disciples to leave Jerusalem and take the gospel to the greater world.

Once these dates have been established, the rest is not difficult to work out. Peter was back in Jerusalem by the mid 40s, followed shortly thereafter by Mark, and both are known to have been in Antioch in the late 40s. It was from Antioch that Mark left with Paul on his first missionary journey around the year 50. Mark could easily have left a copy of his Gospel behind in Antioch at this time for our anonymous translator of Matthew to use. Thus, Greek Matthew could have been produced and published by the early 50s, giving Luke a full decade to read, digest, and memorize it before beginning work on his own Gospel.

If this scenario appears to be unduly precise and detailed, we must remember that it is based not on mere guesses but on well-founded and noncontradicted traditions, and on the known movements of the principals involved as gleaned from Paul's letters and the book of Acts. The main question remaining is simply whether the texts of the Synoptics do indeed support the possibility of such early dates, a question whose answer requires detailed and serious analysis.

Regardless of which of the two possible scenarios and time lines outlined above is more plausible, in either case there appears to be no reason to doubt the traditionally assigned authorship for any of the Synoptics. This in itself suggests that we are in a position to take their portraits of Jesus very seriously indeed. If the bulk of Matthew's Gospel was originally written by one of Jesus's own disciples; if Mark was written by the assistant of another of those disciples; if Luke did carefully investigate everything from top to bottom, personally interviewing eyewitnesses; and if all of these men were deeply involved in the first wave of spreading the gospel throughout the Roman Empire, we can be confident that the three Synoptic Gospels do reflect with complete accuracy the views of the very earliest Christians regarding their new faith, and regarding the person, life, death, and resurrection of Jesus.

# Appendix

## *Special Lukan Material*

This appendix includes tables of the source material incorporated into Luke according to the theory proposed in this work.

### Table 7.1. Luke's Unique Material

A list of the material unique to Luke's Gospel is included here not because it represents a single source of its own but because it represents material not from either Mark or Matthew that Luke chose to include in his Gospel, probably from more than one source, possibly all oral sources. It varies in style and content, from single-sentence sayings of Jesus to long parables and stories about Jesus. Pericopes not separated by a line indicate a continuous passage in Luke. Those separated by a black line have other intervening material between them. This list is inclusive of passages that have loose parallels to pericopes in the other Synoptics, since they represent a different form and hence a probable different source from other similar passages. Such parallel pericopes are indicated in square brackets. The division of Luke's Gospel into sections corresponds to the analogy of sonata form as discussed in the body of this work.

# Luke's Introduction

| Verses | Pericope |
|---|---|
| Luke 1:1–4 | Prologue |
| Luke 1:5–25 | The Birth of John the Baptist Foretold |
| Luke 1:26–38 | The Annunciation [Matt 1:18–25] |
| Luke 1:39–56 | Mary's Visit to Elizabeth |
| Luke 1:57–80 | The Birth of John the Baptist |
| Luke 2:1–7 | The Birth of Jesus |
| Luke 2:8–20 | The Shepherds Adore the Infant Jesus |
| Luke 2:21–38 | The Circumcision and Presentation |
| Luke 2:39–40 | The Childhood of Jesus at Nazareth [Matt 2:22–23] |
| Luke 2:41–52 | The Boy Jesus in the Temple |

# Luke's Exposition

| Verses | Pericope |
|---|---|
| Luke 3:1–2 | The Beginning of John's Ministry [Matt 3:1] |
| Luke 3:10–15 | John the Baptist's Teaching |
| Luke 3:23–38 | The Genealogy of Jesus [Matt 1:1–17] |
| Luke 4:16–30 | Jesus Rejected at Nazareth [Matt 4:16–22] |
| Luke 5:1–9 | The Call of the Disciples [Mark 1:16–20] |
| Luke 6:20–26 | Beatitudes and Woes [Matt 5:3–12] |
| Luke 7:11–17 | The Widow's Son at Nain |
| Luke 7:36–50 | The Woman with the Ointment [Matt 26:6–13] |
| Luke 8:1–3 | The Ministering Women |

# Luke's Development

| Verses | Pericope |
|---|---|
| Luke 9:51 | Decision to Go to Jerusalem |
| Luke 9:52–56 | Jesus Is Rejected by Samaritans |
| Luke 10:1 | Commissioning the Seventy |
| Luke 10:17–20 | The Return of the Seventy |
| Luke 10:30–37 | The Parable of the Good Samaritan |
| Luke 10:38–42 | Mary and Martha |
| (Luke 11:1–4) | (The Lord's Prayer [Matt 6:9–13]) |
| Luke 11:5–8 | The Importunate Friend at Midnight |
| Luke 11:21–22 | The Strong Man [Matt 12:29] |
| Luke 11:27–28 | True Blessedness |
| Luke 11:37–41 | Washing Hands [Matt 15:1–3] |
| Luke 11:53–54 | The Opposition of the Pharisees |
| Luke 12:13–15 | Warning against Avarice |
| Luke 12:16–21 | The Parable of the Rich Fool |
| Luke 12:32 | Fear Not Little Flock |
| Luke 12:35–38 | Watchfulness [Matt 25:1–13] |
| Luke 12:47–48 | Faithfulness |
| Luke 12:49–50 | Baptism in Fire [Mark 10:38] |
| Luke 13:1–5 | Repentance or Destruction |
| Luke 13:6–9 | The Parable of the Barren Fig Tree |
| Luke 13:10–17 | The Healing of the Crippled Woman |
| Luke 13:22–24 | The Narrow Door [Matt 7:13–14] |
| Luke 13:25–28 | Exclusion from the Kingdom [Matt 7:22–23] |
| Luke 13:31–33 | A Warning against Herod |
| Luke 14:1–6 | The Healing of the Man with Dropsy |
| Luke 14:7–15 | Teaching on Humility |

# Luke's Development *(continued)*

| Verses | Pericope |
|--------|----------|
| Luke 14:28–33 | The Conditions of Discipleship |
| Luke 15:8–10 | The Parable of the Lost Coin |
| Luke 15:11–32 | The Parable of the Prodigal Son |
| Luke 16:1–9 | The Parable of the Unjust Steward |
| Luke 16:10–12 | On Faithfulness in What Is Least |
| Luke 16:14–15 | The Pharisees Reproved |
| Luke 16:16–17 | Concerning the Law [Matt 11:12–13] |
| Luke 16:19–31 | The Parable of the Rich Man and Lazarus |
| Luke 17:3–4 | On Forgiveness [Matt 18:15] |
| Luke 17:5–6 | On Faith [Matt 17:19–21] |
| Luke 17:7–10 | We Are Unprofitable Servants |
| Luke 17:11–19 | The Cleansing of the Ten Lepers |
| Luke 17:20–22 | On the Coming of the Kingdom of God |
| Luke 18:1–8 | The Parable of the Unjust Judge |
| Luke 18:9–14 | The Pharisee and the Publican |
| Luke 19:1–10 | Zacchaeus |

# Luke's Recapitulation

| Verses | Pericope |
|---|---|
| Luke 19:41–44 | Jesus Weeps over Jerusalem |
| Luke 21:34–36 | Take Heed to Yourselves |
| Luke 21:37–38 | The Ministry of Jesus in Jerusalem |
| (Luke 22:14–20) | (The Last Supper [Mark 14:22–25]) |
| Luke 22:31–32 | Simon Sifted by Satan [Matt 26:31–35] |
| Luke 22:35–38 | The Two Swords |
| Luke 23:1–16 | Jesus before Pilate and Herod [Mark 15:1–5] |
| Luke 23:27–31 | Daughters of Jerusalem |
| Luke 23:34 | Father Forgive Them |
| Luke 23:39–43 | Today You Will Be with Me in Paradise |
| Luke 23:46 | I Commit My Spirit |

# Luke's Coda

| Verses | Pericope |
|---|---|
| Luke 24:1–9 | The Resurrection [Matt 28:1–8] |
| Luke 24:10–12 | Jesus Appears to the Women [Matt 28:9–10] |
| Luke 24:13–35 | The Way to Emmaus |
| Luke 24:36–43 | Jesus Appears to His Disciples |
| Luke 24:44–53 | Jesus's Last Words and Ascension |

## Table 7.2. Material Omitted by Luke

This list is exclusive of passages that have loose parallels to pericopes in the other Synoptics, since Luke would not be expected to include such parallels if he had already included a variant form from a different source.

| Matthew | Mark | Pericope |
|---|---|---|
| Matt 2:1–12 | | The Magi Adore the Infant Jesus |
| Matt 2:13–21 | | The Flight into Egypt and Return |
| Matt 5:19–20 | | On the Law and the Prophets |
| Matt 5:21–24 | | On Murder and Wrath |
| Matt 5:27–30 | | On Adultery |
| Matt 5:33–37 | | On Oaths |
| Matt 6:1–4 | | On Almsgiving |
| Matt 6:5–6 | | On Prayer |
| Matt 6:16–18 | | On Fasting |
| Matt 7:6 | | On Profaning the Holy |
| Matt 11:28–30 | | Come to Me |
| | Mark 3:20–21 | Jesus Is Thought to be Beside Himself |
| | Mark 4:26–29 | The Parable of the Seed Growing Secretly |
| Matt 13:24–30 | | The Parable of the Tares |
| Matt 13:34–35 | Mark 4:33–34 | Jesus's Use of Parables |
| Matt 13:36–43 | | Interpretation of the Parable of the Tares |
| Matt 13:44–46 | | The Parable of the Hidden Treasure |
| Matt 13:47–50 | | The Parable of the Net |
| Matt 13:51–53 | | Treasures New and Old |
| Matt 14:5–12 | Mark 6:18–29 | The Death of John the Baptist |
| Matt 14:22–33 | Mark 6:45–52 | The Walking on the Water |
| Matt 14:34–36 | Mark 6:53–56 | Healings at Gennesaret |
| Matt 15:4–11 | Mark 7:6–23 | Defilement—Traditional and Real |
| Matt 15:21–28 | Mark 7:24–30 | The Syrophoenician Woman |
| Matt 15:29–31 | Mark 7:31–37 | Jesus Heals a Deaf Mute |
| Matt 15:32–39 | Mark 8:1–10 | Four Thousand are Fed |

| Matthew | Mark | Pericope |
|---|---|---|
| | Mark 8:22–26 | A Blind Man Is Healed at Bethsaida |
| Matt 17:10–13 | Mark 9:11–13 | The Coming of Elijah |
| Matt 17:24–27 | | Payment of the Temple Tax |
| Matt 18:19–20 | | Where Two or Three are Gathered |
| Matt 18:23–35 | | The Parable of the Unforgiving Servant |
| Matt 19:3–8 | Mark 10:2–9 | On Divorce |
| Matt 19:10–12 | | On Celibacy |
| Matt 20:1–16 | | The Parable of the Laborers in the Vineyard |
| Matt 20:20–23 | Mark 10:35–40 | The Sons of Zebedee |
| Matt 21:18–19 | Mark 11:12–14 | The Cursing of the Fig Tree |
| Matt 21:20 | Mark 11:20–22 | The Fig Tree Is Withered |
| Matt 21:28–32 | | The Parable of the Two Sons |
| Matt 23:8–12 | | Call No Man Your Father |
| | Mark 13:33–37 | Take Heed Watch |
| Matt 25:1–13 | | The Parable of the Ten Virgins |
| Matt 25:31–46 | | The Last Judgment |
| Matt 26:59–63 | Mark 14:55–61 | False Witnesses against Jesus |
| Matt 27:3–10 | | The Death of Judas [but see Acts 1:15–20] |
| Matt 27:27–31 | Mark 15:16–20 | Jesus Mocked by the Soldiers |
| Matt 27:46–49 | Mark 15:34–36 | Why Have You Forsaken Me |
| Matt 27:51–53 | | The Earthquake |
| Matt 27:62–66 | | The Guard at the Tomb |
| Matt 28:11–15 | | The Report of the Guard |
| Matt 28:16–20 | | The Great Commission |

**Fig. 7.1. The Composition of Luke**

This figure is available online at
http://fortresspress.com/lukethecomposer.

# Bibliography

## Ancient Sources

Aland, Kurt, ed. *Synopsis of the Four Gospels: English Edition.* New York: American Bible Society, 1982. [Text of the Revised Standard Version © 1946, 1971, and 1973 by the Division of Christian Education of the National Council of Churches of Christ in the U.S.A.]

____. *Synopsis Quattuor Evangeliorum* 4th ed. Stuttgart: Württembergische Bibelanstalt, 1967.

*The Ante-Nicene Fathers: Translations of the Writings of the Fathers Down to A.D. 325.* Edited by Alexander Roberts and James Donaldson. 10 volumes. Buffalo: Christian Literature Company, 1885–96. Reprint, Peabody, MA: Hendrickson, 1994.

Eusebius. *The Ecclesiastical History.* Edited and translated by Kirsopp Lake, H. J. Lawlor, and J. E. L. Oulton. 2 volumes. Loeb Classical Library. London: Heinemann, 1926–32.

*The Holy Bible, Containing the Old and New Testaments: English Standard Version.* Wheaton, IL: Good News, 2001. [ESV]

*The Holy Bible, Containing the Old and New Testaments: New International Version.* Grand Rapids: Zondervan, 1978. [NIV]

*The Holy Bible, Containing the Old and New Testaments with the Apocrypha/Deuterocanonical Books: New Revised Standard Version.* Oxford: Oxford University Press, 1989. [NRSV]

*New American Standard Bible.* La Habra: Lockman Foundation, 1995. [NASB]

*Nicene and Post-Nicene Fathers.* Edited by Philip Schaff. 14 volumes. Buffalo: Christian Literature Publishing Company, 1900.

*Novum Testamentum Graece.* Edited by Erwin Nestle, Kurt Aland, Barbara Aland et al. 28th ed. Stuttgart: Deutsche Bibelgesellschaft, 2012.

## Modern Sources

Alexander, Loveday. "Ancient Book Production and the Circulation of the Gospels." In *The Gospels for All Christians: Rethinking the Gospel Audience*, edited by Richard Bauckham, 71–105. Grand Rapids: Eerdmans, 1998.

Barr, Allan. *A Diagram of Synoptic Relationships: In Four Colors.* 1900. Reprint, Edinburgh: T&T Clark, 1938, 1976.

Bauckham, Richard J. *Jesus and the Eyewitnesses: The Gospels as Eyewitness Testimony.* Grand Rapids: Eerdmans, 2006.

Bradby, E. L. "In Defence of Q." *Expository Times* 68 (1957): 315–18. Reprinted in *The Two-Source Hypothesis: A Critical Appraisal*, edited by Arthur J. Bellinzoni Jr, 287–93. Macon, GA: Mercer University Press, 1985.

Bultmann, Rudolf. *Jesus and the Word.* New York: Scribner's, 1926.

Butler, B. C. *The Originality of St. Matthew: A Critique of the Two-Document Hypothesis.* Cambridge: Cambridge University Press, 1951.

Carlson, Stephen C. "Clement of Alexandria on the 'Order' of the Gospels." *New Testament Studies* 47 (2001): 118–25.

Danker, Frederick W., rev. and ed. *A Greek-English Lexicon of the New Testament and Other Early Christian Literature.* 3rd ed. Based on Walter Bauer's *Griechisch-deutsches Wörterbuch zu den Schriften des Neuen Testaments und der übrigen urchristlichen Literatur*, and on previous English editions by W. F. Arndt and F. W. Gingrich. Chicago: University of Chicago Press, 2000.

Derrenbacker, R. A., Jr. *Ancient Compositional Practices and the Synoptic Problem.* Bibliotheca Ephemeridum theologicarum Lovaniensium 186. Leuven: Peeters, 2005.

Downing, F. G. "Towards a Rehabilitation of Q." *New Testament Studies* 11 (1964): 169–81. Reprinted in *The Two-Source Hypothesis: A Critical Appraisal*, edited by Arthur J. Bellinzoni Jr, 268–85. Macon, GA: Mercer University Press, 1985.

Dunn, James D. G. *Jesus Remembered.* Christianity in the Making 1. Grand Rapids: Eerdmans, 2003.

Ehrman, Bart D. *Lost Christianities: The Battles for Scripture and the Faiths We Never Knew.* Oxford: Oxford University Press, 2003.

Farmer, William R. "Modern Developments of Griesbach's Hypothesis." *New Testament Studies* 23 (1977): 280–93.

———. *The Synoptic Problem: A Critical Analysis.* New York: Macmillan, 1964.

Farrer, Austin. "On Dispensing with Q." In *Studies in the Gospels: Essays in Memory of R. H. Lightfoot,* edited by D. E. Nineham, 55–88. Oxford: Blackwell, 1955.

Fitzmyer, Joseph A. "Luke, The Gospel According to." In *The Oxford Companion to the Bible,* edited by Bruce M. Metzger and Michael D. Coogan, 469–74. Oxford: Oxford University Press.

Fleddermann, Harry T. *Q: A Reconstruction and Commentary.* Biblical Tools and Studies 1. Leuven: Peeters, 2005.

Fuller, Reginald H. *The New Testament in Current Study.* London: SCM, 1963.

Gerhardsson, Birger. *Memory and Manuscript: Oral Tradition and Written Transmission in Rabbinic Judaism and Early Christianity.* Translated by Eric J. Sharpe. Acta Seminarii Neotestamentici Upsaliensis 22. Copenhagen: Munksgaard, 1961.

Goodacre, Mark. *The Case against Q: Studies in Markan Priority and Synoptic Problem.* Harrisburg, PA: Trinity Press International, 2002.

____. *Goulder and the Gospels: An Examination of a New Paradigm.* Journal for the Study of the New Testament: Supplement Series 133. Sheffield: Sheffield Academic Press.

____. "A Monopoly on Marcan Priority? Fallacies at the Heart of *Q*." *Society of Biblical Literature 2000 Seminar Papers,* 538–622. Atlanta: Society of Biblical Literature, 2000.

Goulder, Michael D. *Luke: A New Paradigm.* Journal for the Study of the New Testament: Supplement Series 20. Sheffield: Sheffield Academic Press, 1989.

Goulder, Michael D. "The Order of a Crank." In *Synoptic Studies: The Ampleforth Conferences of 1982 and 1983,* edited by C. M. Tuckett, 111–30. Journal for the Study of the New Testament: Supplement Series 7. Sheffield: JSOT Press, 1984.

Griesbach, Johann Jakob. "A Demonstration That Mark Was Written after Matthew and Luke" (1789). In *J. J. Griesbach: Synoptic and Text-Critical Studies 1776-1976,* edited and translated by Bernard Orchard and Thomas R. W. Longstaff, 103–35. Society for New Testament Studies Monograph 34. Cambridge: Cambridge University Press, 1978.

Hawkins, John C. *Horae Synopticae: Contributions to the Study of the Synoptic Problem.* 2nd rev. ed. Oxford: Clarendon, 1909.

Hengel, Martin. *The Four Gospels and the One Gospel of Jesus Christ: An Investigation of the Collection and Origin of the Canonical Gospels.* Translated by John Bowden. London: SCM, 2000.

Holtzmann, Heinrich Julius. *Die synoptischen Evangelien: Ihr Ursprung und geschichtlicher Charakter.* Leipzig: Wilhelm Engelmann, 1863.

Kamien, Roger. *Music: An Appreciation.* 11th ed. New York: McGraw-Hill, 2015.

Kloppenborg, John S. "On Dispensing with Q? Goodacre on the Relation of Luke to Matthew." *New Testament Studies* 49 (2003): 210–36.

Kloppenborg Verbin, John S. *Excavating Q: The History and Setting of the Sayings Gospel.* Minneapolis: Fortress Press, 2000.

Lindsey, Robert L. *A Hebrew Translation of the Gospel of Mark: Greek-Hebrew Diglot with English Introduction.* Jerusalem: Dugith, 1973.

_____. "A Modified Two-Document Theory of the Synoptic Dependence and Independence." *Novum Testamentum* 6 (1963): 239–63.

Marxsen, W. *Introduction to the New Testament: An Approach to Its Problems.* Translated by G. Buswell. Philadelphia: Fortress Press, 1968.

Mason, Steve. *Life of Josephus: Translation and Commentary.* Leiden: Brill, 2003.

Matson, Mark A. "Luke's Rewriting of the Sermon on the Mount." In *Questioning Q: A Multidimensional Critique,* edited by Mark Goodacre and Nicholas Perrin, 43–70.London: SPCK, 2004.

Mauck, John W. *Paul on Trial: The Book of Acts as a Defense of Christianity.* Nashville: Thomas Nelson, 2001.

Metzger, Bruce M. *The Text of the New Testament: Its Transmission, Corruption and Restoration.* 2nd ed. Oxford: Oxford University Press, 1968.

_____. *A Textual Commentary on the Greek New Testament: A Companion Volume to the United Bible Societies' Greek New Testament (3d ed.).* Stuttgart: United Bible Societies, 1971.

Olson, Ken. "The Lord's Prayer (Abridged Edition)." In *Marcan Priority without Q: Explorations in the Farrer Hypothesis,* edited by John C. Poirier and Jeffrey Peterson, 101–18. Library of New Testament Studies 455. London: Bloomsbury T&T Clark, 2015.

_____. "Unpicking on the Farrer Theory." In *Questioning Q: A Multidimensional Critique,* edited by Mark Goodacre and Nicholas Perrin, 127–50. London: SPCK, 2004.

Orchard, Bernard, and Harold Riley. *The Order of the Synoptics: Why Three Synoptic Gospels?* Macon, GA: Mercer University Press, 1987.

Richards, E. Randolph. *Paul and First-Century Letter Writing: Secretaries, Composition, and Collection.* Downers Grove, IL: InterVarsity Press, 2004.

Robinson, James M., Paul Hoffmann, and John S. Kloppenborg, eds. *The Critical Edition of Q: Synopsis Including the Gospels of Matthew and Luke, Mark and Thomas, with English, German, and French Translations of Q and Thomas.* Minneapolis: Fortress Press, 2000.

_____. *The Sayings Gospel Q in Greek and English: With Parallels from the Gospels of Mark and Thomas.* Minneapolis: Fortress Press, 2002.

Robinson, John A. T. *Redating the New Testament.* London: SCM, 1976.

_____. *The Priority of John.* Oak Park: Meyer-Stone Books, 1987.

Shellard, Barbara. *New Light on Luke: Its Purpose, Sources, and Literary Context.* Journal for the Study of the New Testament: Supplement Series 215. London: Sheffield Academic Press, 2004.

Stone, Michael E., ed. *Jewish Writings of the Second Temple Period: Apocrypha, Pseudepigrapha, Qumran Sectarian Writings, Philo, Josephus.* Compendia rerum

Iudaicarum ad Novum Testamentum, section 2. Minneapolis: Fortress Press, 1984.

Streeter, Burnett Hillman. *The Four Gospels: A Study of Origins, Treating of the Manuscript Tradition, Sources, Authorship and Dates.* London: Macmillan, 1924.

Styler, G. M. "Synoptic Problem." In *The Oxford Companion to the Bible*, edited by Bruce M. Metzger and Michael D. Coogan, 724–27. Oxford: Oxford University Press, 1993.

Tajra, H. W. *The Trial of St. Paul: A Juridical Exegesis of the Second Half of the Acts of the Apostles.* Wissenschaftliche Untersuchungen zum Neuen Testament 2/55. Tübingen: Mohr Siebeck, 1989.

Thompson, Michael B. "The Holy Internet: Communication between Churches in the First Christian Generation." In *The Gospels for All Christians: Rethinking the Gospel Audience*, edited by Richard Bauckham, 49–70. Grand Rapids: Eerdmans, 1998.

Watson, Francis. "Q as Hypothesis: A Study in Methodology." *New Testament Studies* 55 (2009): 397–415.

Weisse, Christian Hermann. *Die evangelische Geschichte, kritisch und philosophisch bearbeitet.* 2 volumes. Leipzig: Breitkopf & Hartel, 1838.

Wenham, John. *Redating Matthew, Mark and Luke: A Fresh Assault on the Synoptic Problem.* Downers Grove, IL: InterVarsity Press, 1992.

Wright, N. T. *The Scriptures, the Cross and the Power of God.* London: SPCK, 2005.

Zahn, Theodor. *Introduction to the New Testament.* Translated by John Moore Trout et al. Edinburgh: T&T Clark, 1909. Reprint, Minneapolis: Klock & Klock, 1977.

## Copyright Notices

Unmarked Scripture quotations have been translated by the author.

*The Holy Bible, Containing the Old and New Testaments: English Standard Version.* Wheaton, IL: Good News, 2001. [ESV]

*The Holy Bible, Containing the Old and New Testaments: New International Version.* Grand Rapids: Zondervan, 1978. [NIV]

*The Holy Bible, Containing the Old and New Testaments with the Apocrypha/Deuterocanonical Books: New Revised Standard Version.* Oxford: Oxford University Press, 1989. [NRSV]

*New American Standard Bible.* La Habra: Lockman Foundation, 1995. [NASB]

*Nicene and Post-Nicene Fathers.* Edited by Philip Schaff. 14 volumes. Buffalo: Christian Literature Publishing Company, 1900.

*Novum Testamentum Graece.* Edited by Erwin Nestle, Kurt Aland, Barbara Aland et al. 28th ed. Stuttgart: Deutsche Bibelgesellschaft, 2012.

# Author Index

Great Omission 149
Naz. Synagogue 129